MARK CRILLEY

FLIGHTS of FANCY

Selected Strips & Bonus Features
from Issues 1 ~ 46

SIRIUS ENTERTAINMENT   ANDOVER, N. J.

This book is dedicated to
John Walter
with gratitude for many years of friendship

AKIKO TRADE PAPERBACK 'FLIGHTS OF FANCY'. MAY, 2002. FIRST PRINTING
PUBLISHED BY SIRIUS ENTERTAINMENT, INC. LAWRENCE SALAMONE, PRESIDENT.
ROBB HORAN, PUBLISHER. MARK BELLIS, EDITOR-IN-CHIEF. KEITH DAVIDSEN, ASSISTANT EDITOR.
MCNABB STUDIOS, PRODUCTION. CORRESPONDENCE: P.O. BOX 834, DOVER, NJ 07802.
AKIKO AND ALL RELATED CHARACTERS ARE TM & © 2002 MARK CRILLEY. SIRIUS AND
THE DOGSTAR LOGO ARE ® SIRIUS ENTERTAINMENT, INC. ALL RIGHTS RESERVED. ANY
SIMILARITY TO PERSONS LIVING OR DEAD IS PURELY COINCIDENTAL.
PRINTED IN THE USA.

Table of Contents

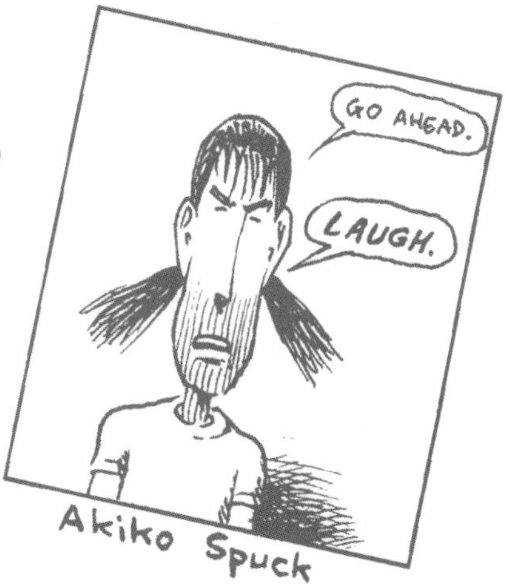

GO AHEAD.
LAUGH.
Akiko Spuck

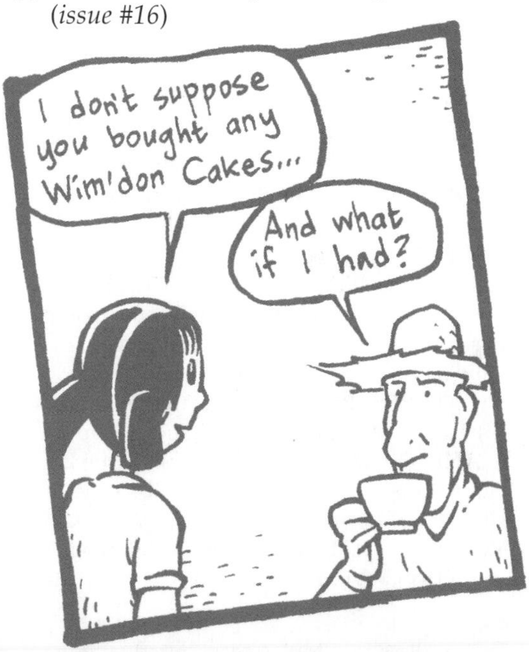

I don't suppose you bought any Wim'don Cakes...
And what if I had?

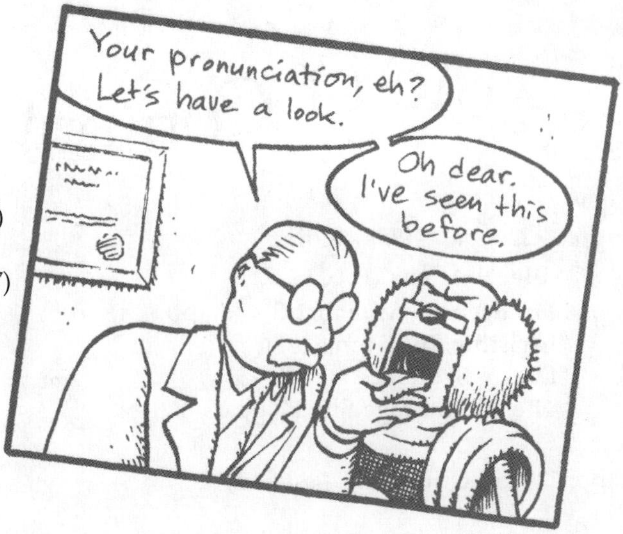
Your pronunciation, eh? Let's have a look.
Oh dear. I've seen this before.

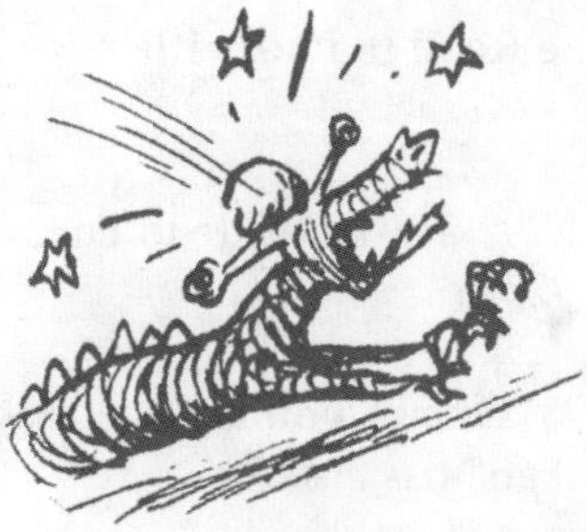

NOTE: This volume omits the following back-up material, which has already been reprinted in previous trade paperback collections: *"The Story So Far"* (from issue 12), reprinted in **AKIKO VOL. 2**; *"Abnug & the Gope Fish"* (issue 14) and *"A Nice, Long Walk"* (issue 25) reprinted in **AKIKO VOL. 3**; *"A 'Kiko Xmas"* (issue 21), *"East Meets West"* (issue 24), and *"24 Ways to Draw Poog"* (issue 31), reprinted in **AKIKO VOL. 4**; and *"Small World"* (issue 28), reprinted in **AKIKO VOL. 5**.

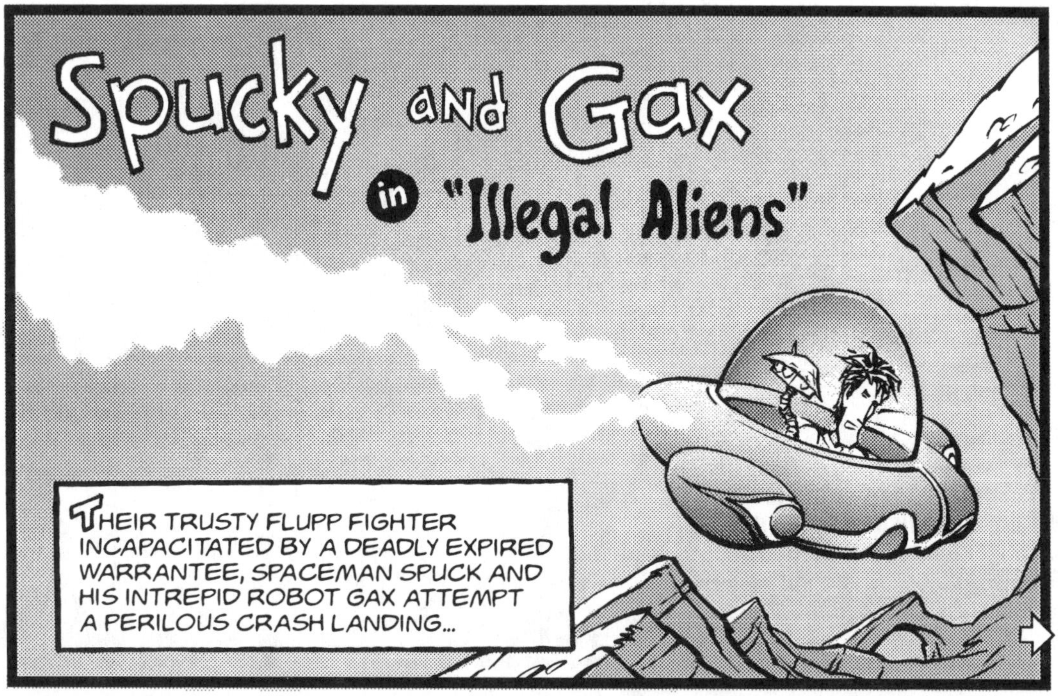
Spucky and Gax
in "Illegal Aliens"
THEIR TRUSTY FLUPP FIGHTER INCAPACITATED BY A DEADLY EXPIRED WARRANTEE, SPACEMAN SPUCK AND HIS INTREPID ROBOT GAX ATTEMPT A PERILOUS CRASH LANDING...

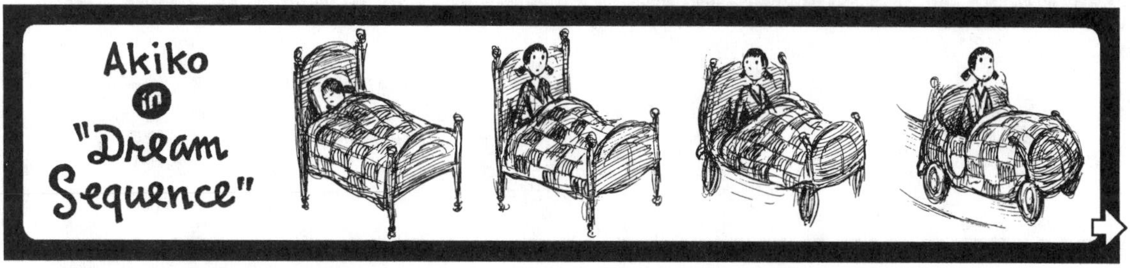
Akiko
in
"Dream Sequence"

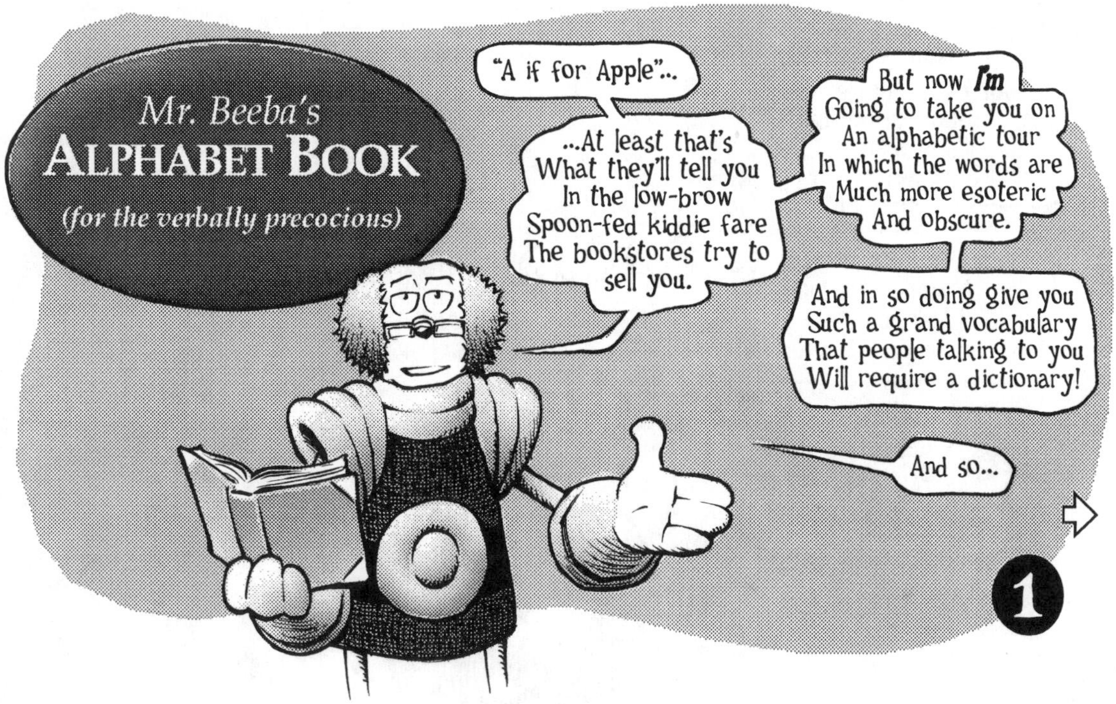
Mr. Beeba's
ALPHABET BOOK
(for the verbally precocious)
"A if for Apple"..
...At least that's What they'll tell you In the low-brow Spoon-fed kiddie fare The bookstores try to sell you.
But now I'm Going to take you on An alphabetic tour In which the words are Much more esoteric And obscure.
And in so doing give you Such a grand vocabulary That people talking to you Will require a dictionary!
And so...

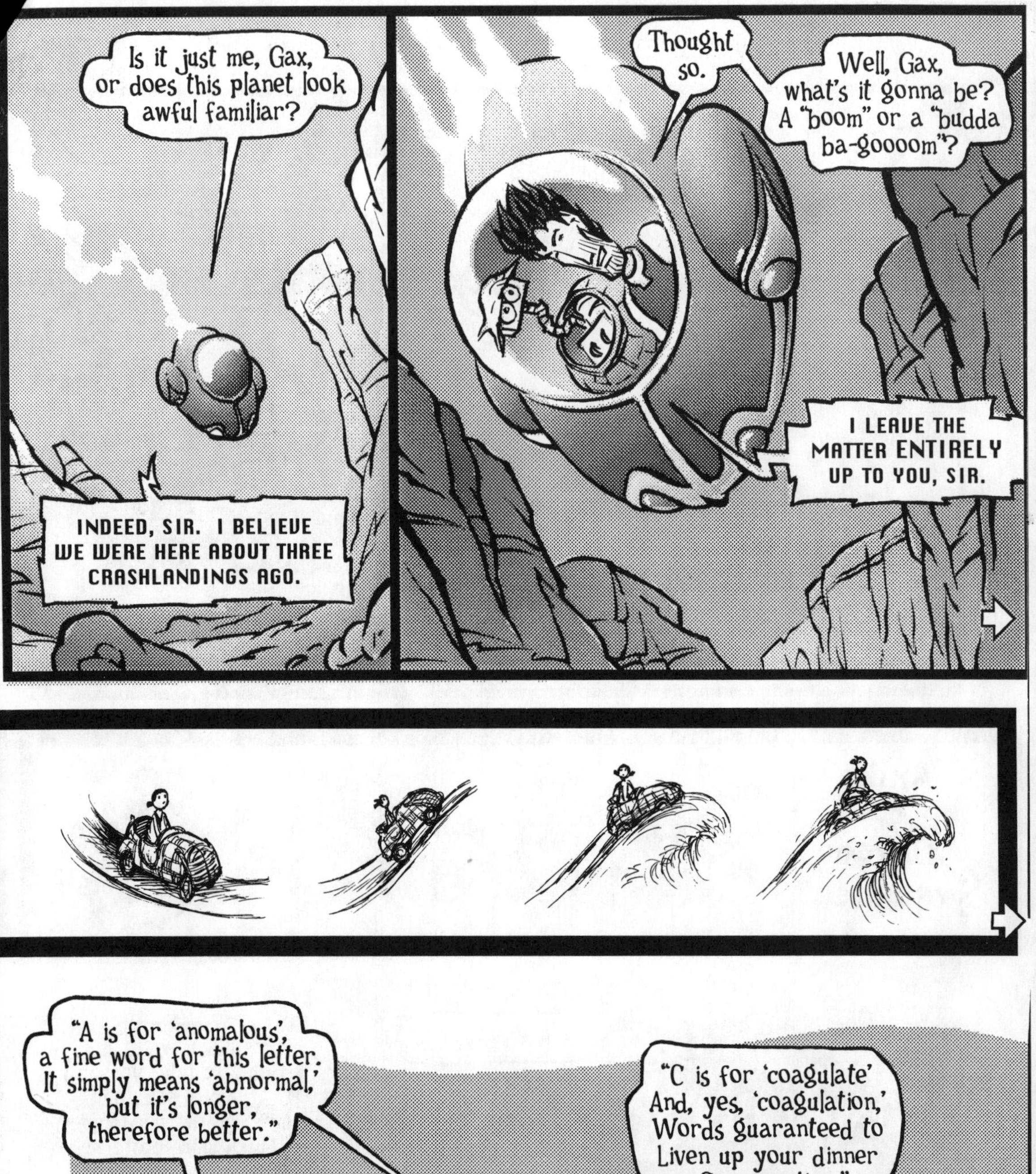

Is it just me, Gax, or does this planet look awful familiar?
INDEED, SIR. I BELIEVE WE WERE HERE ABOUT THREE CRASHLANDINGS AGO.
Thought so.
Well, Gax, what's it gonna be? A "boom" or a "budda ba-goooom"?
I LEAVE THE MATTER ENTIRELY UP TO YOU, SIR.
"A is for 'anomalous', a fine word for this letter. It simply means 'abnormal,' but it's longer, therefore better."
"B is for 'bituminous,' a most impressive word. I learned it in the second grade."
"All right, perhaps the third."
"C is for 'coagulate' And, yes, 'coagulation,' Words guaranteed to Liven up your dinner Conversation."
"And D is for 'dreptilious,' A word you do not know. How could you? After all, I made it up an hour ago."

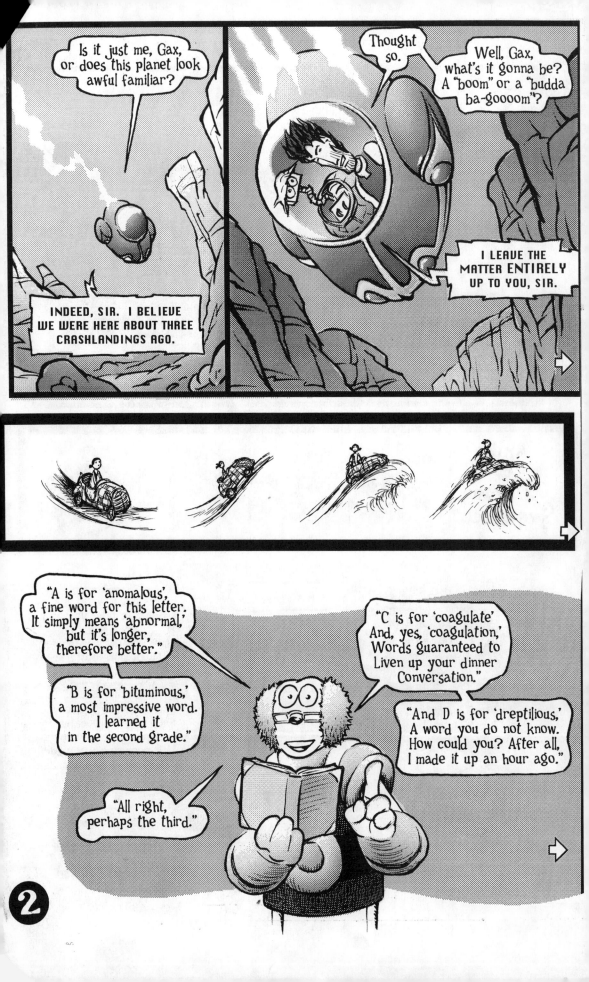

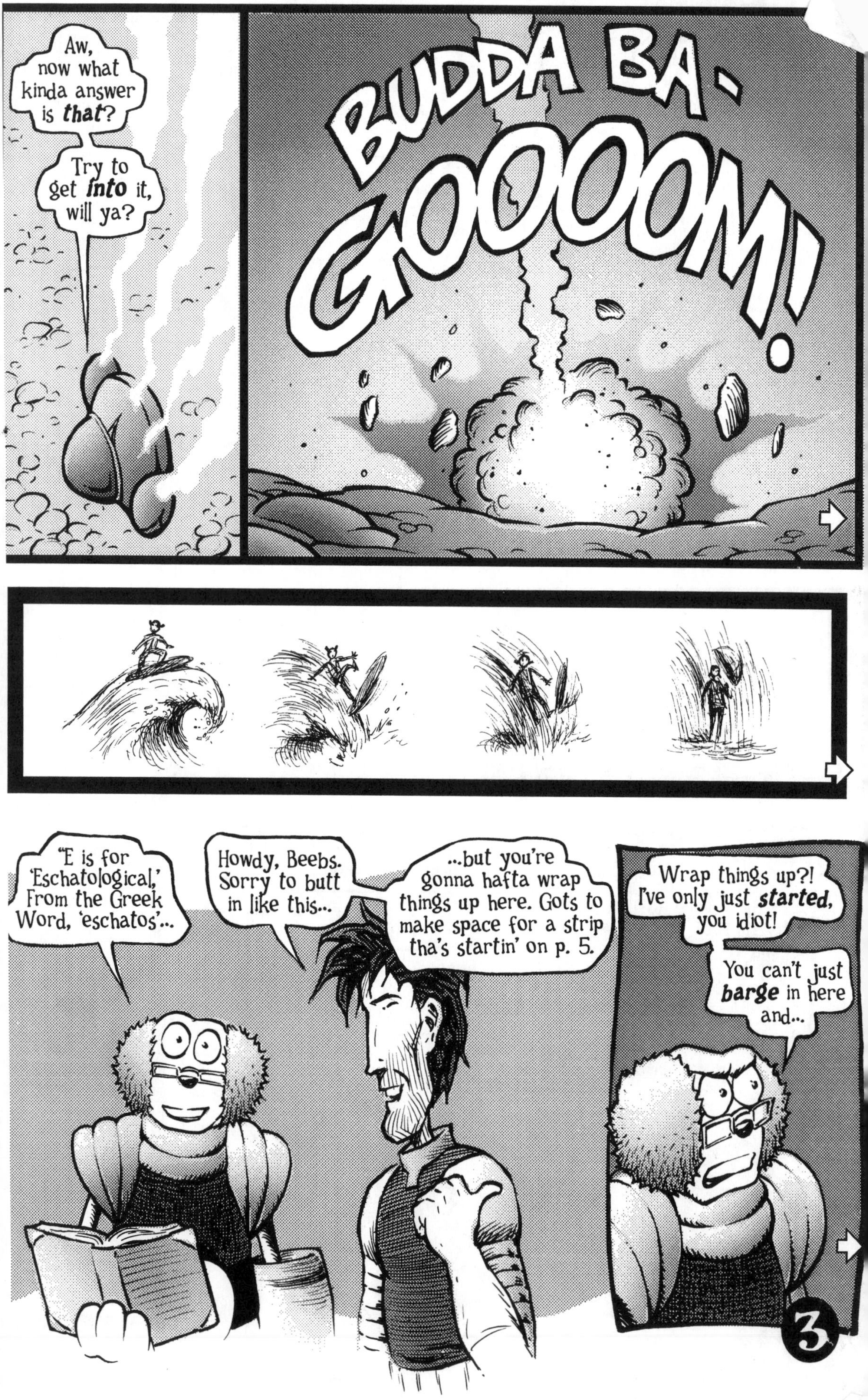

Aw, now what kinda answer is *that*?
Try to get *into* it, will ya?
BUDDA BA-GOOOOM!
"E is for 'Eschatological,' From the Greek Word, 'eschatos'...
Howdy, Beebs. Sorry to butt in like this...
...but you're gonna hafta wrap things up here. Gots to make space for a strip tha's startin' on p. 5.
Wrap things up?! I've only just *started*, you idiot!
You can't just *barge* in here and...

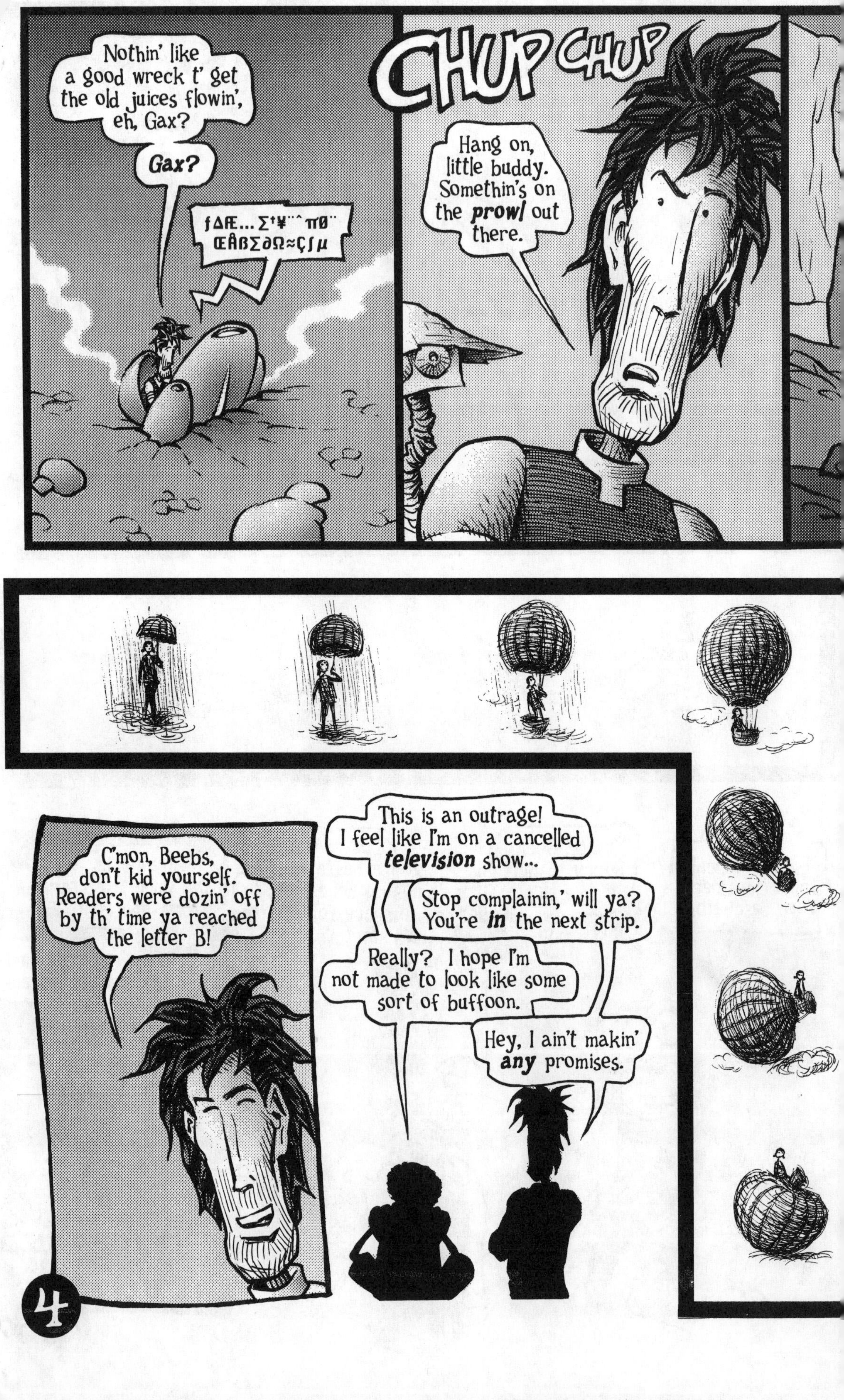

Nothin' like a good wreck t' get the old juices flowin', eh, Gax?
Gax?
ƒ∆Æ... Σ†¥¨ˆπØ¨ ŒÅßΣ∂Ω≈Ç∫µ
CHUP CHUP
Hang on, little buddy. Somethin's on the prowl out there.
C'mon, Beebs, don't kid yourself. Readers were dozin' off by th' time ya reached the letter B!
This is an outrage! I feel like I'm on a cancelled television show...
Stop complainin,' will ya? You're in the next strip.
Really? I hope I'm not made to look like some sort of buffoon.
Hey, I ain't makin' any promises.

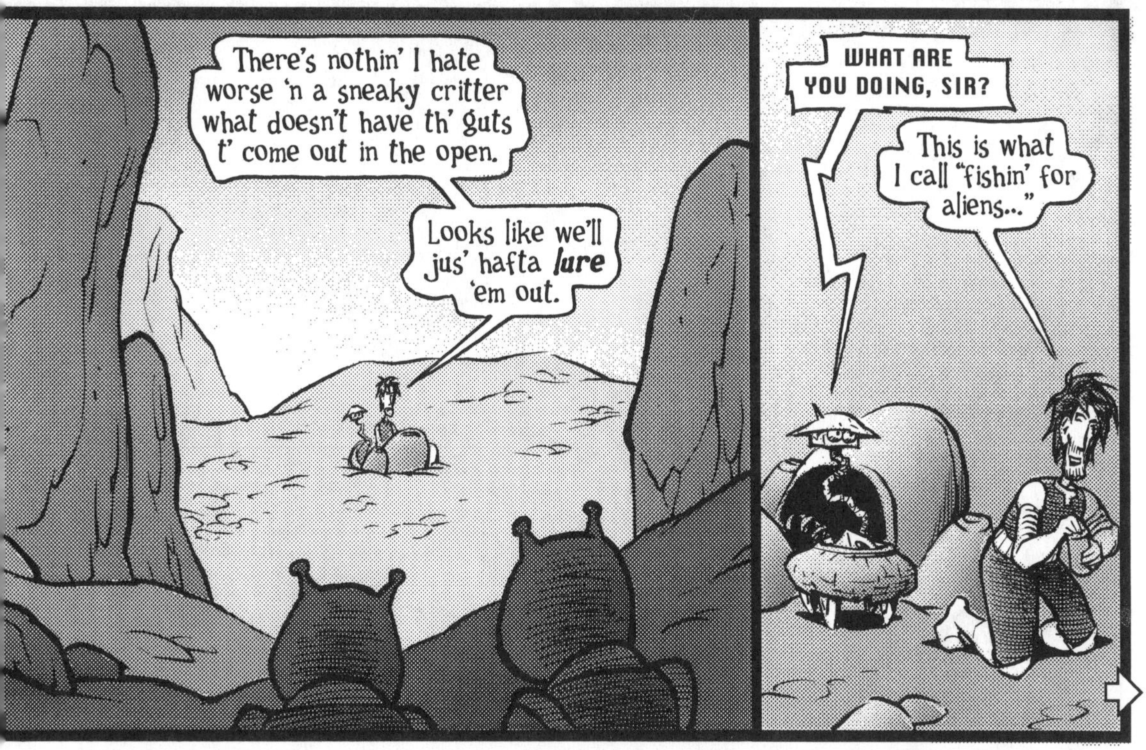
There's nothin' I hate worse 'n a sneaky critter what doesn't have th' guts t' come out in the open.
Looks like we'll jus' hafta *lure* 'em out.
WHAT ARE YOU DOING, SIR?
This is what I call "fishin' for aliens..."

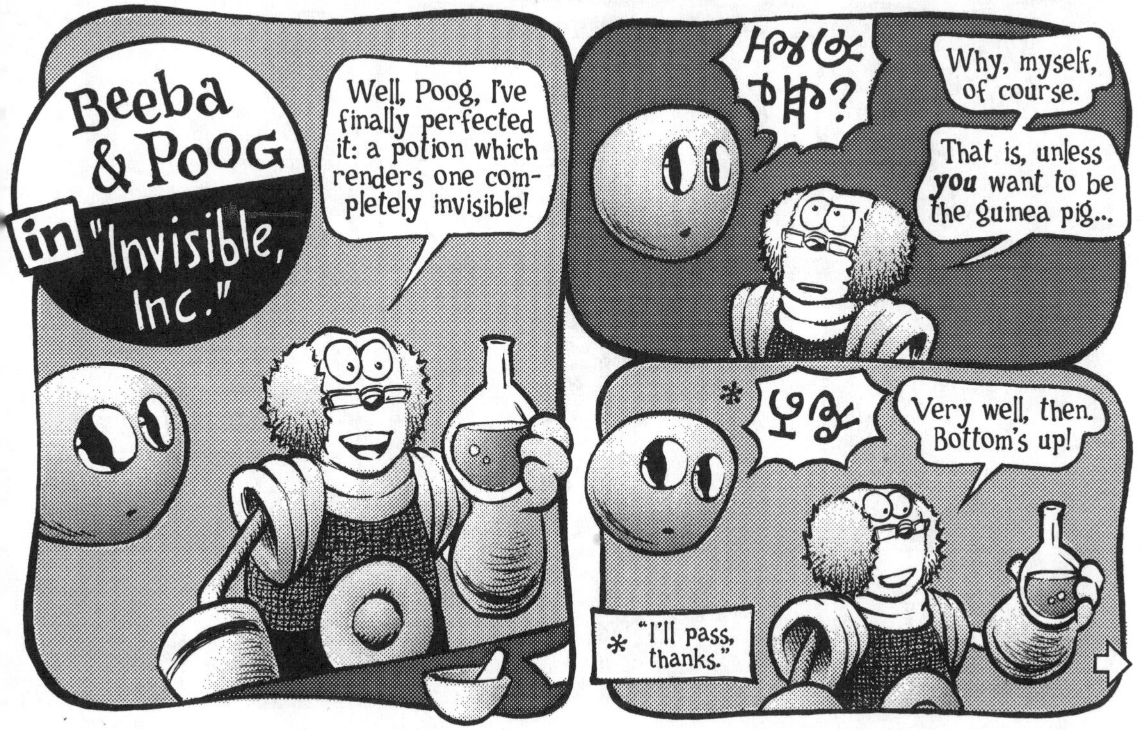
Beeba & Poog in "Invisible, Inc."
Well, Poog, I've finally perfected it: a potion which renders one completely invisible!
Why, myself, of course.
That is, unless *you* want to be the guinea pig...
Very well, then. Bottom's up!
* "I'll pass, thanks."

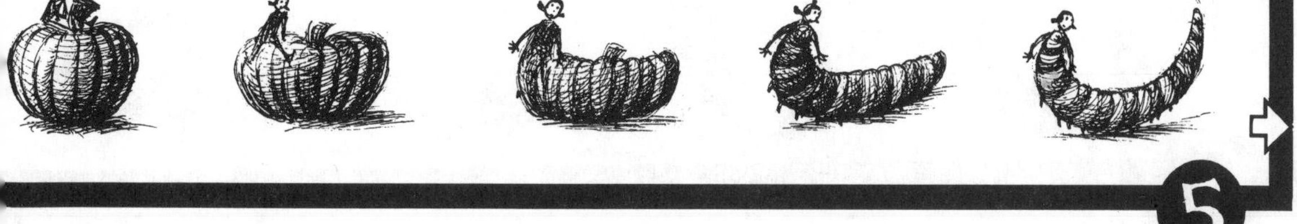

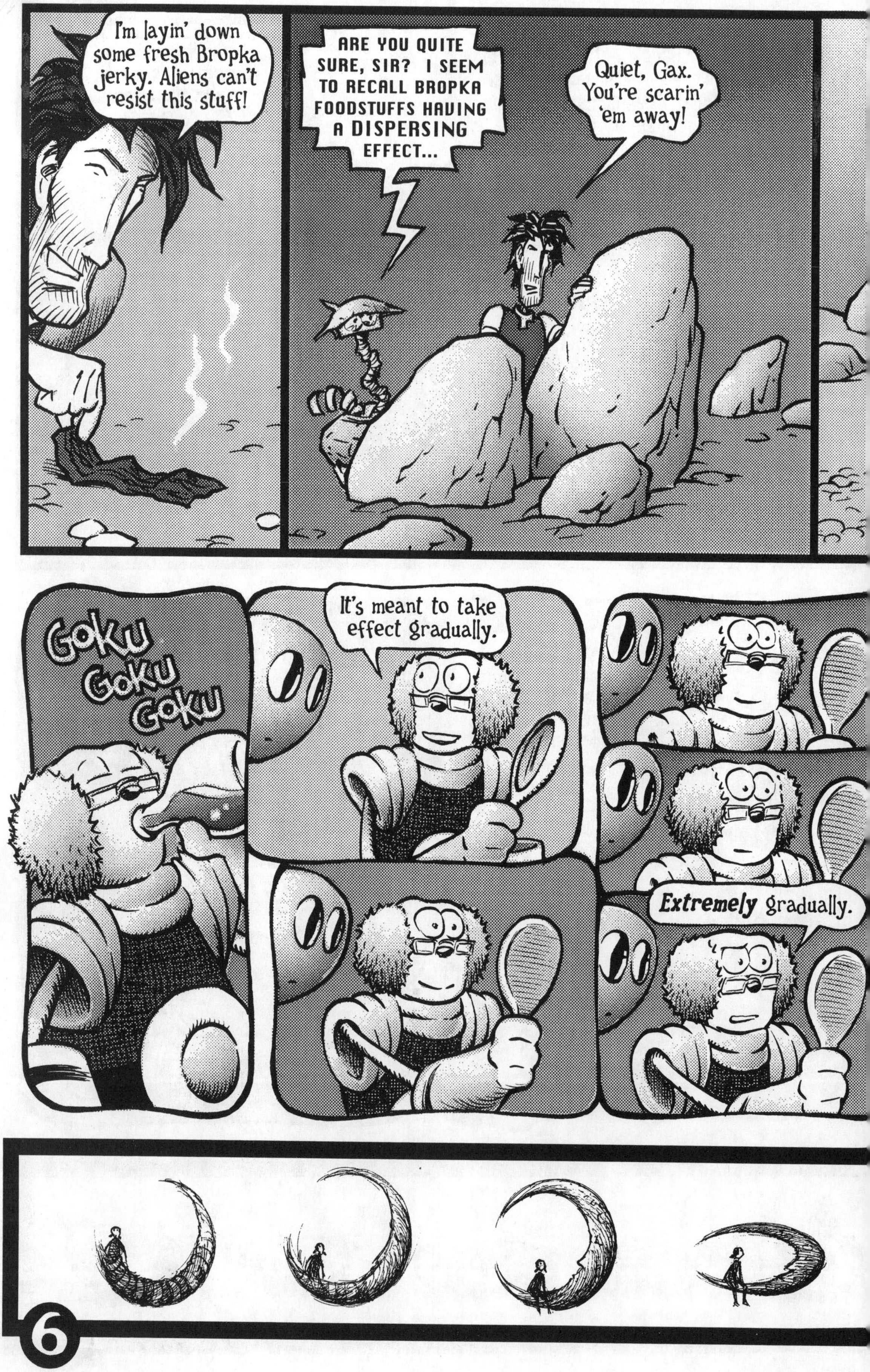
I'm layin' down some fresh Bropka jerky. Aliens can't resist this stuff!
ARE YOU QUITE SURE, SIR? I SEEM TO RECALL BROPKA FOODSTUFFS HAVING A DISPERSING EFFECT...
Quiet, Gax. You're scarin' 'em away!
GOKU GOKU GOKU
It's meant to take effect gradually.
Extremely gradually.

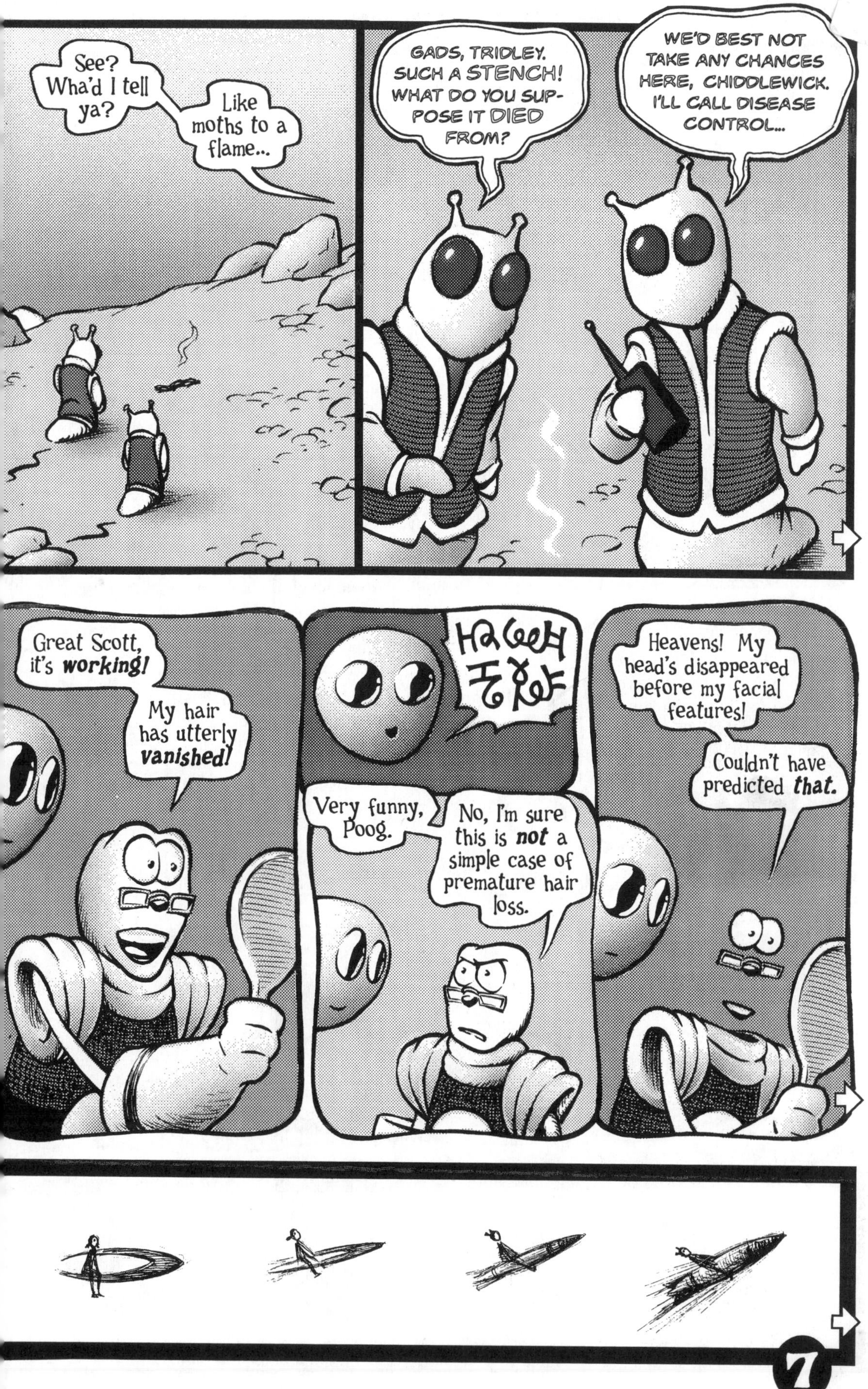

See? What'd I tell ya?
Like moths to a flame...
GADS, TRIDLEY. SUCH A STENCH! WHAT DO YOU SUPPOSE IT DIED FROM?
WE'D BEST NOT TAKE ANY CHANCES HERE, CHIDDLEWICK. I'LL CALL DISEASE CONTROL...
Great Scott, it's **working!**
My hair has utterly ***vanished!***
Very funny, Poog.
No, I'm sure this is ***not*** a simple case of premature hair loss.
Heavens! My head's disappeared before my facial features!
Couldn't have predicted ***that.***

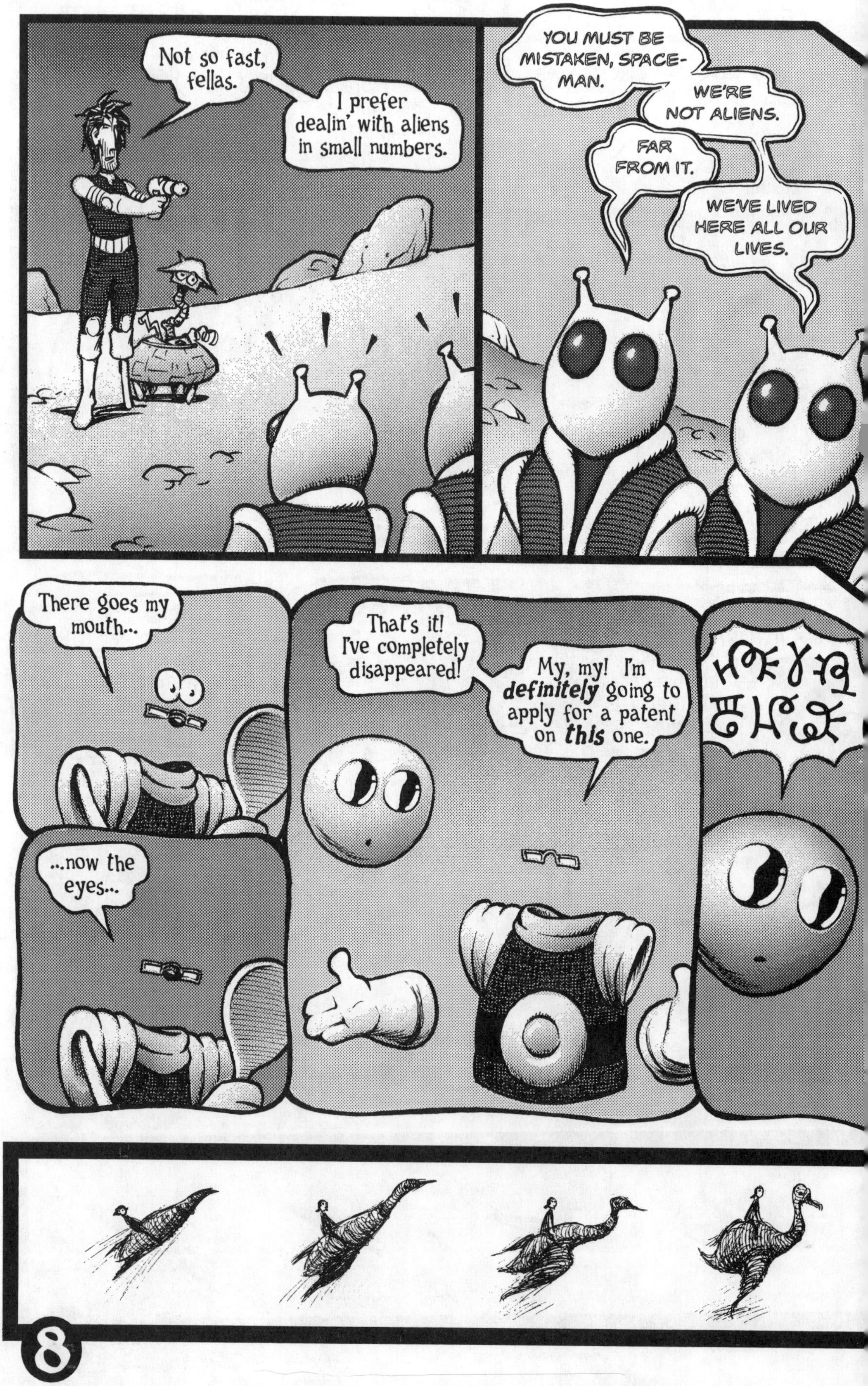
Not so fast, fellas.
I prefer dealin' with aliens in small numbers.
YOU MUST BE MISTAKEN, SPACE-MAN.
WE'RE NOT ALIENS.
FAR FROM IT.
WE'VE LIVED HERE ALL OUR LIVES.
There goes my mouth...
...now the eyes...
That's it! I've completely disappeared!
My, my! I'm **definitely** going to apply for a patent on **this** one.

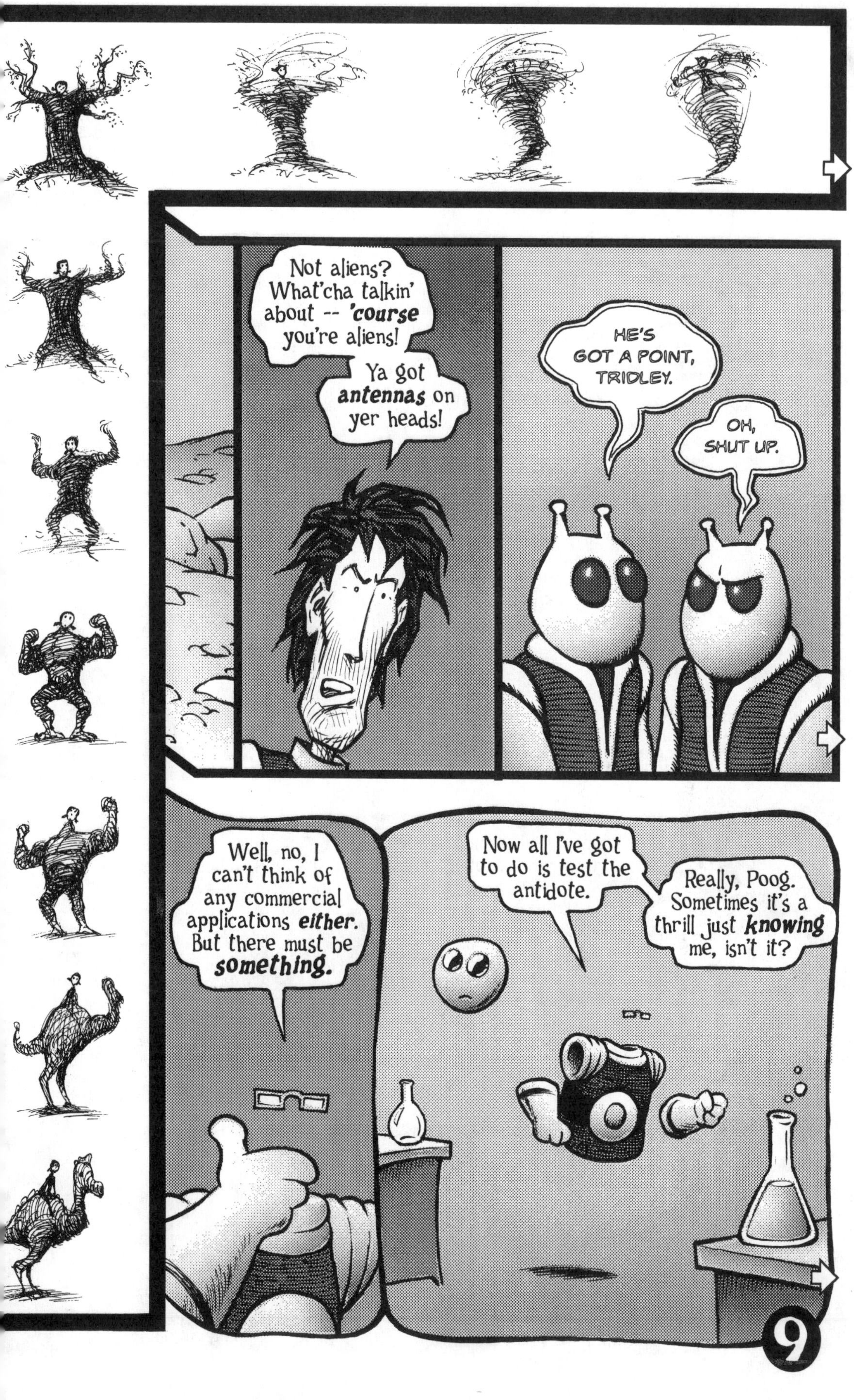

Not aliens? What'cha talkin' about -- **'course** you're aliens!
Ya got **antennas** on yer heads!
HE'S GOT A POINT, TRIDLEY.
OH, SHUT UP.
Well, no, I can't think of any commercial applications **either**. But there must be **something.**
Now all I've got to do is test the antidote.
Really, Poog. Sometimes it's a thrill just **knowing** me, isn't it?

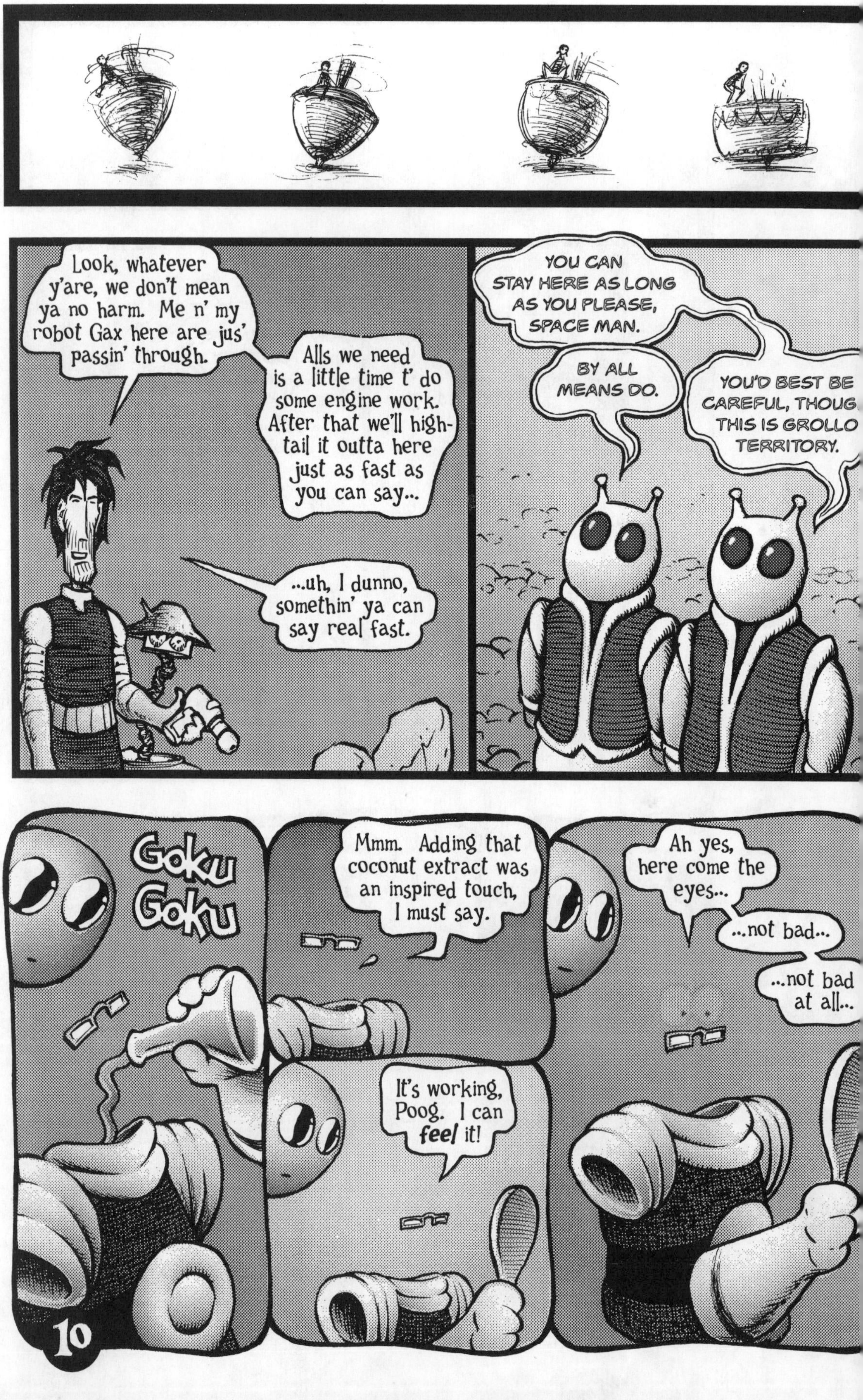

Look, whatever y'are, we don't mean ya no harm. Me n' my robot Gax here are jus' passin' through.
Alls we need is a little time t' do some engine work. After that we'll high-tail it outta here just as fast as you can say...
...uh, I dunno, somethin' ya can say real fast.
YOU CAN STAY HERE AS LONG AS YOU PLEASE, SPACE MAN.
BY ALL MEANS DO.
YOU'D BEST BE CAREFUL, THOUG THIS IS GROLLO TERRITORY.
Goku Goku
Mmm. Adding that coconut extract was an inspired touch, I must say.
It's working, Poog. I can *feel* it!
Ah yes, here come the eyes...
...not bad...
...not bad at all...

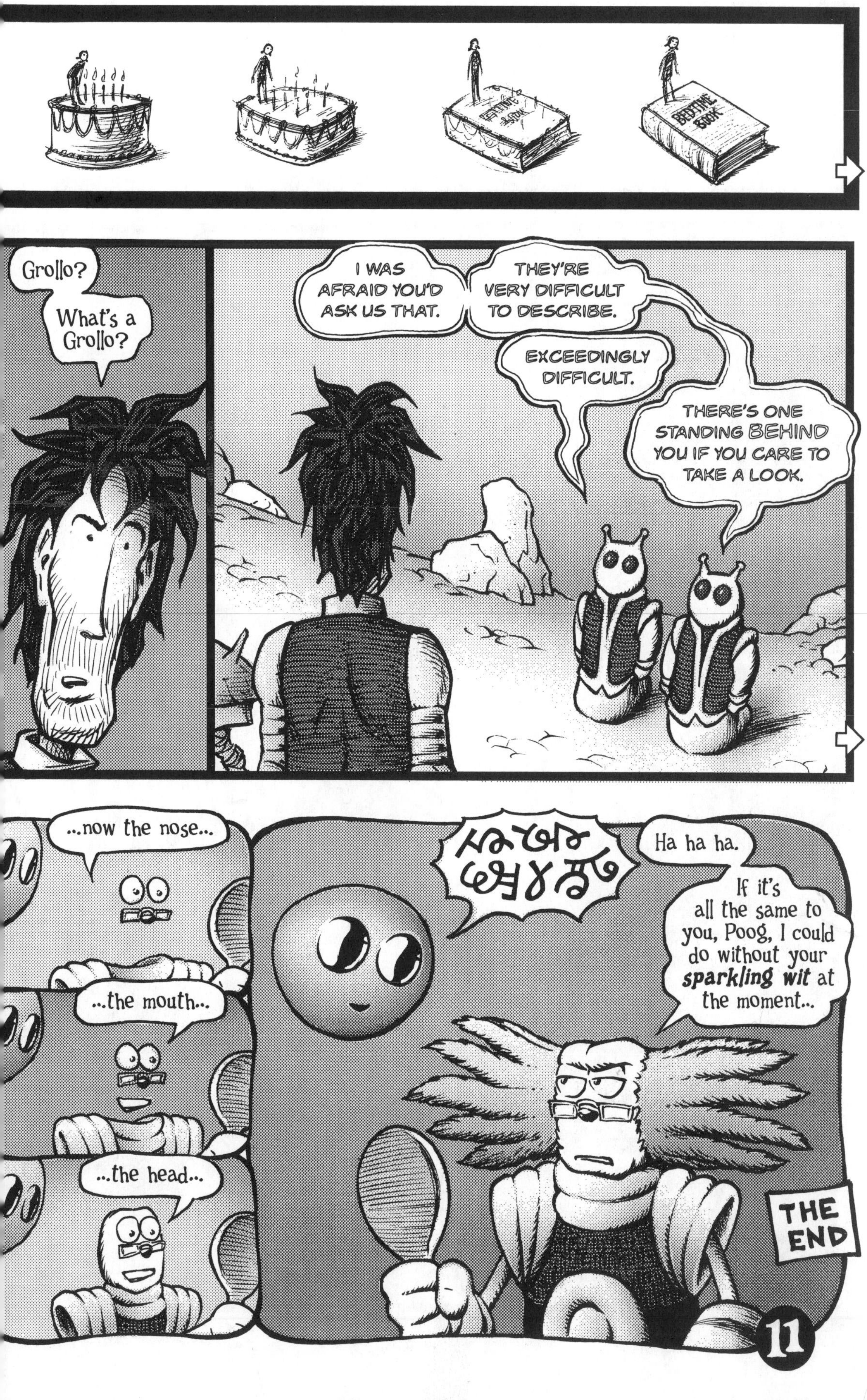
BEDTIME BOOK
Grollo?
What's a Grollo?
I WAS AFRAID YOU'D ASK US THAT.
THEY'RE VERY DIFFICULT TO DESCRIBE.
EXCEEDINGLY DIFFICULT.
THERE'S ONE STANDING BEHIND YOU IF YOU CARE TO TAKE A LOOK.
...now the nose...
...the mouth...
...the head...
Ha ha ha.
If it's all the same to you, Poog, I could do without your *sparkling wit* at the moment...
THE END

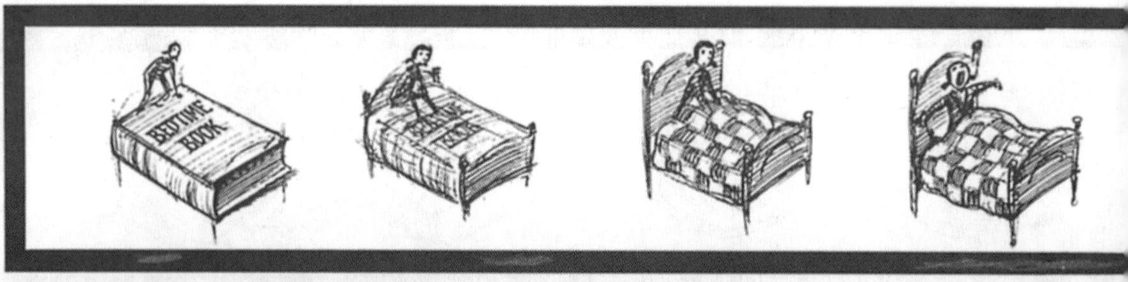
BEDTIME BOOK

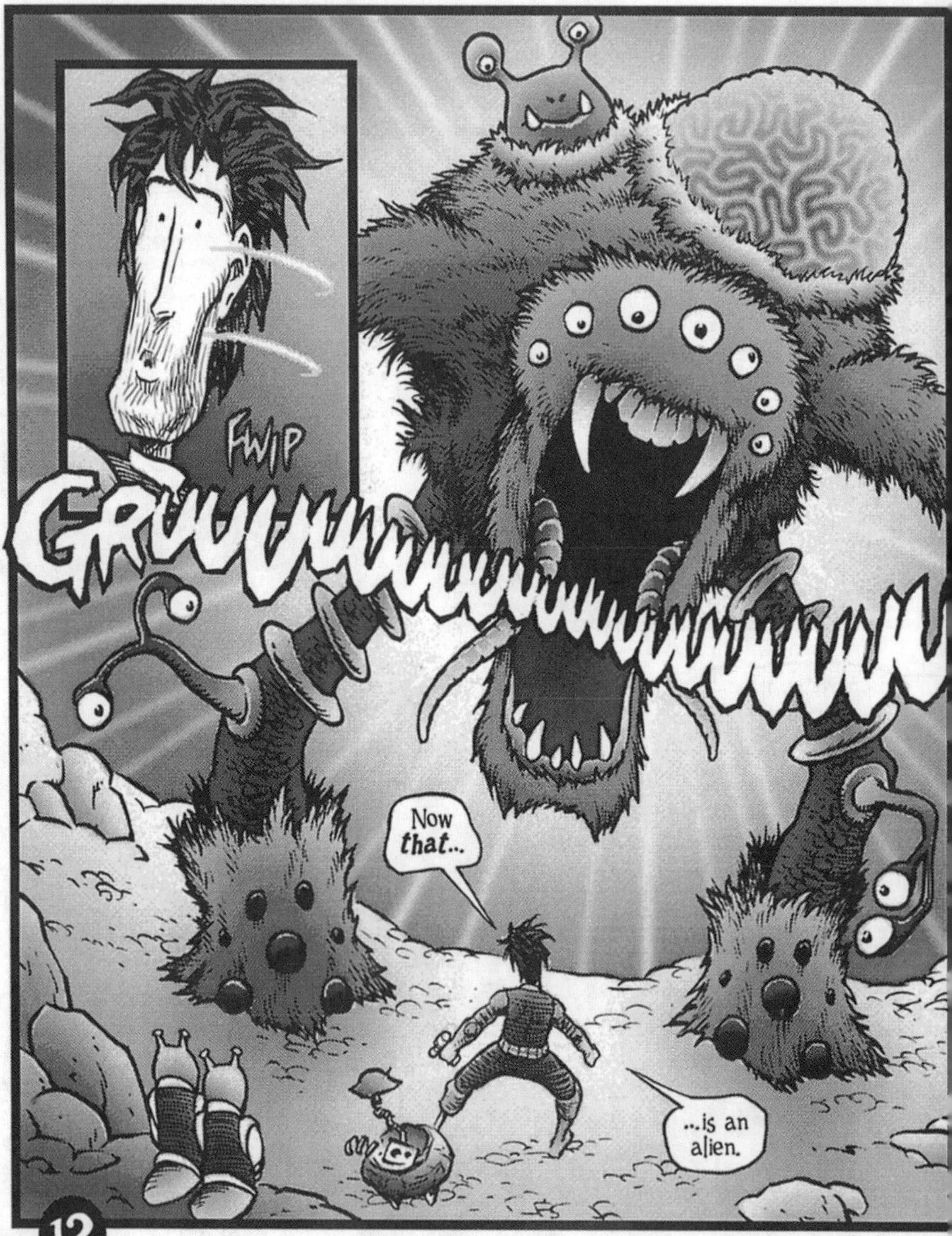
FWIP
GRUUUUUUUUUUUUUUUUUUU
Now that...
...is an alien.

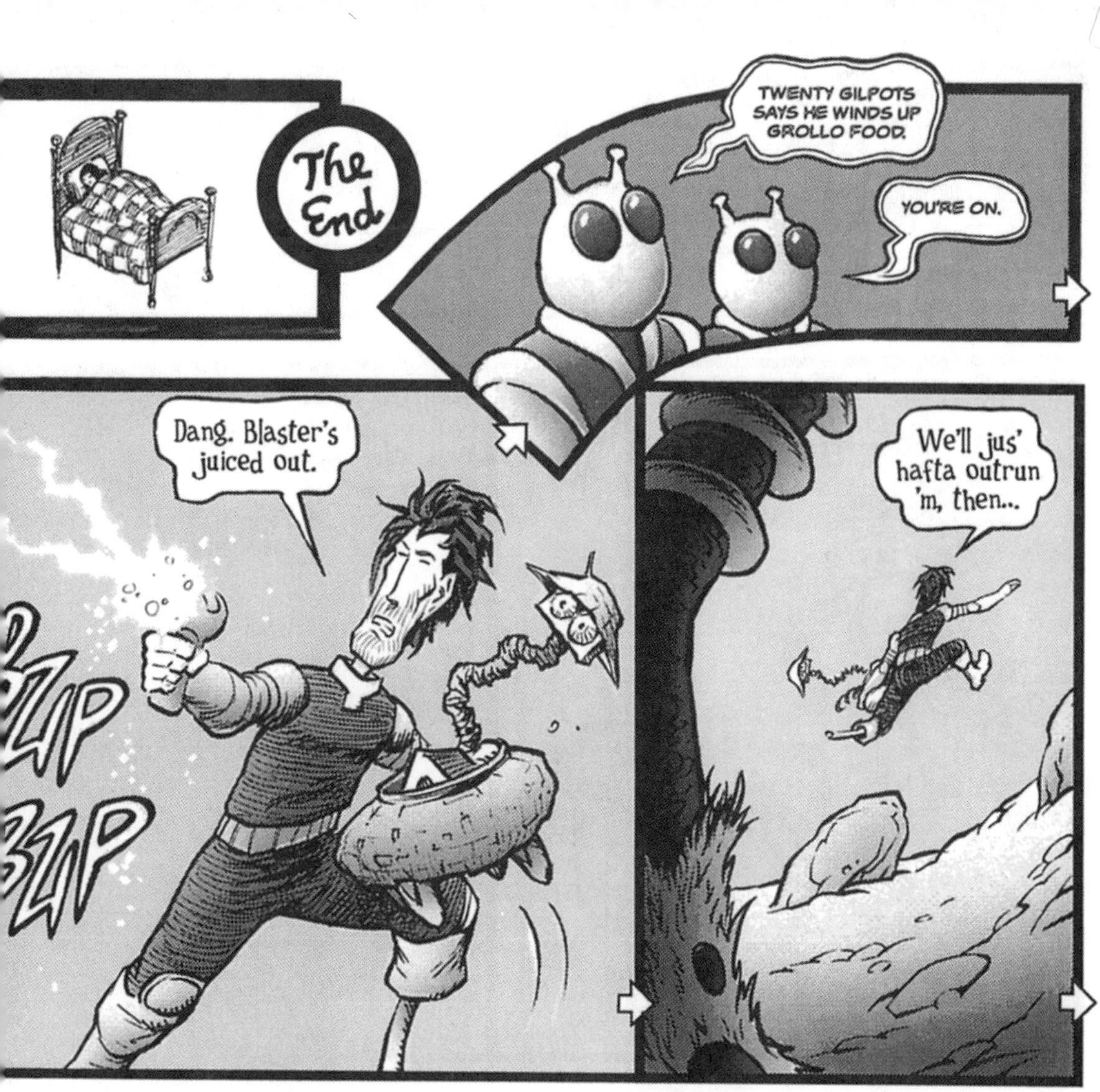

The End
TWENTY GILPOTS SAYS HE WINDS UP GROLLO FOOD.
YOU'RE ON.
Dang. Blaster's juiced out.
We'll jus' hafta outrun 'm, then...

Akiko & P.Q. Goybi in "The Old Storage Shed"

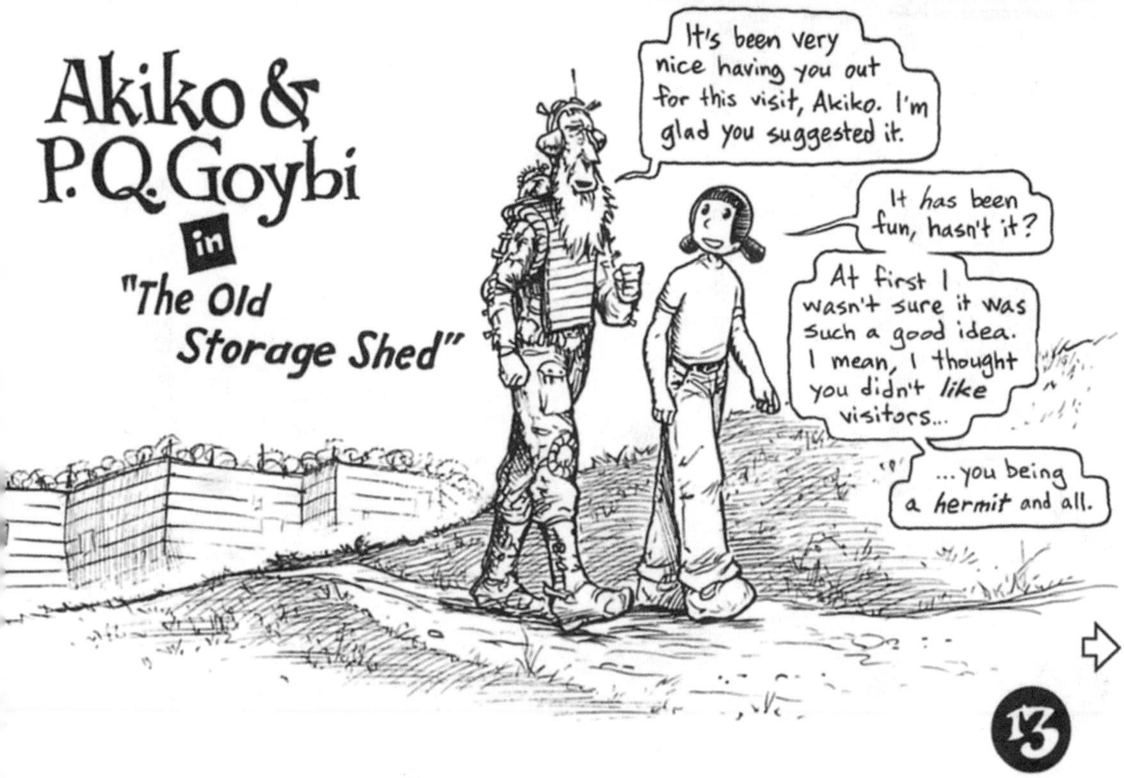

It's been very nice having you out for this visit, Akiko. I'm glad you suggested it.
It *has* been fun, hasn't it?
At first I wasn't sure it was such a good idea. I mean, I thought you didn't *like* visitors...
...you being a *hermit* and all.

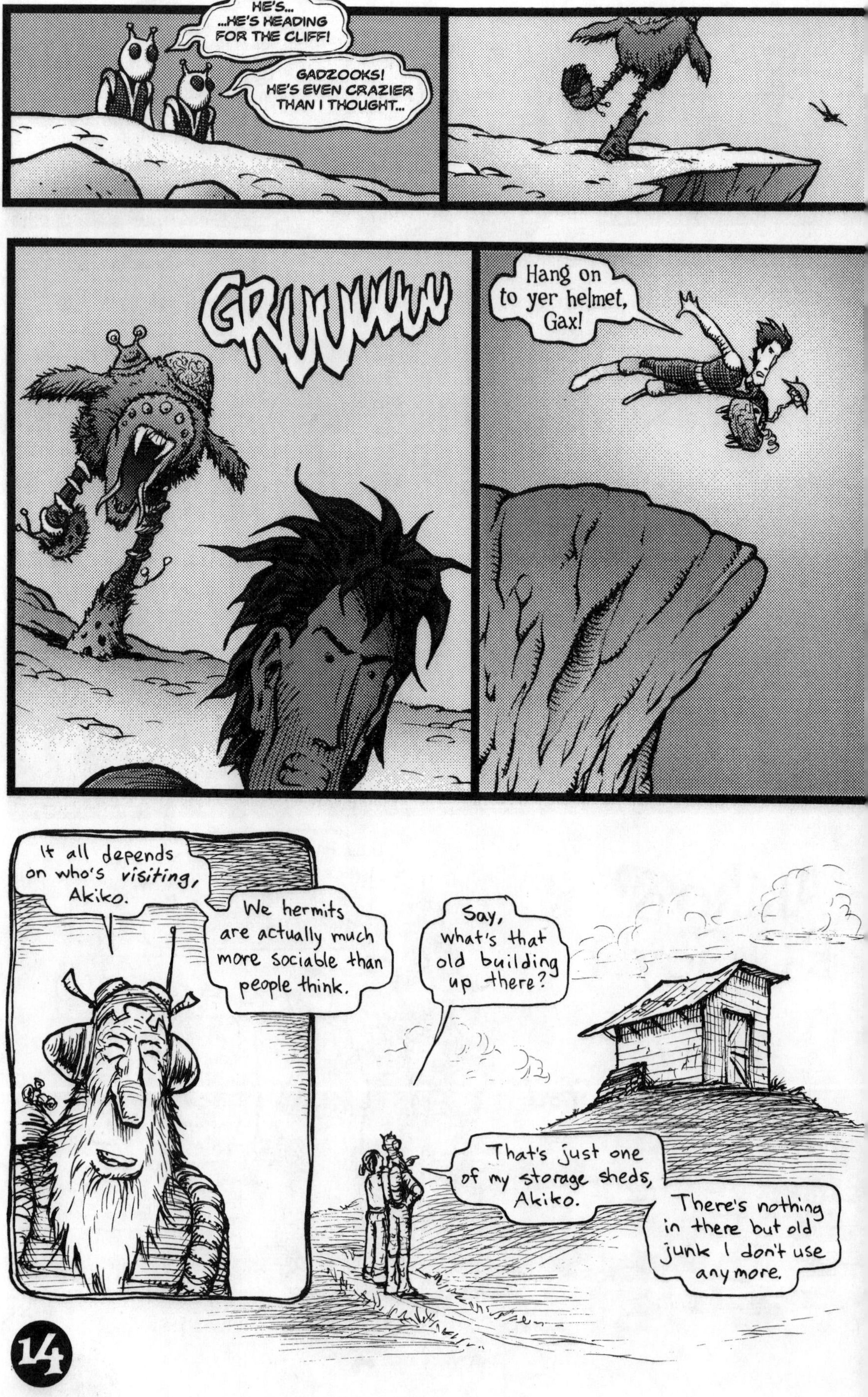
HE'S... ...HE'S HEADING FOR THE CLIFF!
GADZOOKS! HE'S EVEN CRAZIER THAN I THOUGHT...
GRUUUUU
Hang on to yer helmet, Gax!
It all depends on who's visiting, Akiko.
We hermits are actually much more sociable than people think.
Say, what's that old building up there?
That's just one of my storage sheds, Akiko.
There's nothing in there but old junk I don't use anymore.

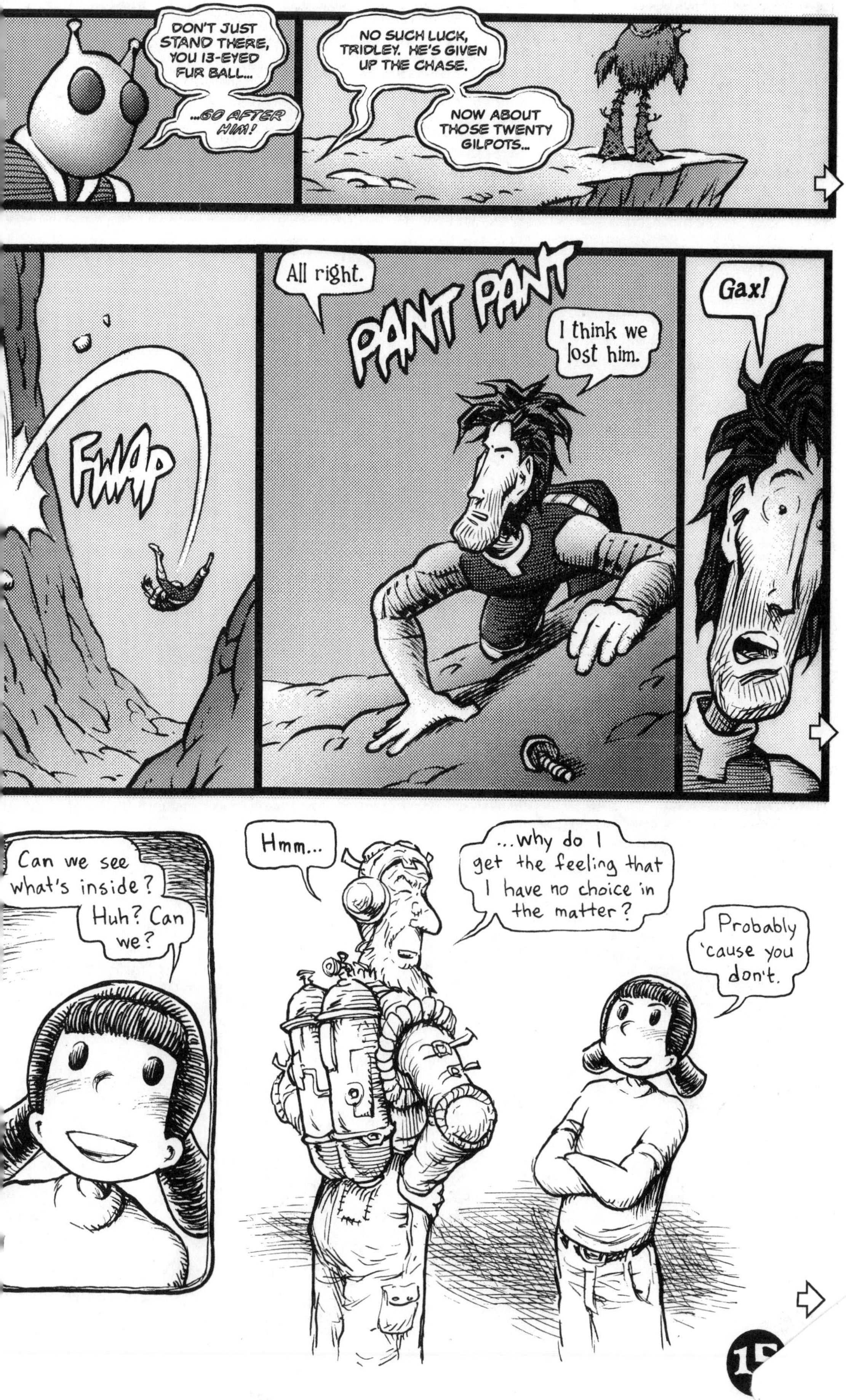
DON'T JUST STAND THERE, YOU 13-EYED FUR BALL...
...GO AFTER HIM!
NO SUCH LUCK, TRIDLEY. HE'S GIVEN UP THE CHASE.
NOW ABOUT THOSE TWENTY GILPOTS...
FWAP
All right.
PANT PANT
I think we lost him.
Gax!
Can we see what's inside?
Huh? Can we?
Hmm...
...why do I get the feeling that I have no choice in the matter?
Probably 'cause you don't.

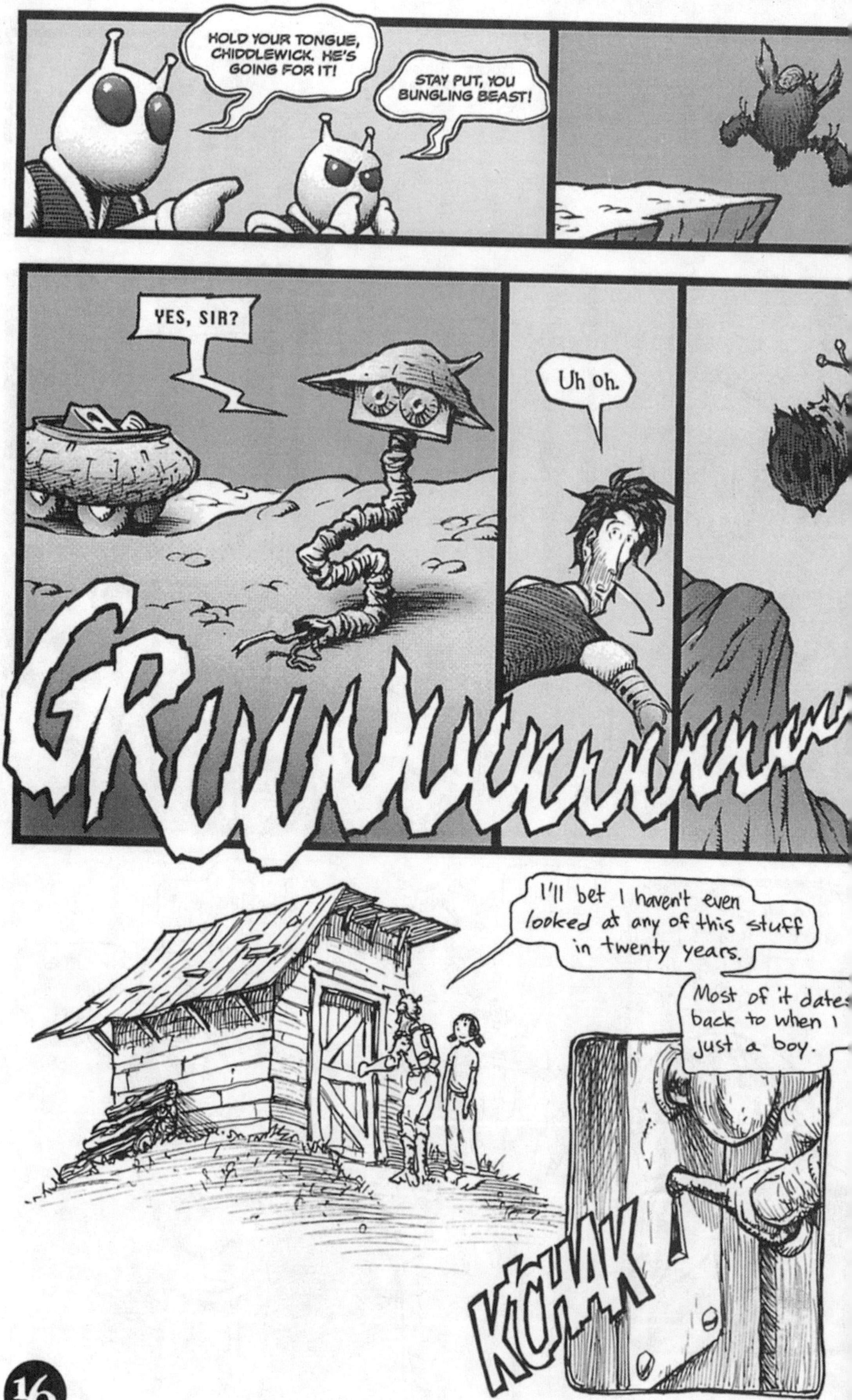
HOLD YOUR TONGUE, CHIDDLEWICK. HE'S GOING FOR IT!
STAY PUT, YOU BUNGLING BEAST!
YES, SIR?
Uh oh.
GRUUUUUUUUU
I'll bet I haven't even looked at any of this stuff in twenty years.
Most of it dates back to when I just a boy.
KCHAK

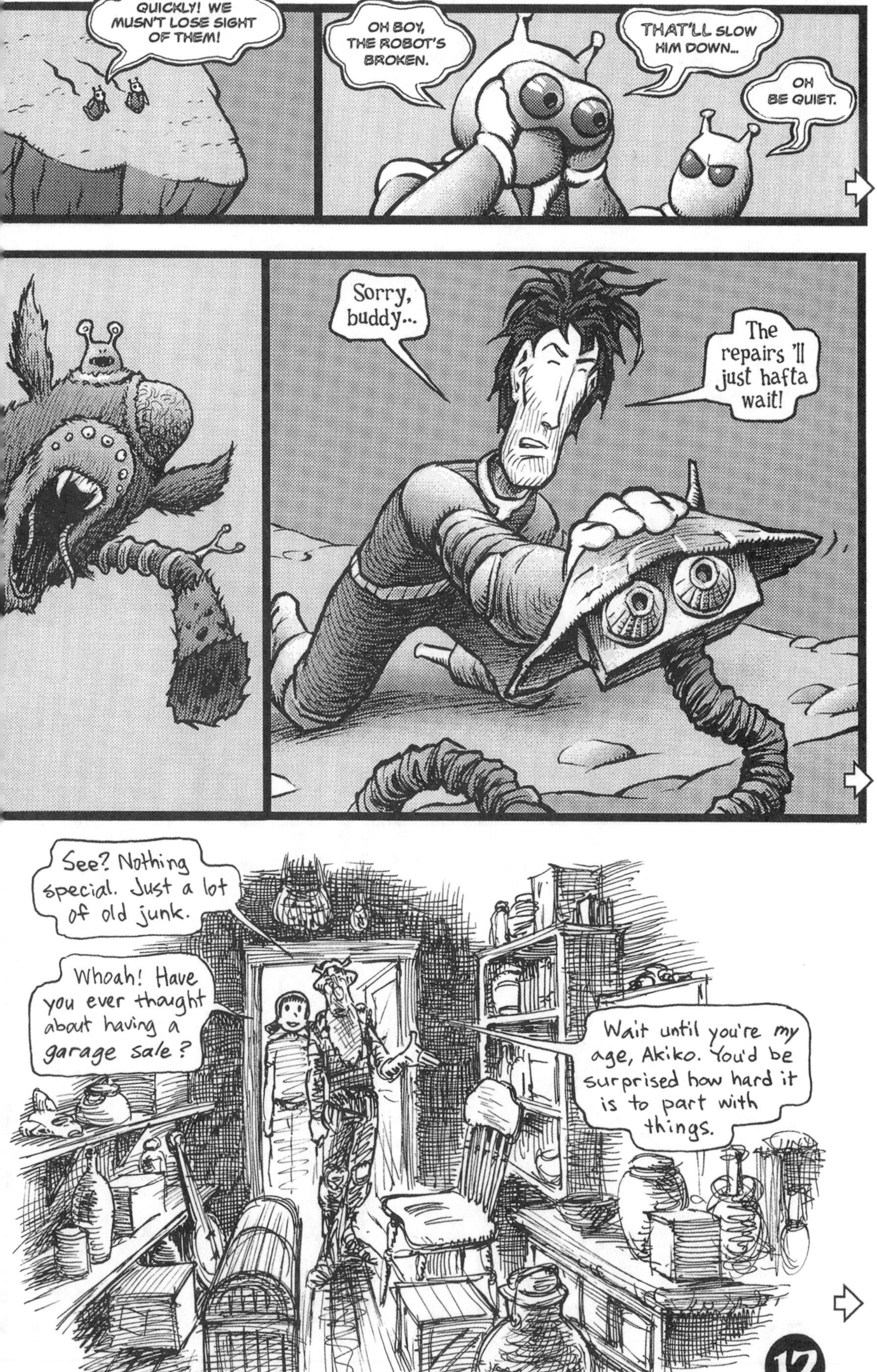
QUICKLY! WE MUSN'T LOSE SIGHT OF THEM!
OH BOY, THE ROBOT'S BROKEN.
THAT'LL SLOW HIM DOWN...
OH BE QUIET.
Sorry, buddy...
The repairs 'll just hafta wait!
See? Nothing special. Just a lot of old junk.
Whoah! Have you ever thought about having a garage sale?
Wait until you're my age, Akiko. You'd be surprised how hard it is to part with things.

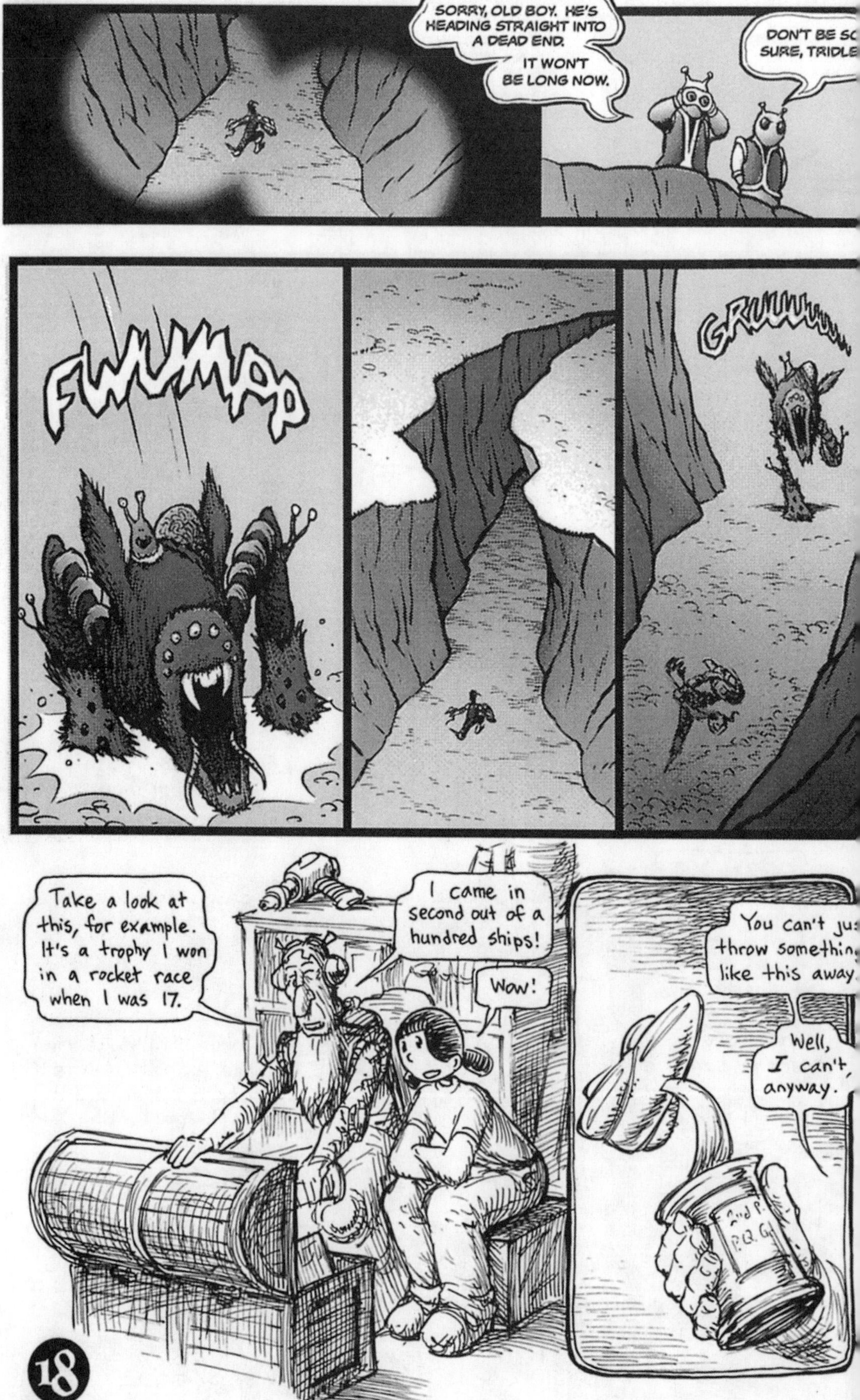

SORRY, OLD BOY. HE'S HEADING STRAIGHT INTO A DEAD END.
IT WON'T BE LONG NOW.
DON'T BE SO SURE, TRIDLE
FWUMP
GRUUUU
Take a look at this, for example. It's a trophy I won in a rocket race when I was 17.
I came in second out of a hundred ships!
Wow!
You can't just throw something like this away.
Well, I can't, anyway.

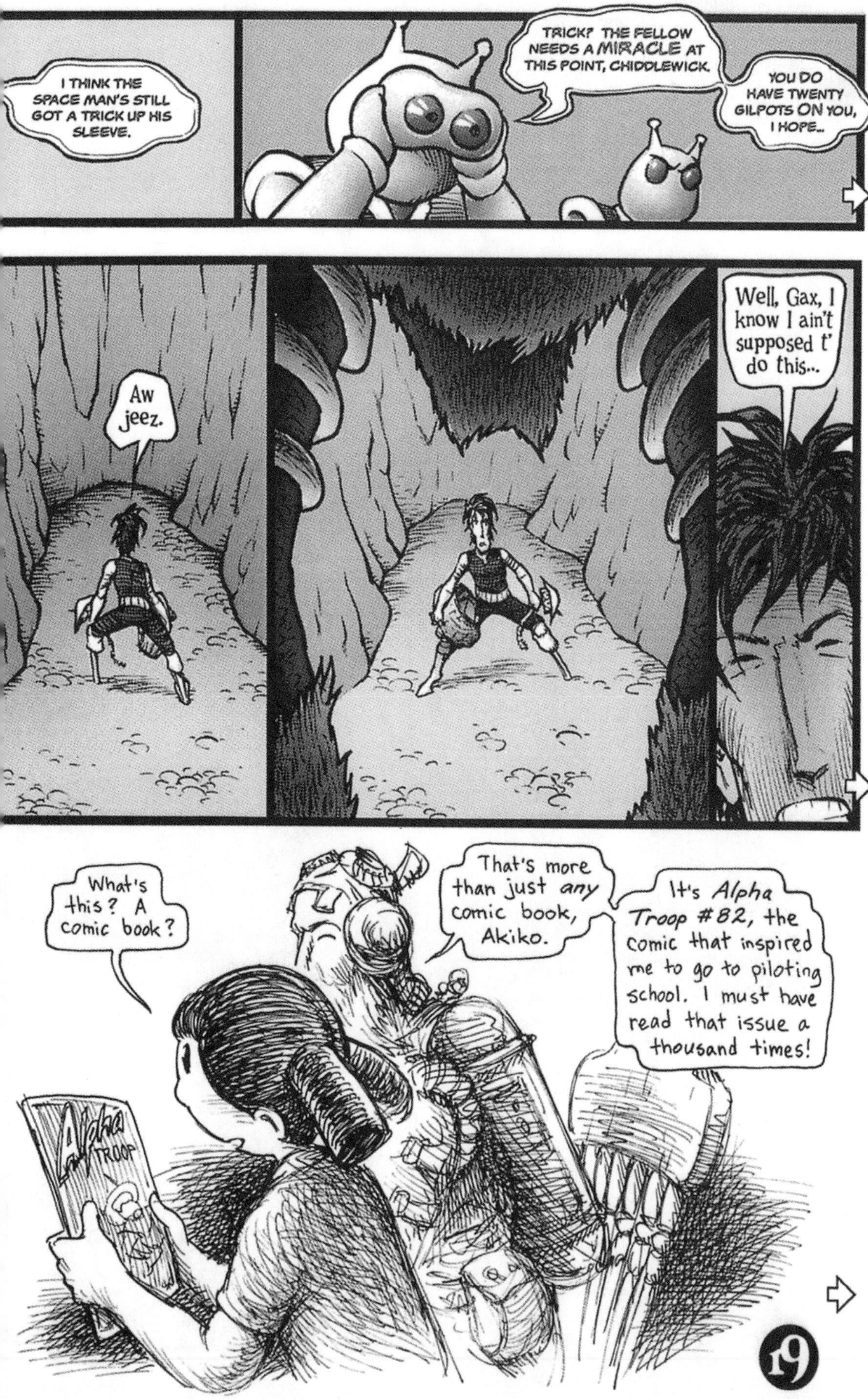
I THINK THE SPACE MAN'S STILL GOT A TRICK UP HIS SLEEVE.
TRICK? THE FELLOW NEEDS A MIRACLE AT THIS POINT, CHIDDLEWICK.
YOU DO HAVE TWENTY GILPOTS ON YOU, I HOPE..
Aw jeez.
Well, Gax, I know I ain't supposed t' do this..
What's this? A comic book?
That's more than just any comic book, Akiko.
It's Alpha Troop #82, the comic that inspired me to go to piloting school. I must have read that issue a thousand times!
Alpha TROOP

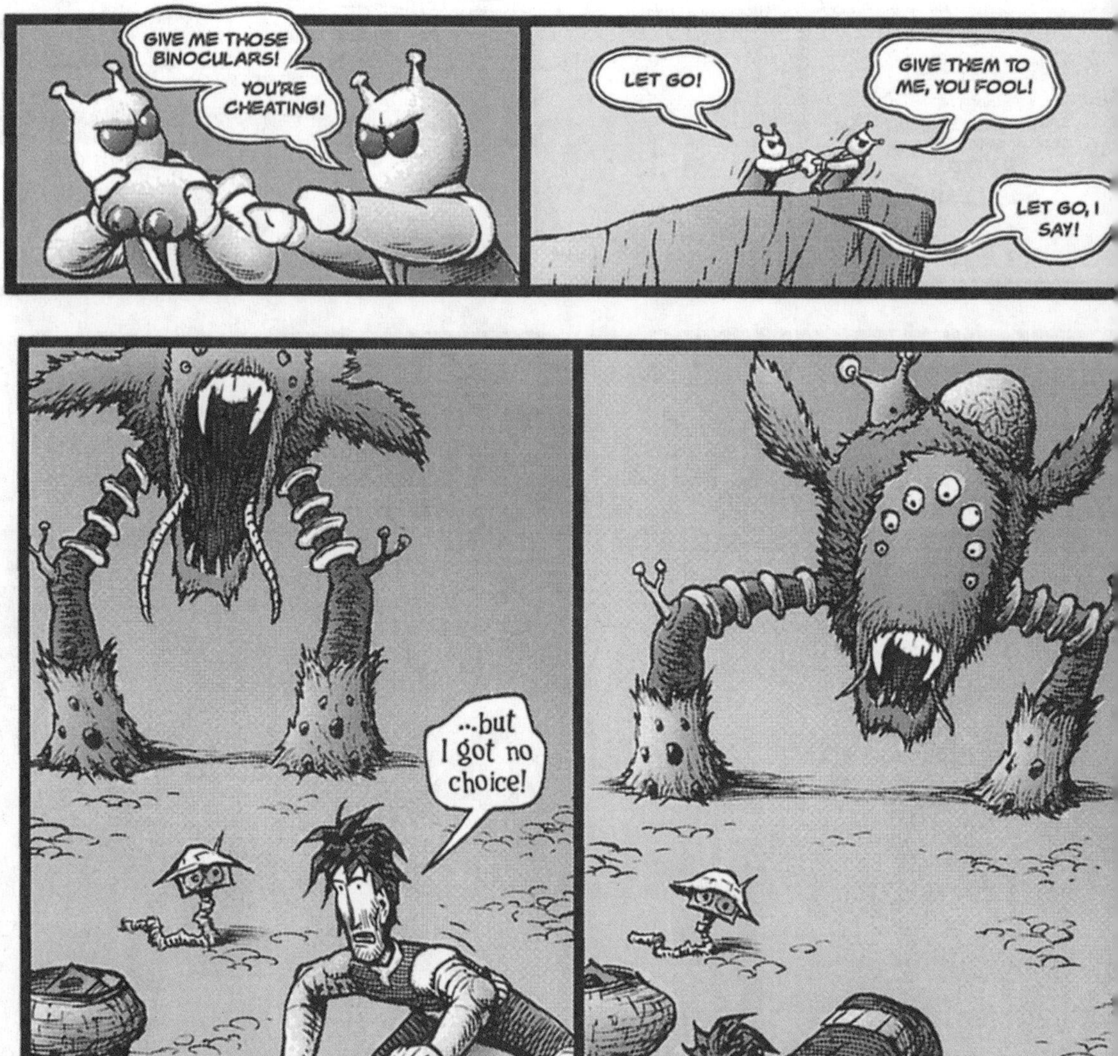
GIVE ME THOSE BINOCULARS!
YOU'RE CHEATING!
LET GO!
GIVE THEM TO ME, YOU FOOL!
LET GO, I SAY!
...but I got no choice!
Number 82, eh? On Earth a comic's not worth very much unless it's issue #1.
Yes, they have the same idea here on Smoo.
Look at the artwork, though. I used to stare at this page for hours.
Cool.

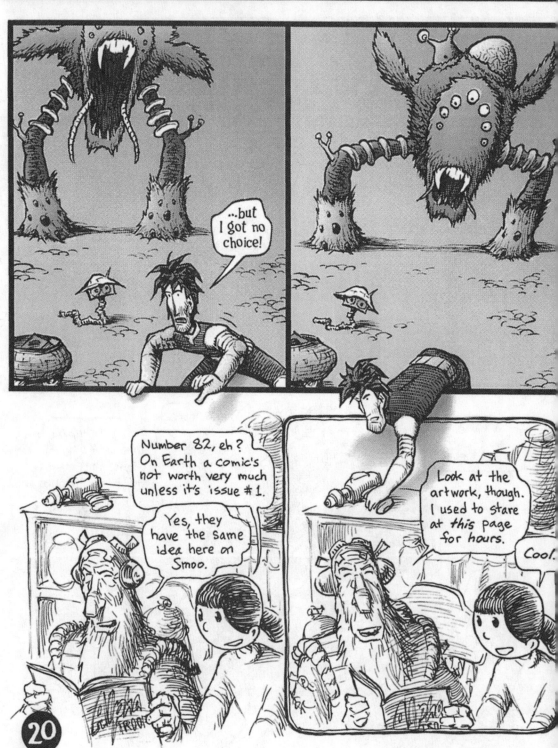

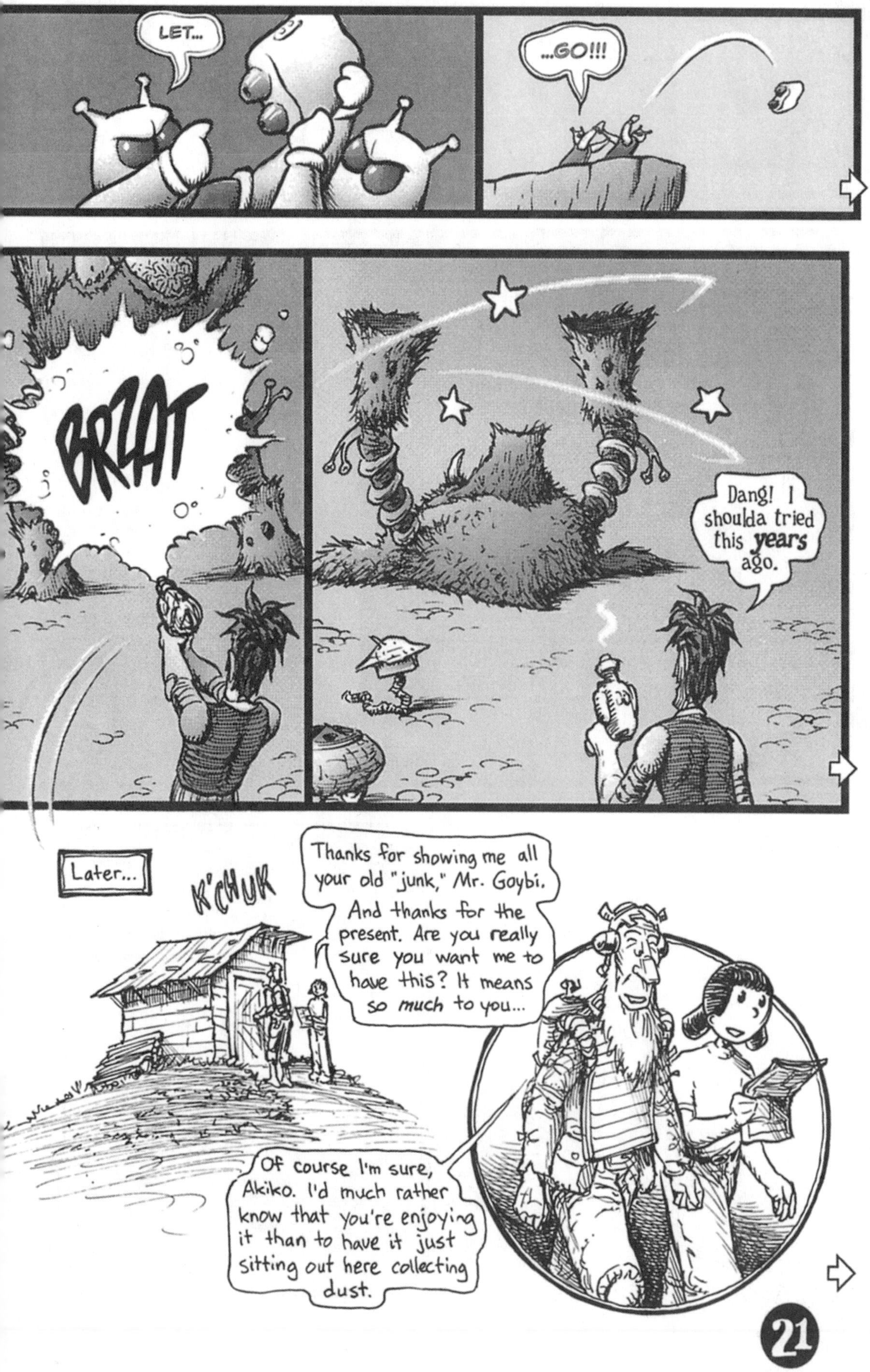

LET...
...GO!!!
BRZAT
Dang! I shoulda tried this years ago.
Later...
K'CHUK
Thanks for showing me all your old "junk," Mr. Goybi.
And thanks for the present. Are you really sure you want me to have this? It means so much to you...
Of course I'm sure, Akiko. I'd much rather know that you're enjoying it than to have it just sitting out here collecting dust.

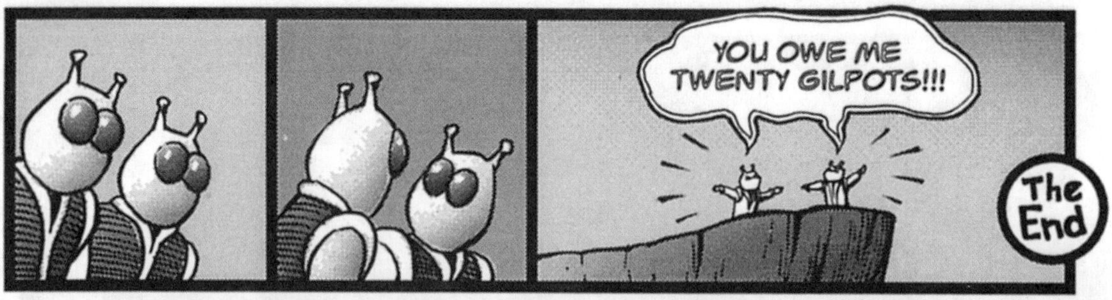
YOU OWE ME TWENTY GILPOTS!!!
The End

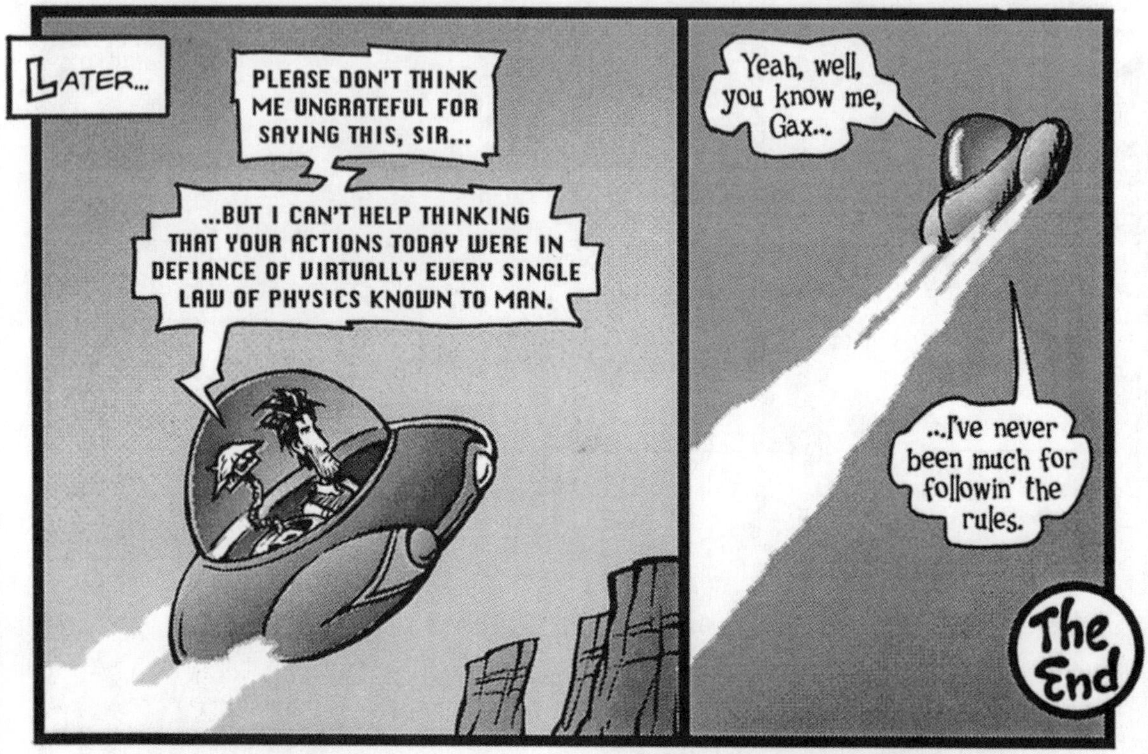
LATER...
PLEASE DON'T THINK ME UNGRATEFUL FOR SAYING THIS, SIR...
...BUT I CAN'T HELP THINKING THAT YOUR ACTIONS TODAY WERE IN DEFIANCE OF VIRTUALLY EVERY SINGLE LAW OF PHYSICS KNOWN TO MAN.
Yeah, well, you know me, Gax...
...I've never been much for followin' the rules.
The End

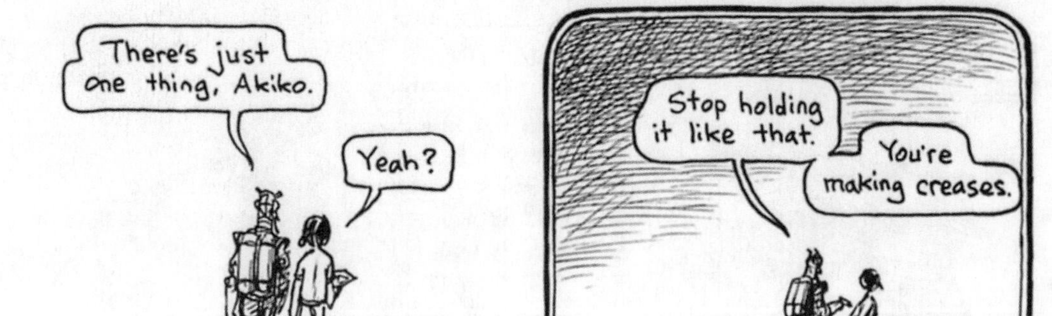
There's just one thing, Akiko.
Yeah?
Stop holding it like that.
You're making creases.
The End

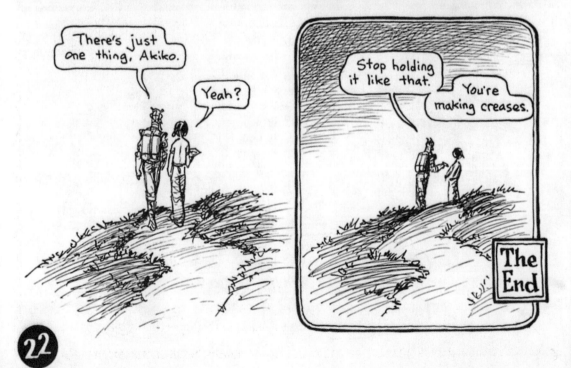

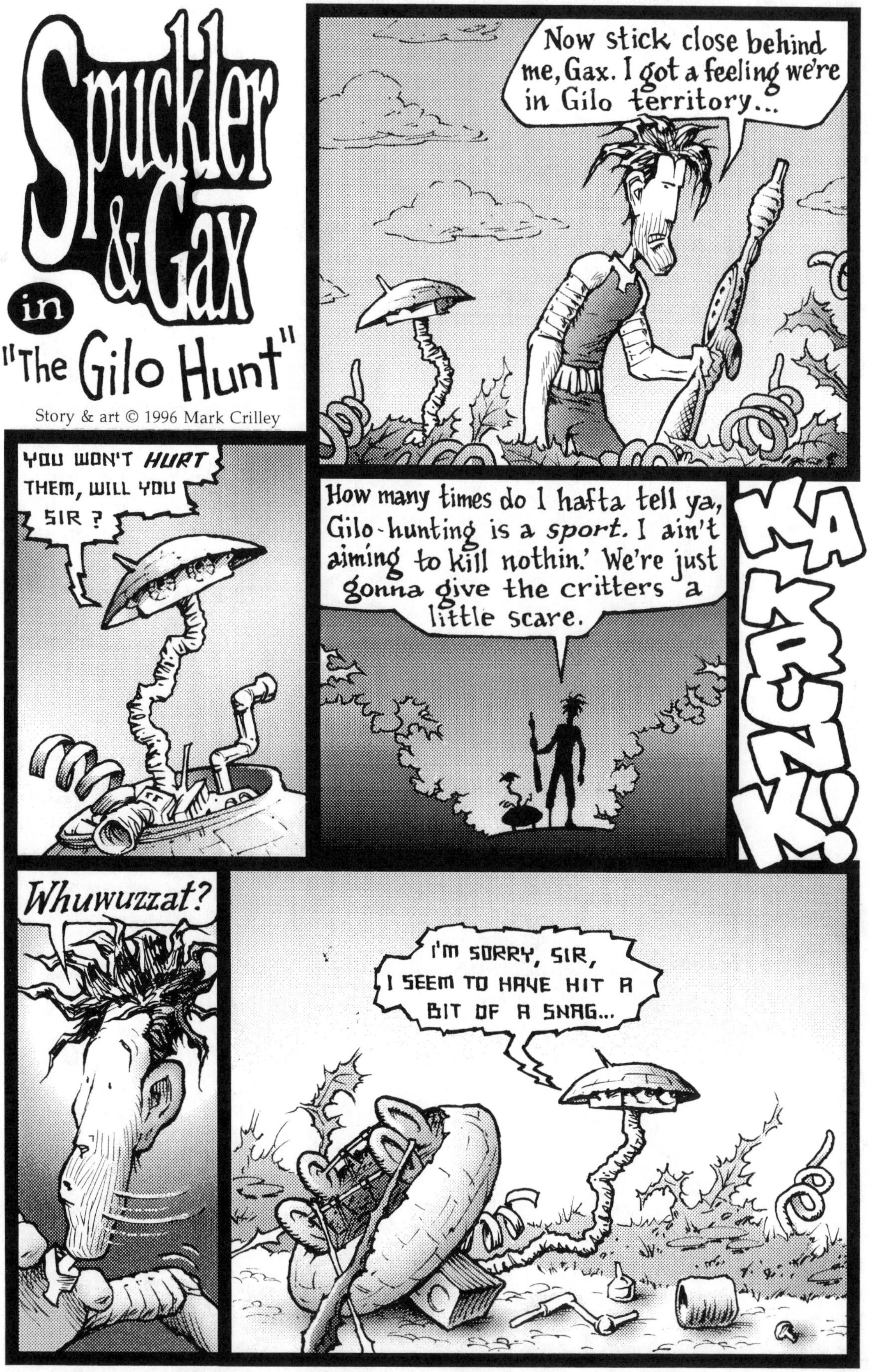
Spuckler & Gax
in
"The Gilo Hunt"
Story & art © 1996 Mark Crilley
Now stick close behind me, Gax. I got a feeling we're in Gilo territory...
YOU WON'T *HURT* THEM, WILL YOU SIR ?
How many times do I hafta tell ya, Gilo-hunting is a *sport.* I ain't aiming to kill nothin.' We're just gonna give the critters a little scare.
KA KRUNK!
Whuwuzzat?
I'M SORRY, SIR, I SEEM TO HAVE HIT A BIT OF A SNAG...

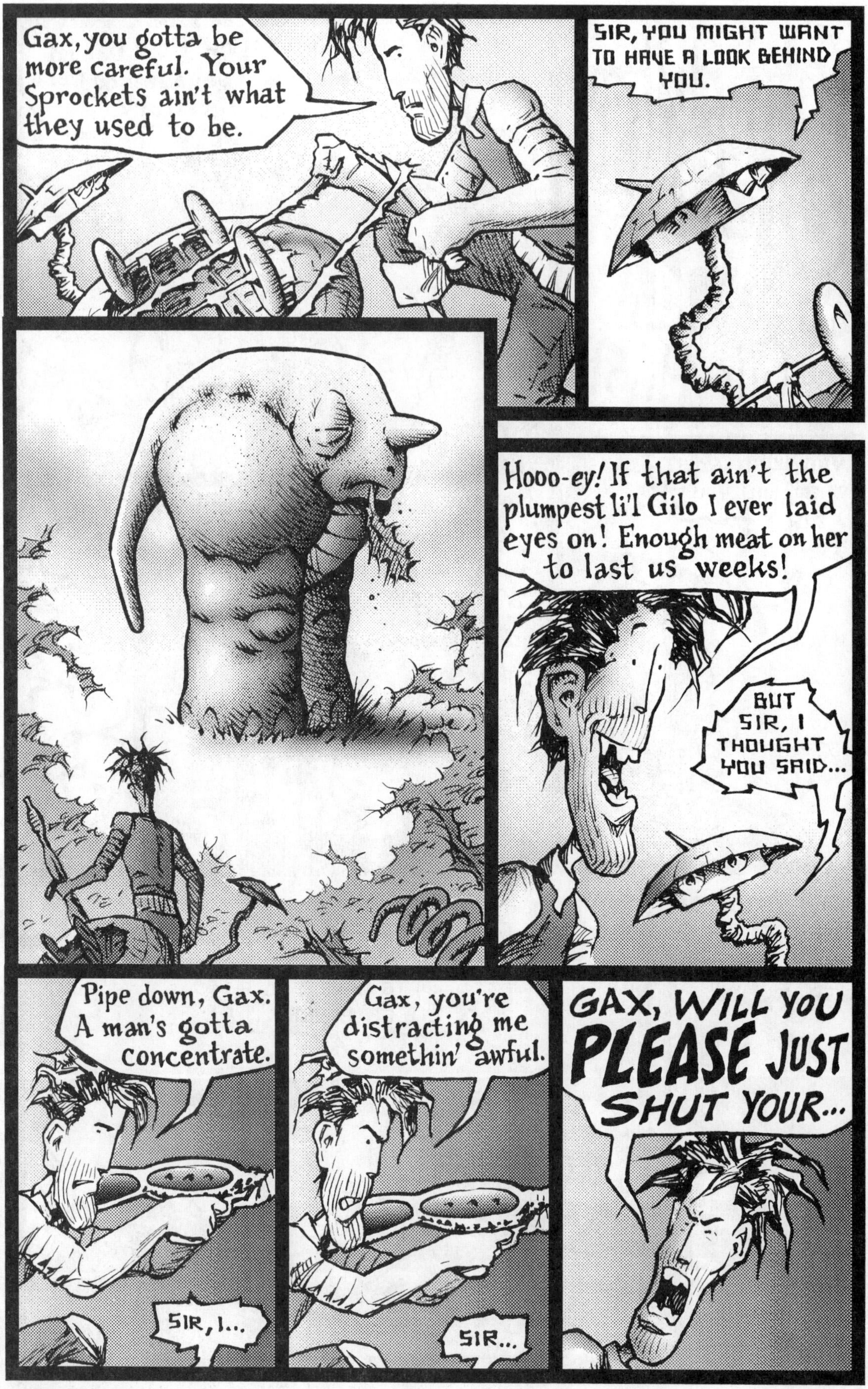
Gax, you gotta be more careful. Your Sprockets ain't what they used to be.
SIR, YOU MIGHT WANT TO HAVE A LOOK BEHIND YOU.
Hooo-ey! If that ain't the plumpest li'l Gilo I ever laid eyes on! Enough meat on her to last us weeks!
BUT SIR, I THOUGHT YOU SAID...
Pipe down, Gax. A man's gotta concentrate.
SIR, I...
Gax, you're distracting me somethin' awful.
SIR...
GAX, WILL YOU PLEASE JUST SHUT YOUR...

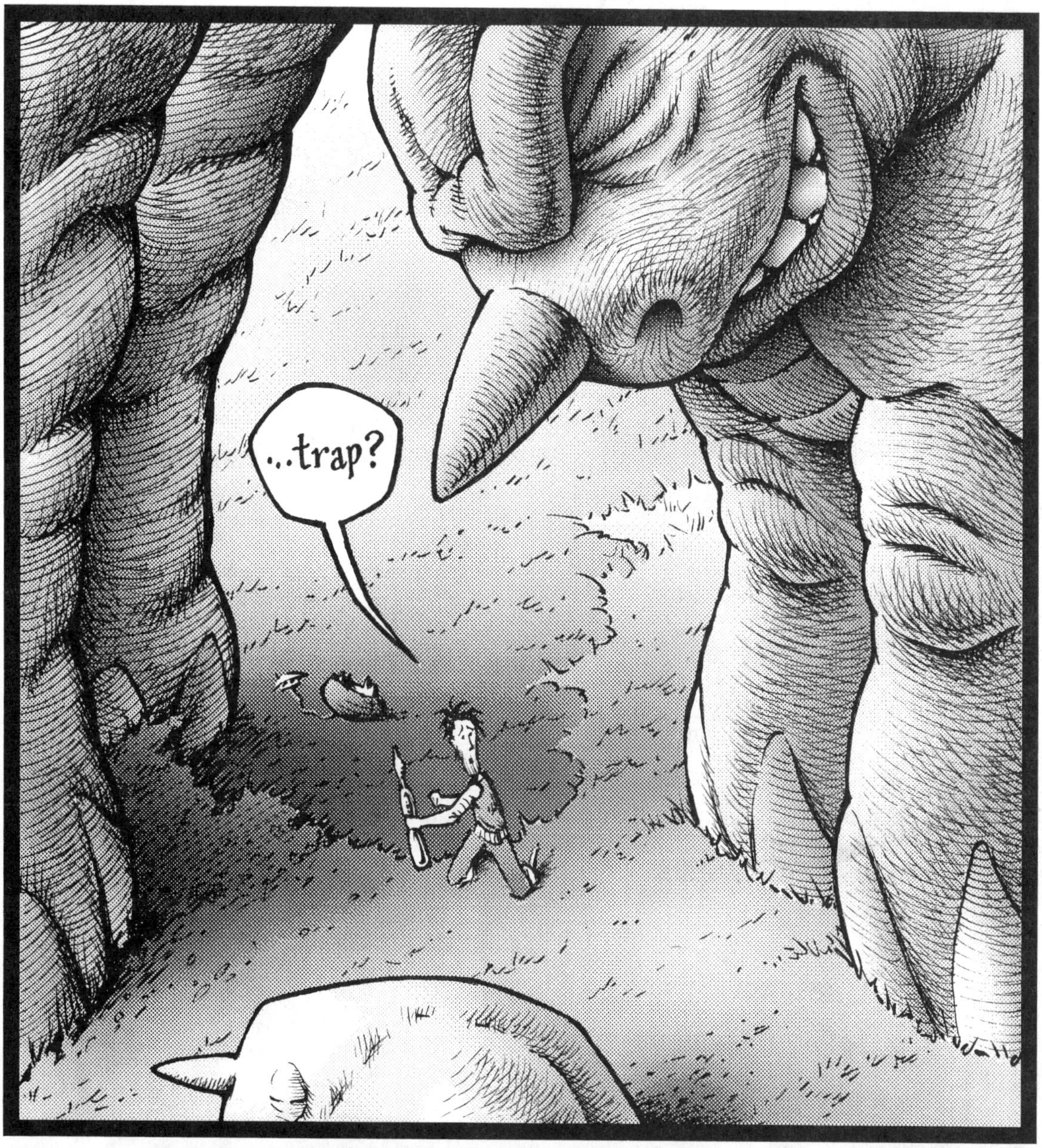
...trap?

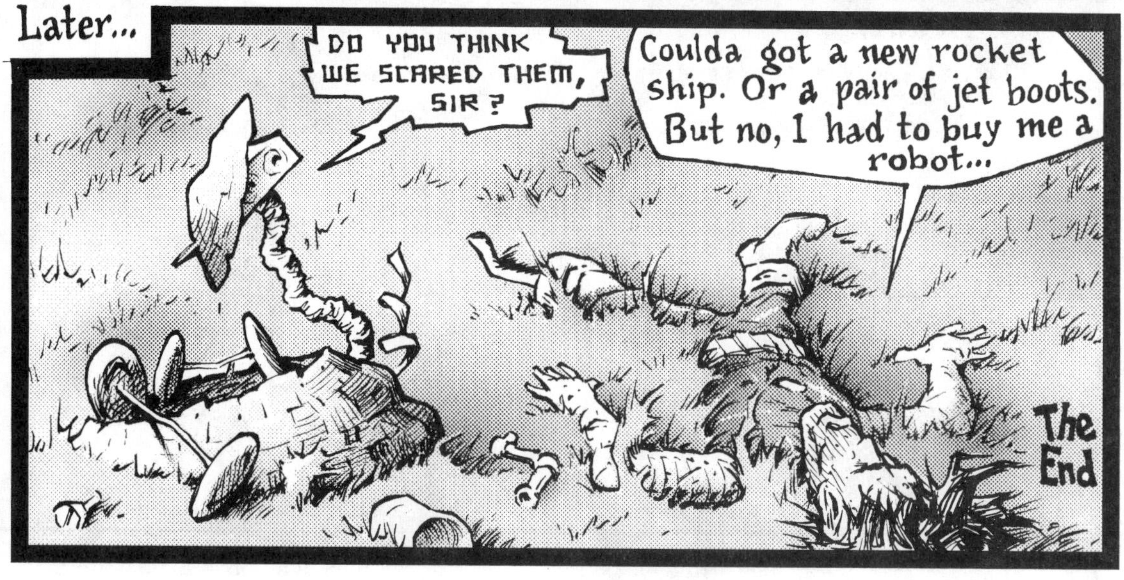
Later...
DO YOU THINK WE SCARED THEM, SIR?
Coulda got a new rocket ship. Or a pair of jet boots. But no, I had to buy me a robot...
The End

Akiko in "Everyone's a Critic"

Whatcha workin' on there, Akiko?

I'm making a comic book. It's all about the adventures I've had with you and Mr. Beeba and everybody.

Who's *that* supposed to be?

Poog.

He's all lopsided... did someone punch him or somethin'?

I was tracing a quarter and it slipped.

Hello, Akiko. What have we here?

It's my new comic book. What do you think?

There's no "h" in "Smoo."

Oh.

I hope that's not supposed to be *me*.

There's something wrong with the hair, isn't there?

Well for starters, I don't part my hair to the side like that.

Now when you draw me, Akiko, make sure you remember these little bumps on my head.

What are they?

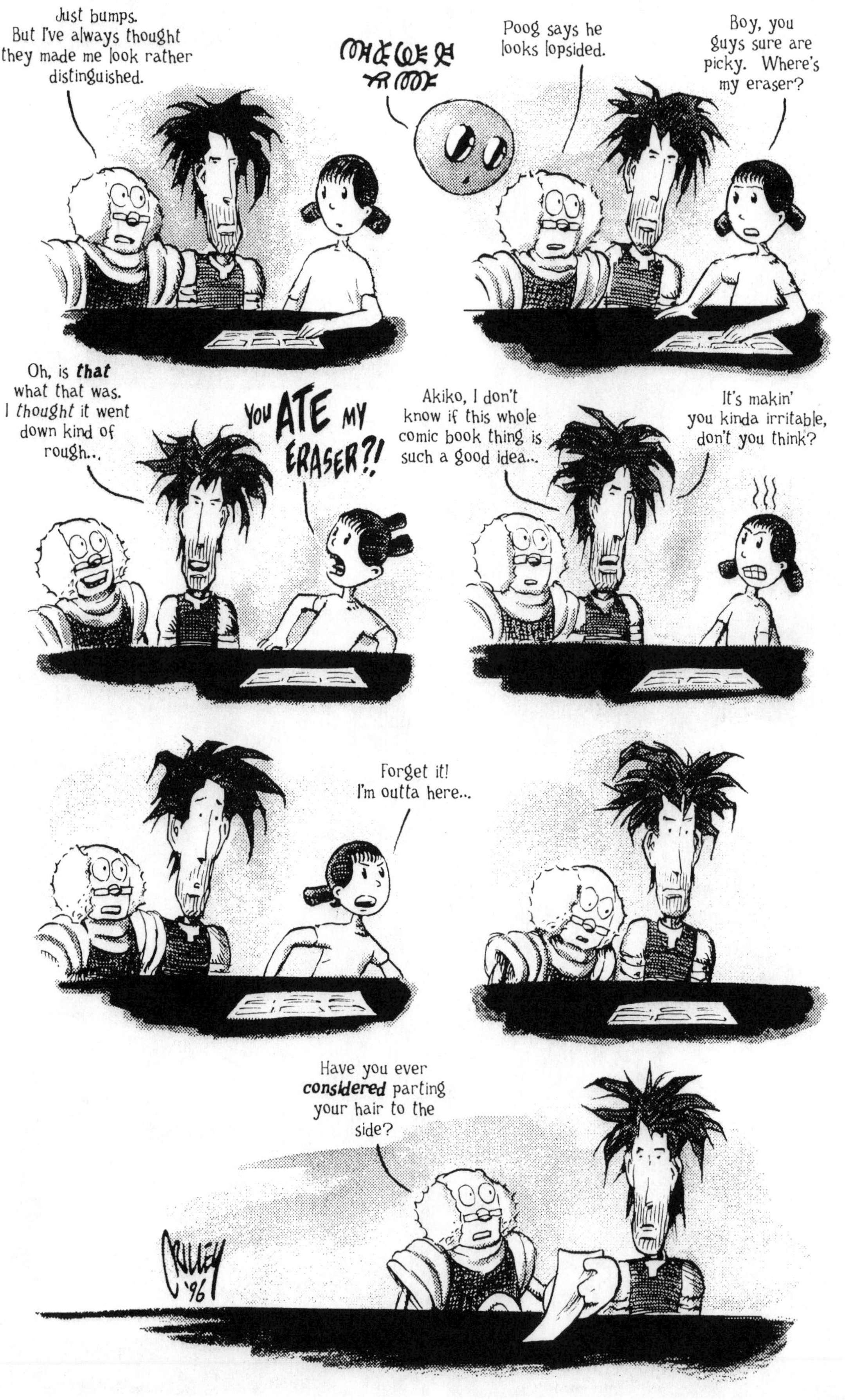

Just bumps. But I've always thought they made me look rather distinguished.
Poog says he looks lopsided.
Boy, you guys sure are picky. Where's my eraser?
Oh, is **that** what that was. I *thought* it went down kind of rough...
YOU ATE MY ERASER?!
Akiko, I don't know if this whole comic book thing is such a good idea...
It's makin' you kinda irritable, don't you think?
Forget it! I'm outta here...
Have you ever **considered** parting your hair to the side?
CRILLEY '96

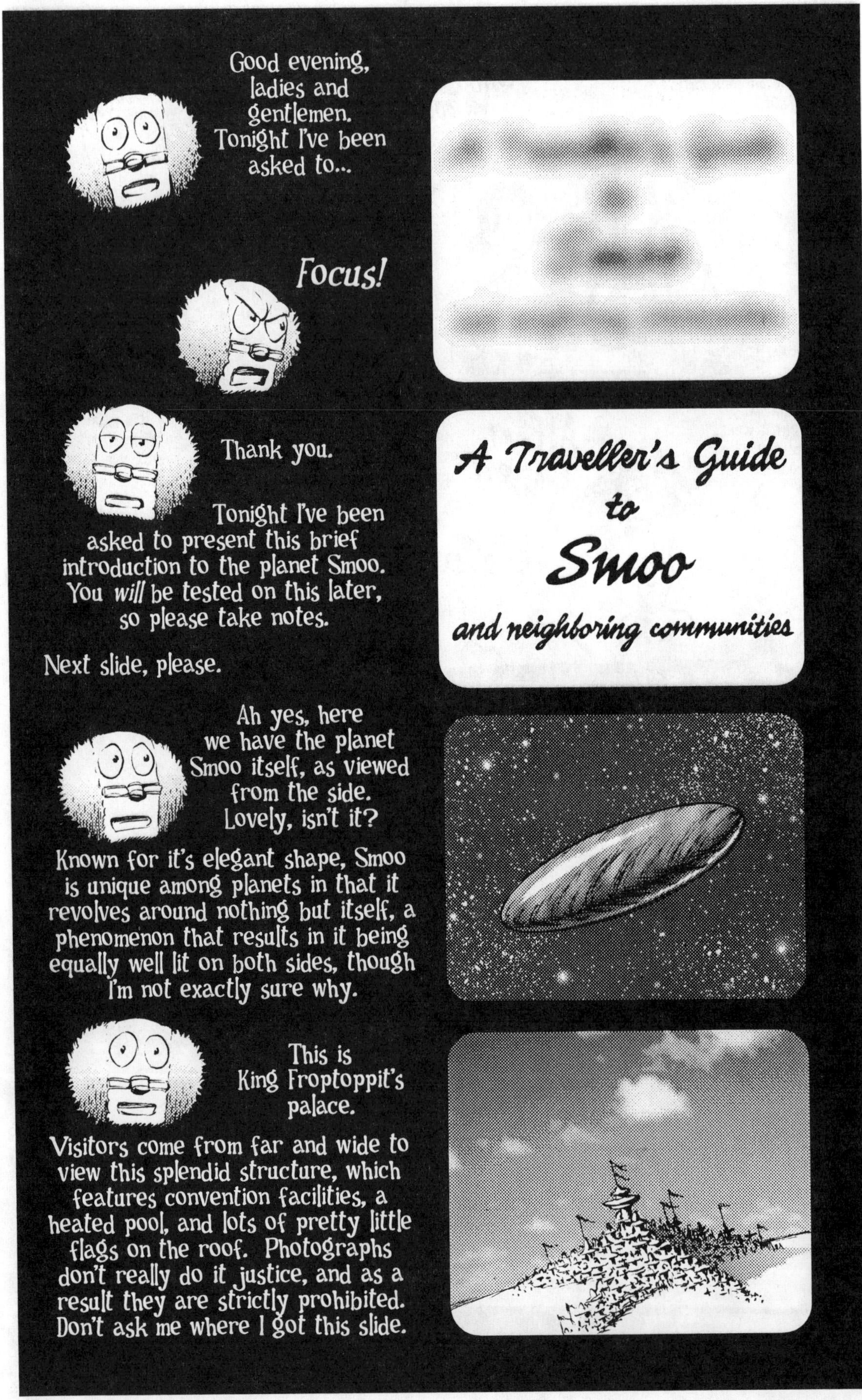
Good evening, ladies and gentlemen. Tonight I've been asked to...
Focus!
Thank you.
A Traveller's Guide to Smoo and neighboring communities
Tonight I've been asked to present this brief introduction to the planet Smoo. You *will* be tested on this later, so please take notes.
Next slide, please.
Ah yes, here we have the planet Smoo itself, as viewed from the side. Lovely, isn't it?
Known for it's elegant shape, Smoo is unique among planets in that it revolves around nothing but itself, a phenomenon that results in it being equally well lit on both sides, though I'm not exactly sure why.
This is King Froptoppit's palace.
Visitors come from far and wide to view this splendid structure, which features convention facilities, a heated pool, and lots of pretty little flags on the roof. Photographs don't really do it justice, and as a result they are strictly prohibited. Don't ask me where I got this slide.

Here is King Froptoppit, famed humorist and beloved ruler of Smoo.

His Majesty invited me to Smoo many years ago to serve as his personal tutor, and though he hasn't excelled in any particular subject, his handwriting has improved considerably.

This is his son, the Prince. Now that he is of marriageable age, his father has been searching the universe for a suitable bride. We have in fact located an excellent candidate, but the wedding has had to be postponed until she has completed what is known on her planet as "the 6th grade."

 Now for some of the sights.

No holiday on Smoo would be complete without a visit to the Floating River of Hebbadoy. This natural marvel has flowed above the surface of Smoo for several centuries. Riverboat tours are available, except during the rainy season when they are cancelled due to the possibility of floods.

Then there is the legendary Upside Down City of Gollarondo, where people live on the underside of a cliff overlooking the Moonguzzit Sea. It's a charming town with a spectacular view, though one must be sure that all articles of clothing are firmly attached before going there, since fallen hats and such can be very difficult to retrieve.

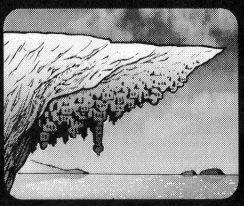

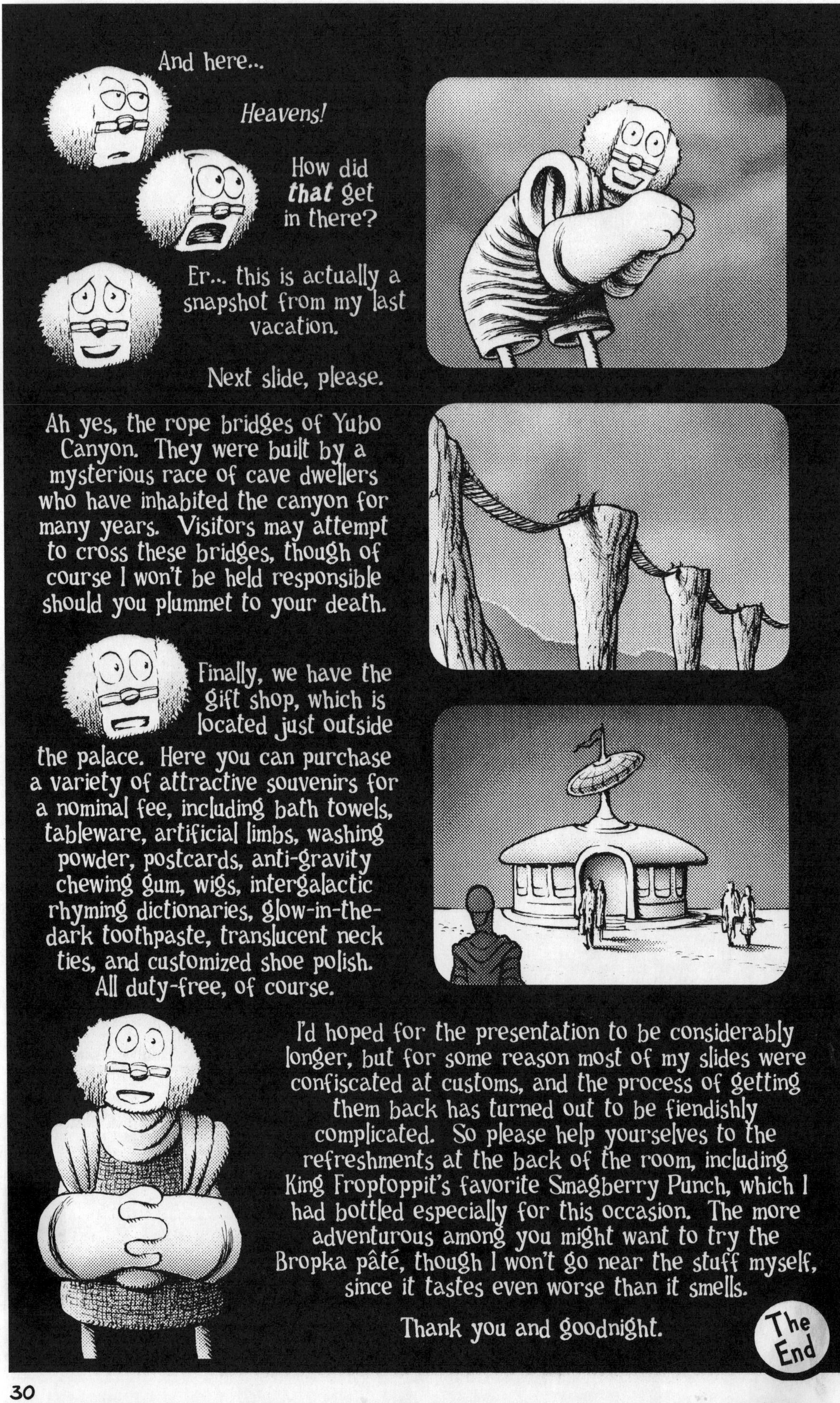
And here...
Heavens!
How did *that* get in there?
Er... this is actually a snapshot from my last vacation.
Next slide, please.
Ah yes, the rope bridges of Yubo Canyon. They were built by a mysterious race of cave dwellers who have inhabited the canyon for many years. Visitors may attempt to cross these bridges, though of course I won't be held responsible should you plummet to your death.
Finally, we have the gift shop, which is located just outside the palace. Here you can purchase a variety of attractive souvenirs for a nominal fee, including bath towels, tableware, artificial limbs, washing powder, postcards, anti-gravity chewing gum, wigs, intergalactic rhyming dictionaries, glow-in-the-dark toothpaste, translucent neck ties, and customized shoe polish. All duty-free, of course.
I'd hoped for the presentation to be considerably longer, but for some reason most of my slides were confiscated at customs, and the process of getting them back has turned out to be fiendishly complicated. So please help yourselves to the refreshments at the back of the room, including King Froptoppit's favorite Smagberry Punch, which I had bottled especially for this occasion. The more adventurous among you might want to try the Bropka pâté, though I won't go near the stuff myself, since it tastes even worse than it smells.
Thank you and goodnight.
The End

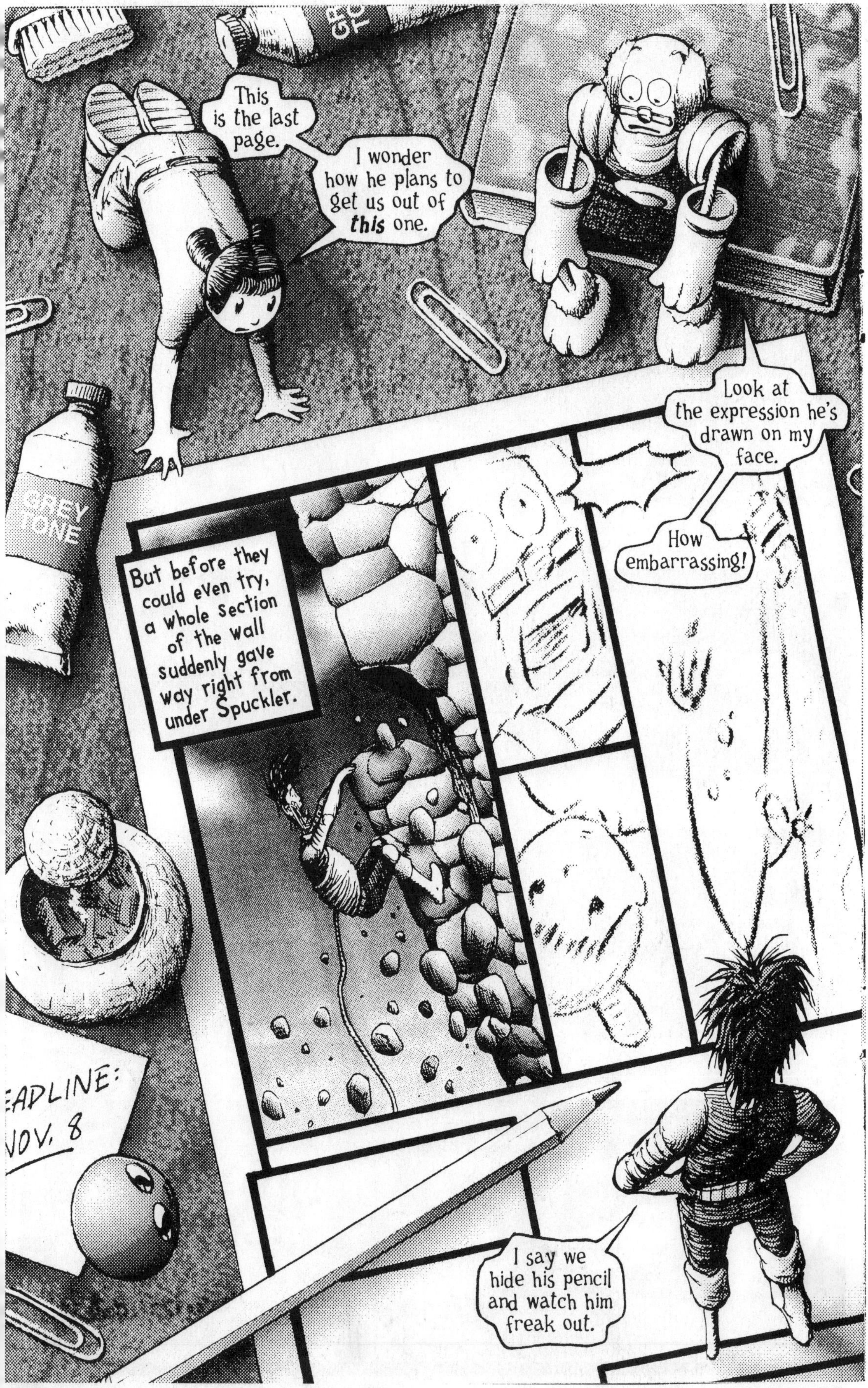

This is the last page.
I wonder how he plans to get us out of *this* one.
Look at the expression he's drawn on my face.
How embarrassing!
But before they could even try, a whole section of the wall suddenly gave way right from under Spuckler.
I say we hide his pencil and watch him freak out.
GREY TONE
EADLINE: NOV. 8

Akiko and the Gang in "MOVIE MAYHEM"

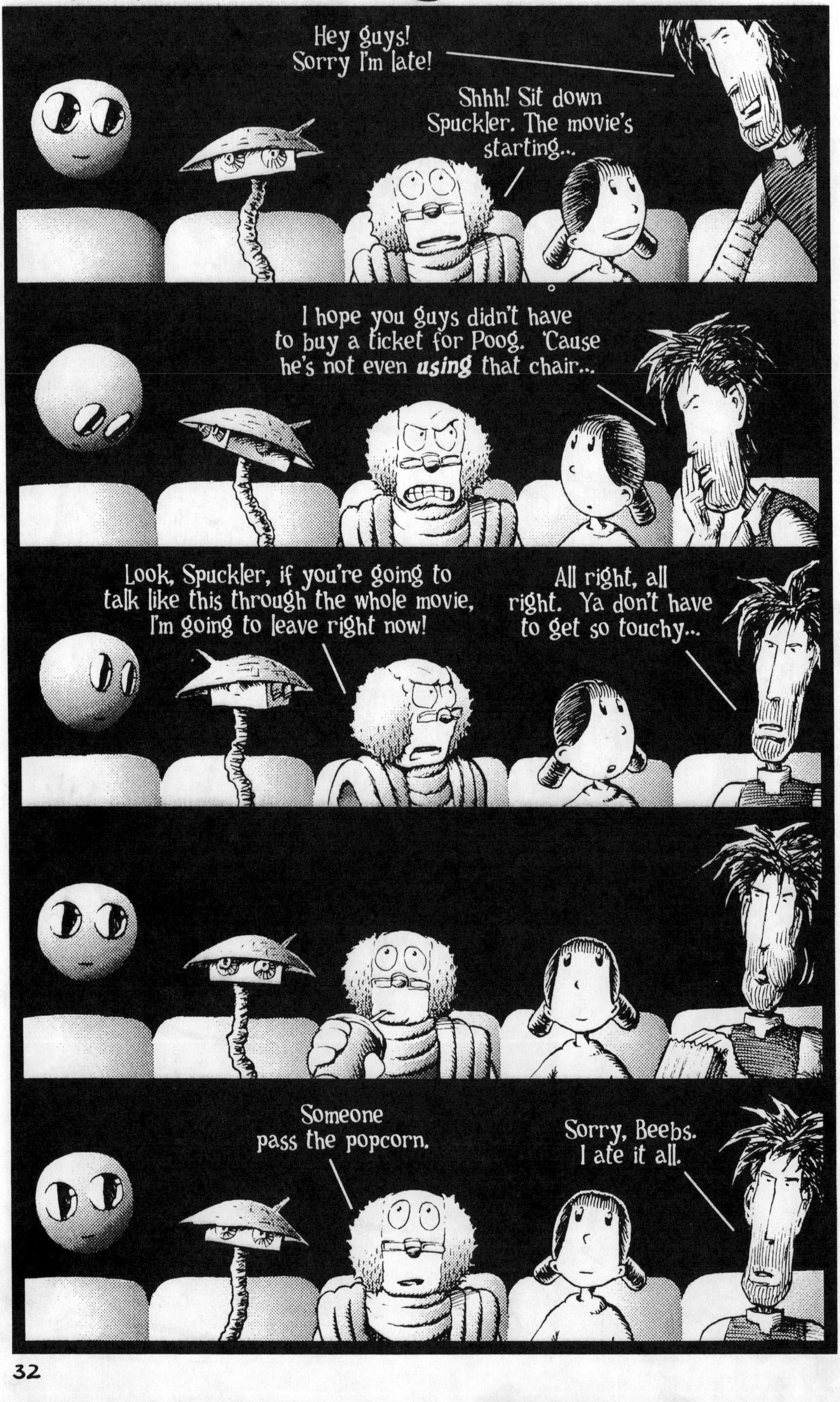

Hey guys! Sorry I'm late!
Shhh! Sit down Spuckler. The movie's starting...
I hope you guys didn't have to buy a ticket for Poog. 'Cause he's not even *using* that chair...
Look, Spuckler, if you're going to talk like this through the whole movie, I'm going to leave right now!
All right, all right. Ya don't have to get so touchy...
Someone pass the popcorn.
Sorry, Beebs. I ate it all.

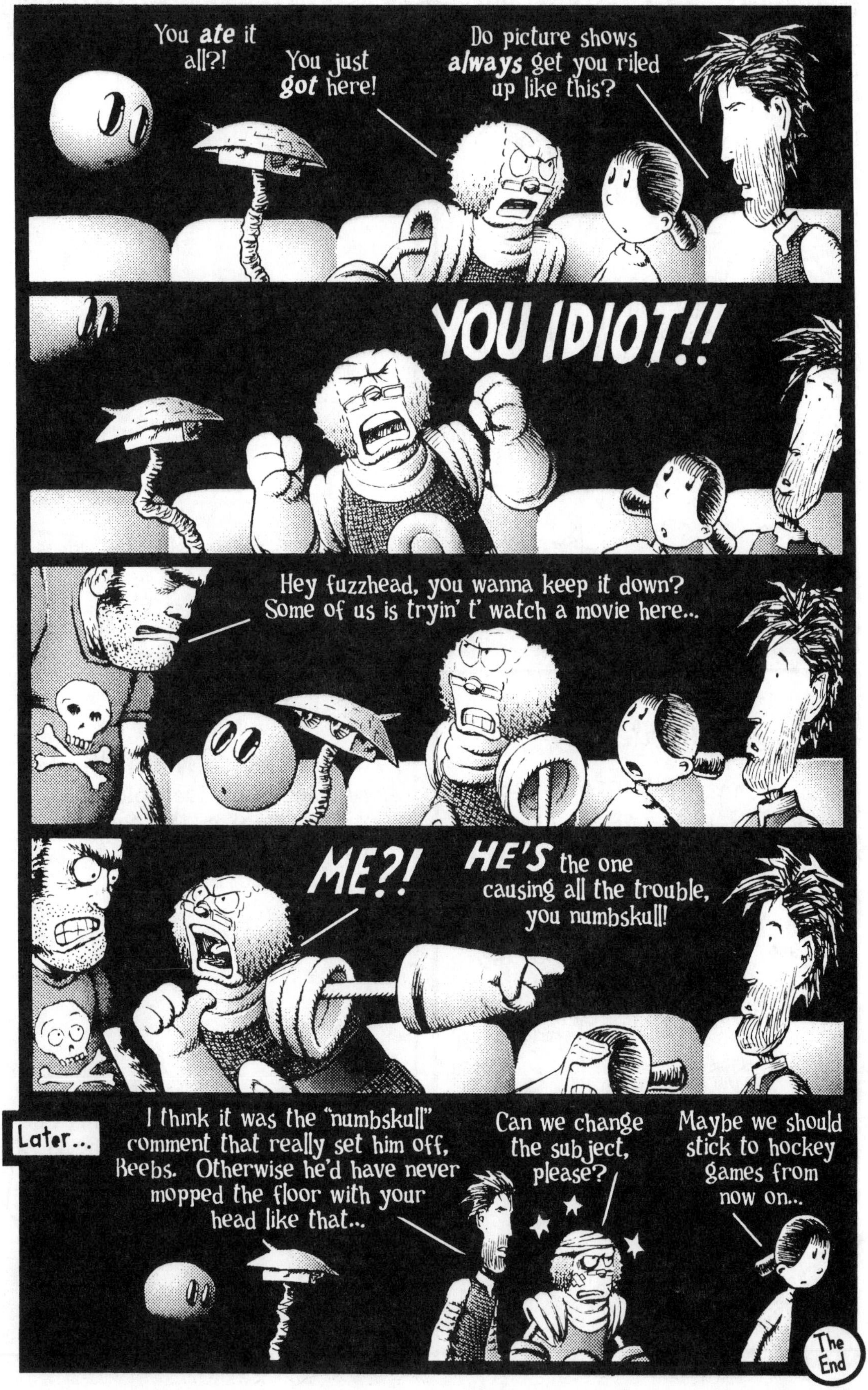
You **ate** it all?!
You just **got** here!
Do picture shows **always** get you riled up like this?
YOU IDIOT!!
Hey fuzzhead, you wanna keep it down? Some of us is tryin' t' watch a movie here...
ME?!
HE'S the one causing all the trouble, you numbskull!
Later...
I think it was the "numbskull" comment that really set him off, Beebs. Otherwise he'd have never mopped the floor with your head like that...
Can we change the subject, please?
Maybe we should stick to hockey games from now on...
The End

Me 'N 'Kiko in "Return to Sender"

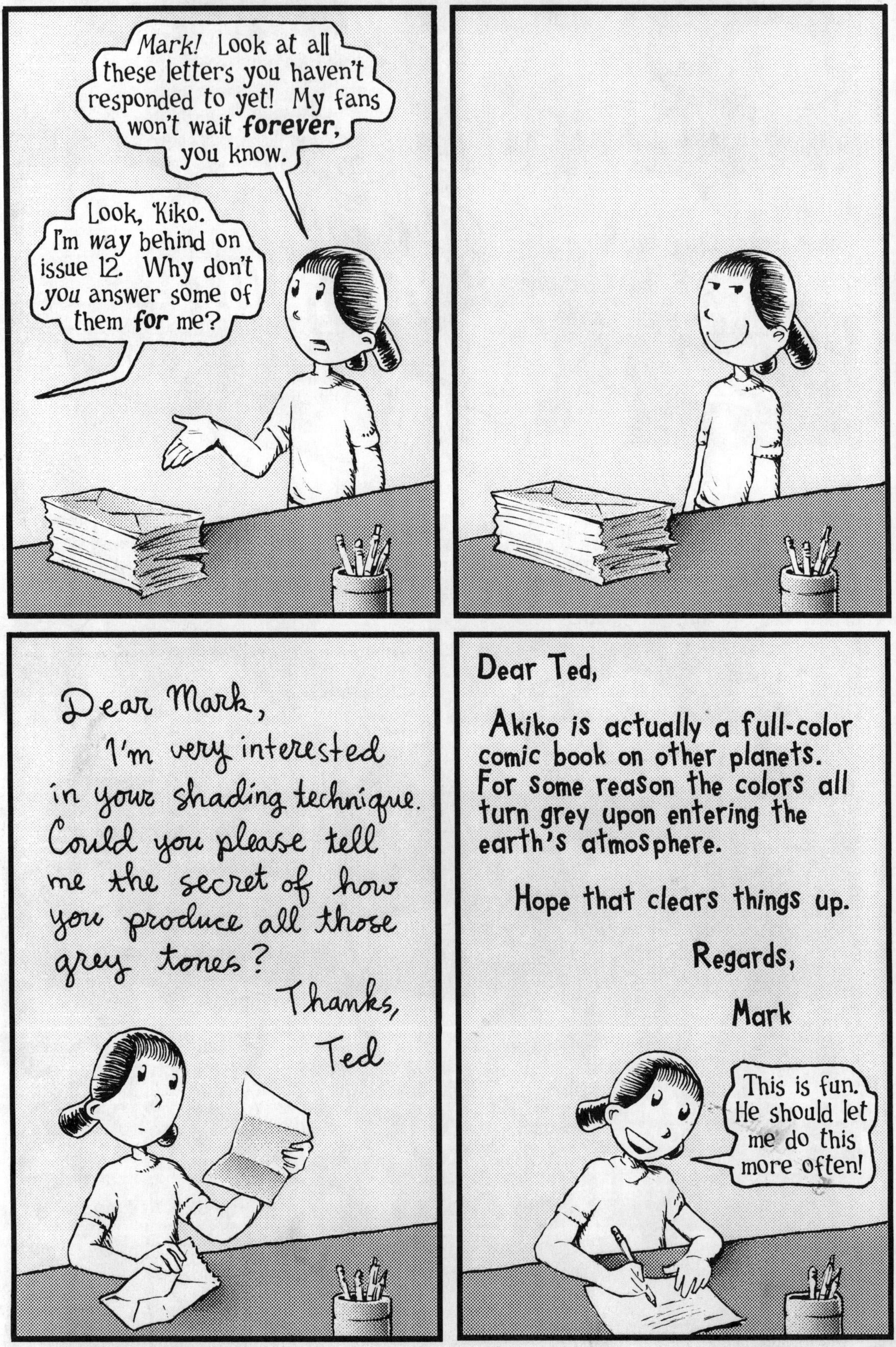
Mark! Look at all these letters you haven't responded to yet! My fans won't wait **forever**, you know.
Look, 'Kiko. I'm *way* behind on issue 12. Why don't *you* answer some of them **for** me?
Dear Mark,
I'm very interested in your shading technique. Could you please tell me the secret of how you produce all those grey tones?
Thanks,
Ted
Dear Ted,
Akiko is actually a full-color comic book on other planets. For some reason the colors all turn grey upon entering the earth's atmosphere.
Hope that clears things up.
Regards,
Mark
This is fun. He should let me do this more often!

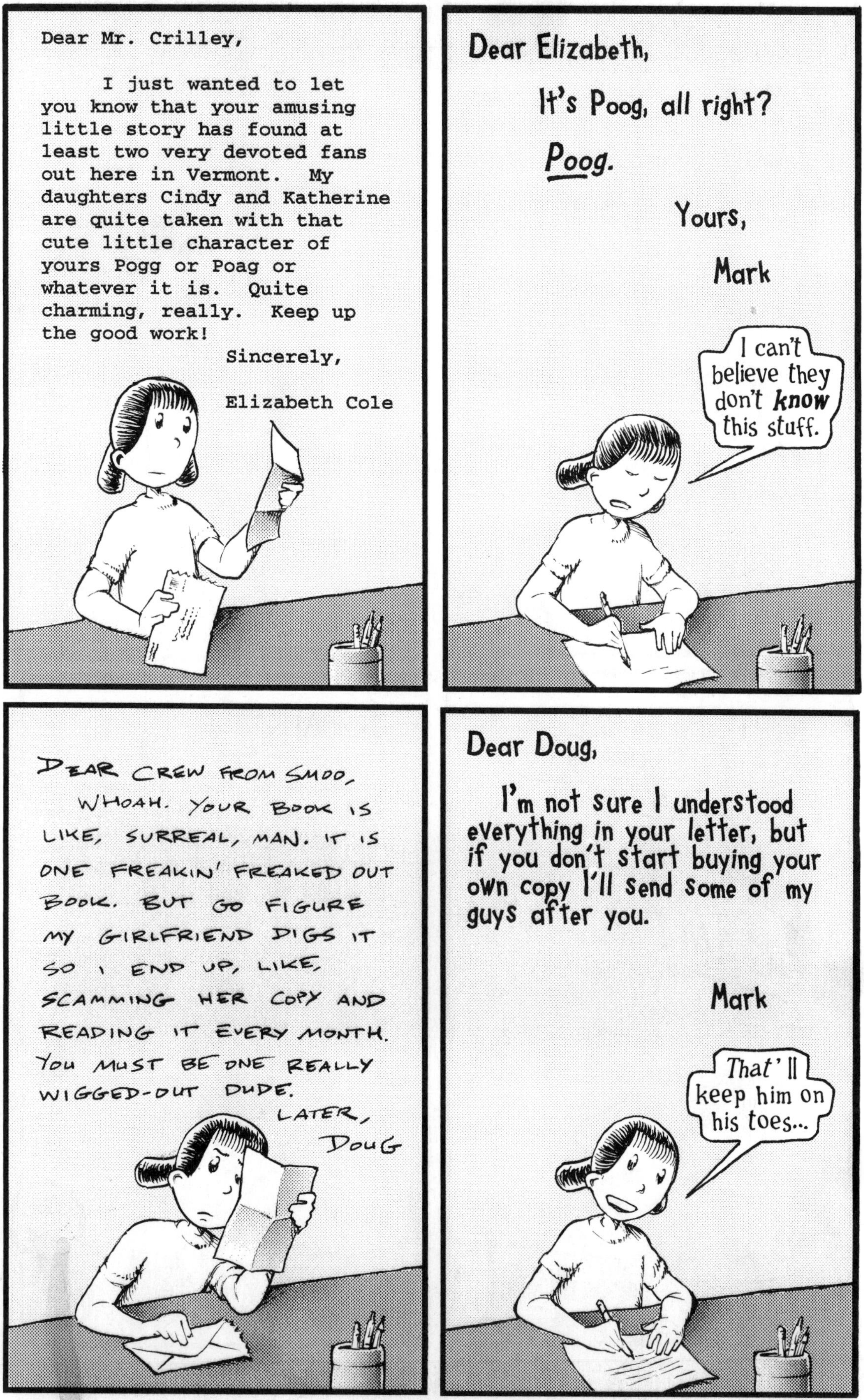
Dear Mr. Crilley,
I just wanted to let you know that your amusing little story has found at least two very devoted fans out here in Vermont. My daughters Cindy and Katherine are quite taken with that cute little character of yours Pogg or Poag or whatever it is. Quite charming, really. Keep up the good work!
Sincerely,
Elizabeth Cole
Dear Elizabeth,
It's Poog, all right?
Poog.
Yours,
Mark
I can't believe they don't know this stuff.
DEAR CREW FROM SMOO,
WHOAH. YOUR BOOK IS LIKE, SURREAL, MAN. IT IS ONE FREAKIN' FREAKED OUT BOOK. BUT GO FIGURE MY GIRLFRIEND DIGS IT SO I END UP, LIKE, SCAMMING HER COPY AND READING IT EVERY MONTH. YOU MUST BE ONE REALLY WIGGED-OUT DUDE.
LATER,
DOUG
Dear Doug,
I'm not sure I understood everything in your letter, but if you don't start buying your own copy I'll send some of my guys after you.
Mark
That'll keep him on his toes...

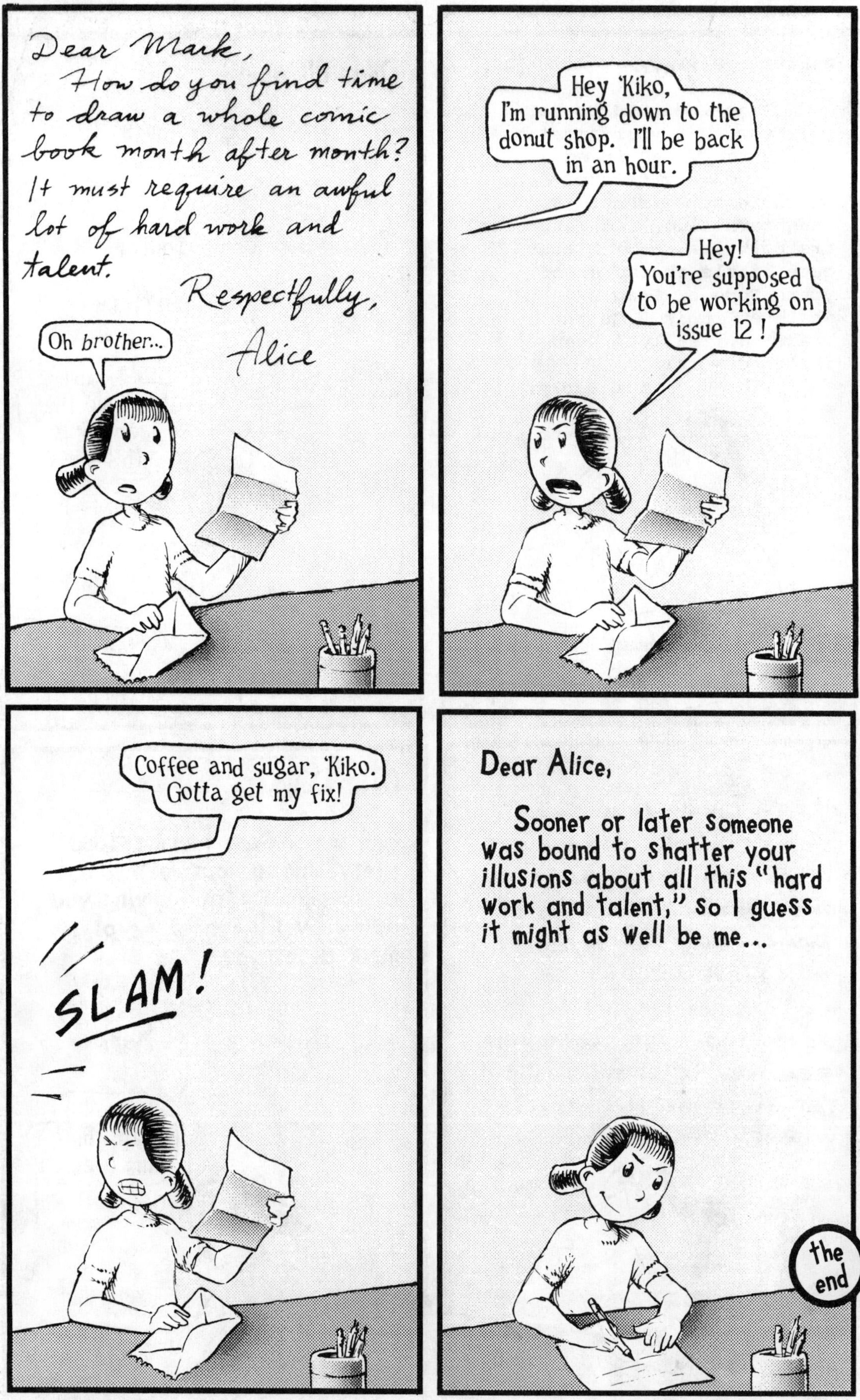
Dear Mark,
How do you find time to draw a whole comic book month after month? It must require an awful lot of hard work and talent.
Respectfully,
Alice
Oh brother...
Hey 'Kiko,
I'm running down to the donut shop. I'll be back in an hour.
Hey!
You're supposed to be working on issue 12!
Coffee and sugar, 'Kiko.
Gotta get my fix!
SLAM!
Dear Alice,
Sooner or later someone was bound to shatter your illusions about all this "hard work and talent," so I guess it might as well be me...
the end

DISCLAIMER: Any similarity to real letters I've received is purely coincidental. I mean, okay, I do *get letters about the grey tones like that. But no one's ever called me a "wigged-out dude" before, I swear.*

Spucky N' Beebs in "The Experiment"

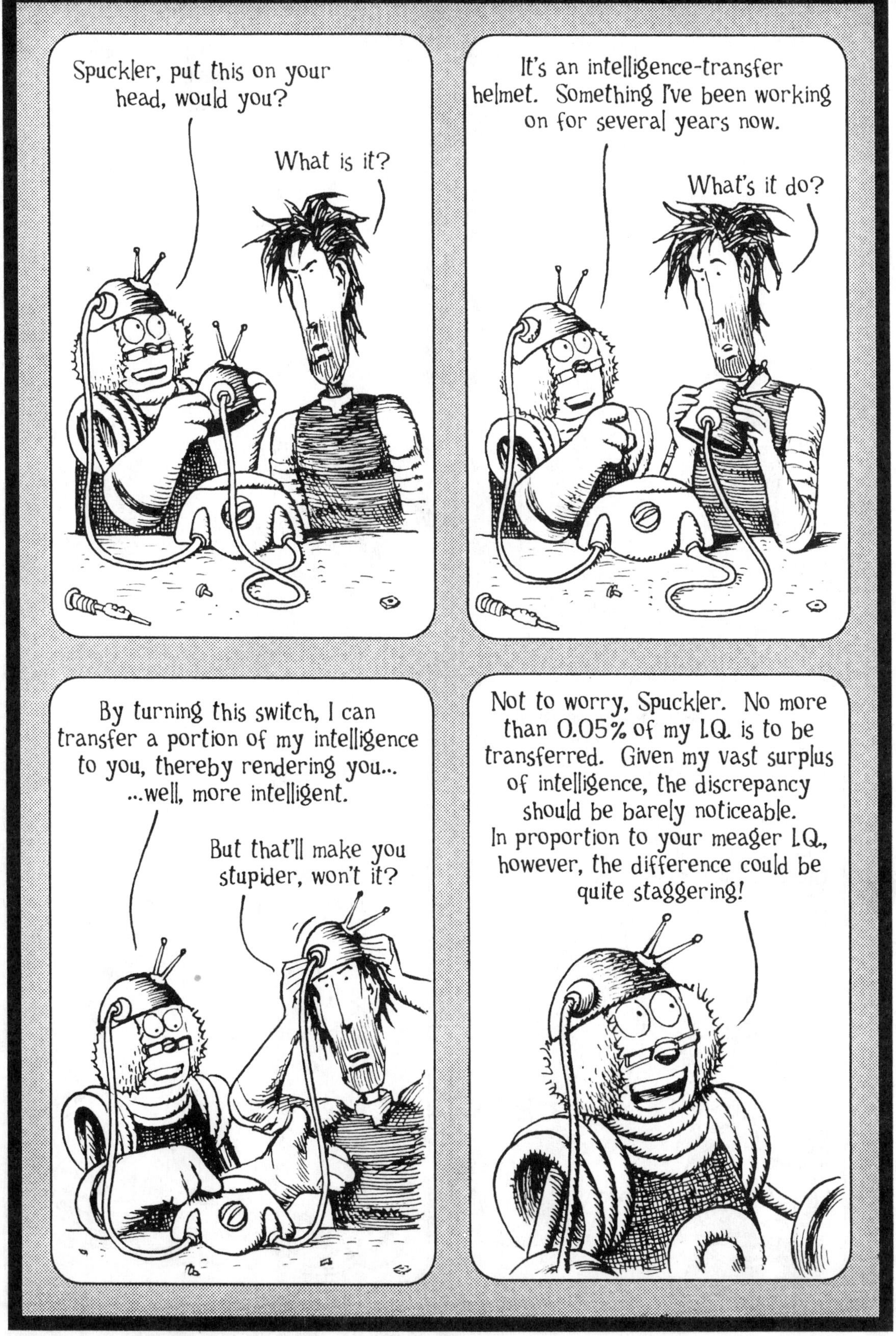
Spuckler, put this on your head, would you?
What is it?
It's an intelligence-transfer helmet. Something I've been working on for several years now.
What's it do?
By turning this switch, I can transfer a portion of my intelligence to you, thereby rendering you... ...well, more intelligent.
But that'll make you stupider, won't it?
Not to worry, Spuckler. No more than 0.05% of my I.Q. is to be transferred. Given my vast surplus of intelligence, the discrepancy should be barely noticeable. In proportion to your meager I.Q., however, the difference could be quite staggering!

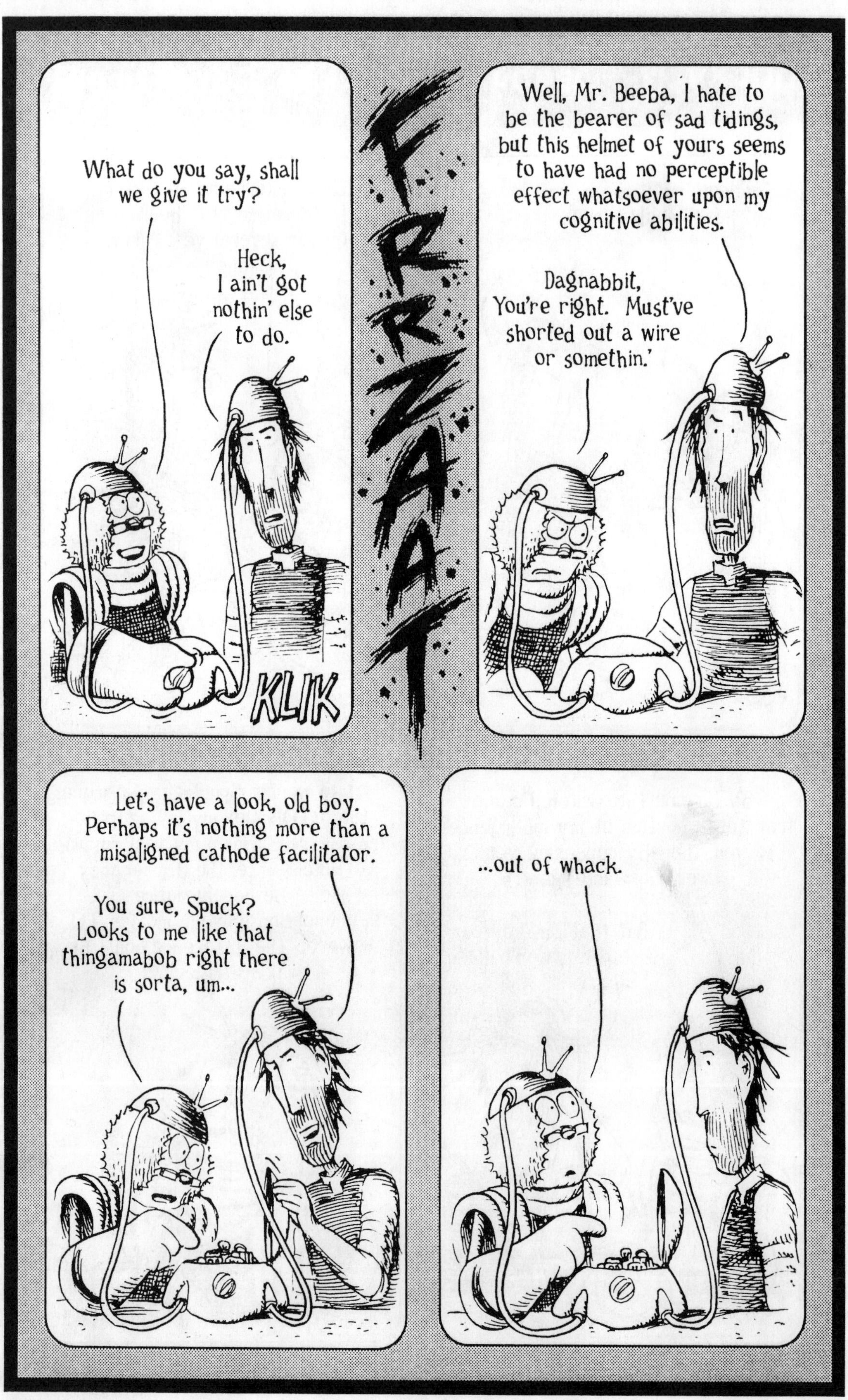

What do you say, shall we give it try?
Heck, I ain't got nothin' else to do.
KLIK
FRRZZAT
Well, Mr. Beeba, I hate to be the bearer of sad tidings, but this helmet of yours seems to have had no perceptible effect whatsoever upon my cognitive abilities.
Dagnabbit, You're right. Must've shorted out a wire or somethin.'
Let's have a look, old boy. Perhaps it's nothing more than a misaligned cathode facilitator.
You sure, Spuck? Looks to me like that thingamabob right there is sorta, um...
...out of whack.

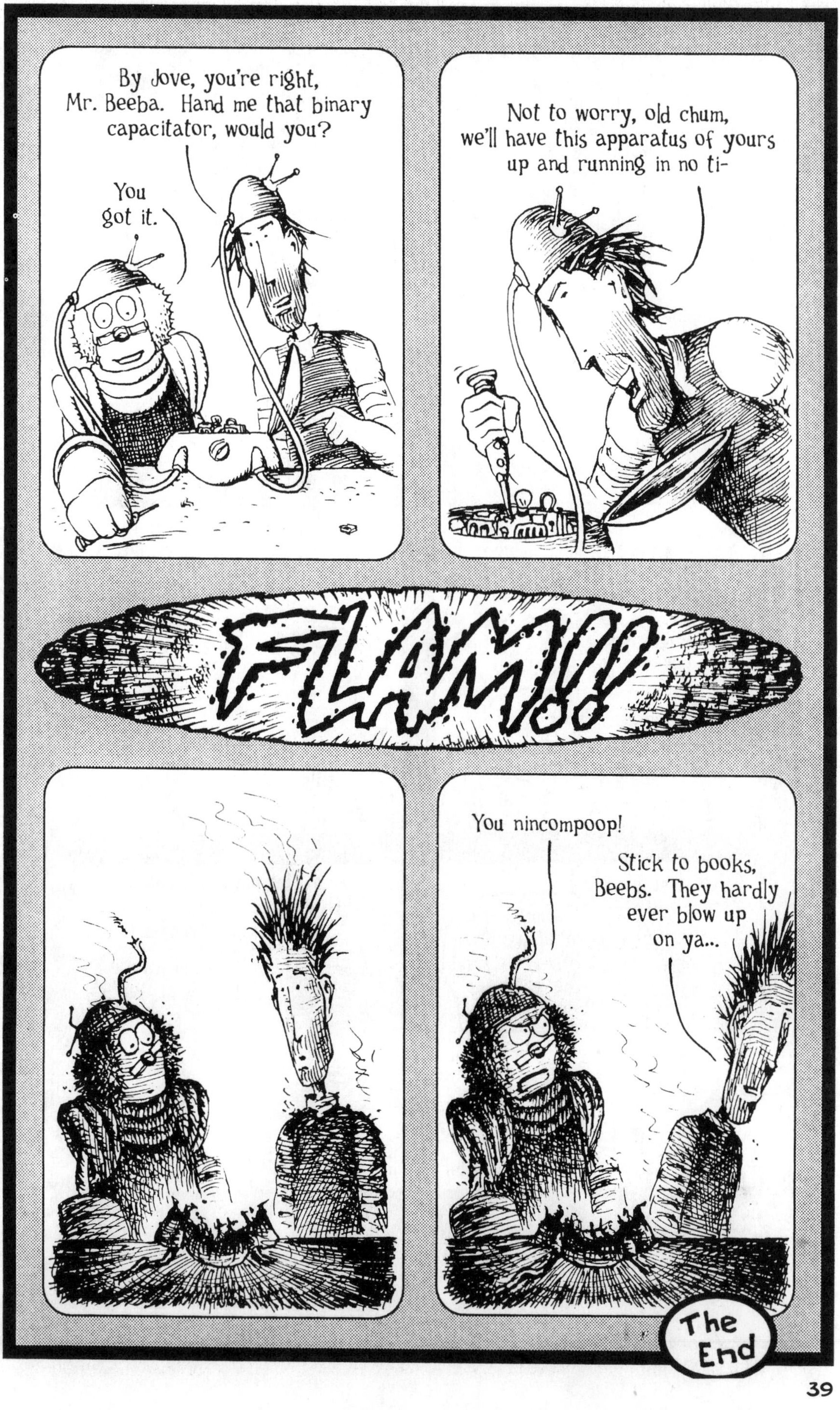
By Jove, you're right, Mr. Beeba. Hand me that binary capacitator, would you?
You got it.
Not to worry, old chum, we'll have this apparatus of yours up and running in no ti-
FLAM!!
You nincompoop!
Stick to books, Beebs. They hardly ever blow up on ya...
The End

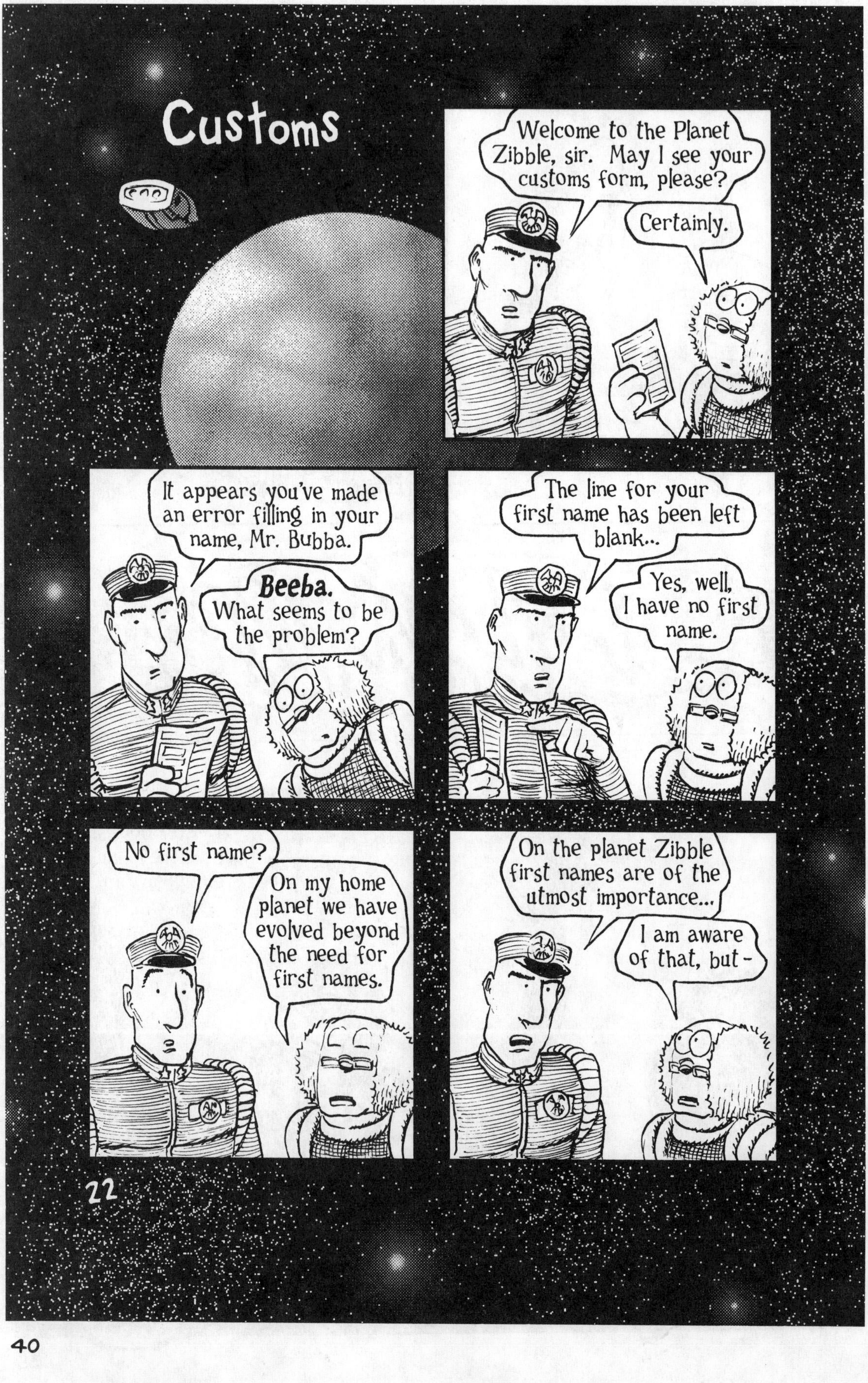
Customs
Welcome to the Planet Zibble, sir. May I see your customs form, please?
Certainly.
It appears you've made an error filling in your name, Mr. Bubba.
Beeba. What seems to be the problem?
The line for your first name has been left blank...
Yes, well, I have no first name.
No first name?
On my home planet we have evolved beyond the need for first names.
On the planet Zibble first names are of the utmost importance...
I am aware of that, but -
22

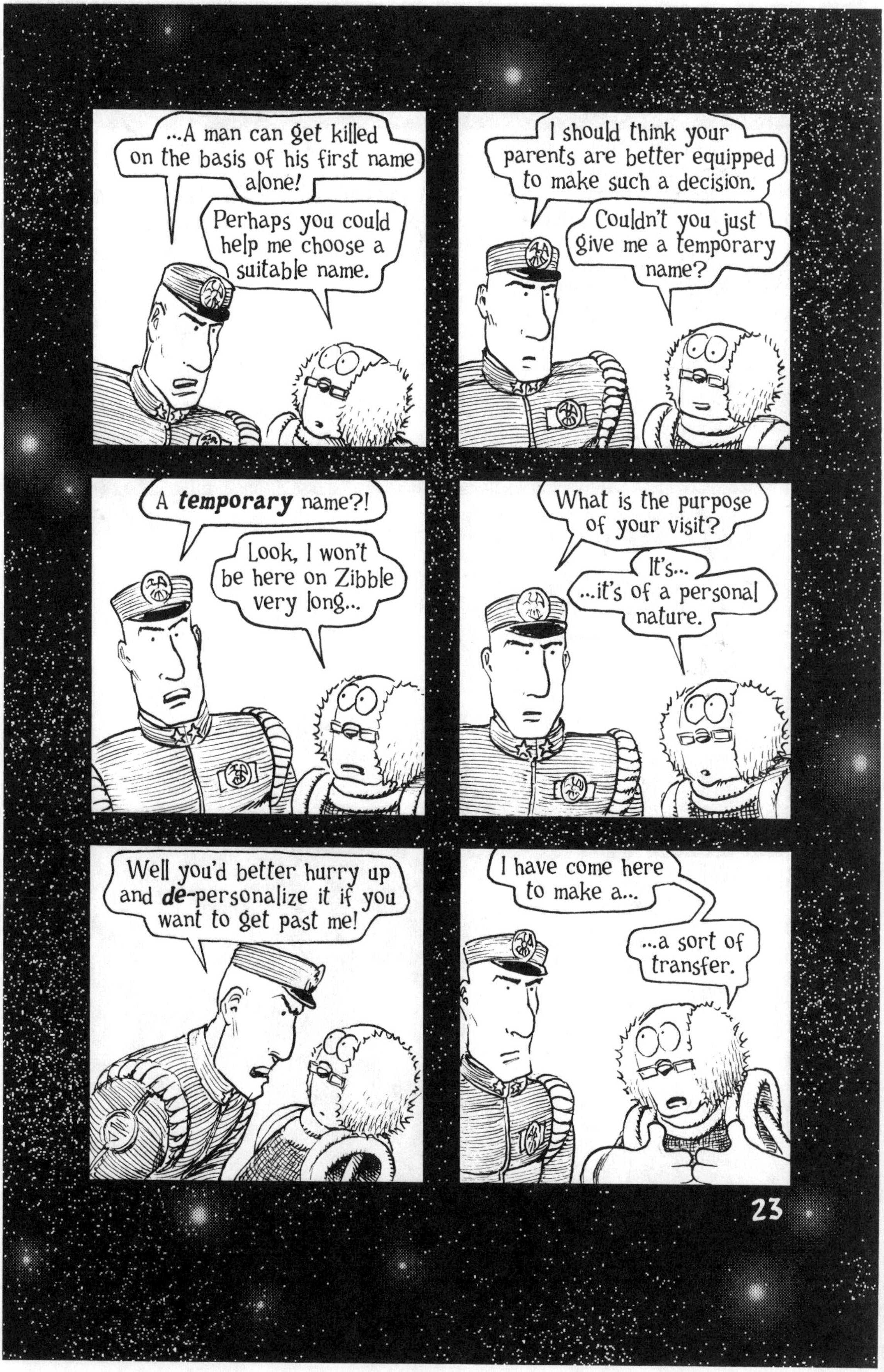

...A man can get killed on the basis of his first name alone!
Perhaps you could help me choose a suitable name.
I should think your parents are better equipped to make such a decision.
Couldn't you just give me a temporary name?
A **temporary** name?!
Look, I won't be here on Zibble very long...
What is the purpose of your visit?
It's... ...it's of a personal nature.
Well you'd better hurry up and **de**-personalize it if you want to get past me!
I have come here to make a...
...a sort of transfer.
23

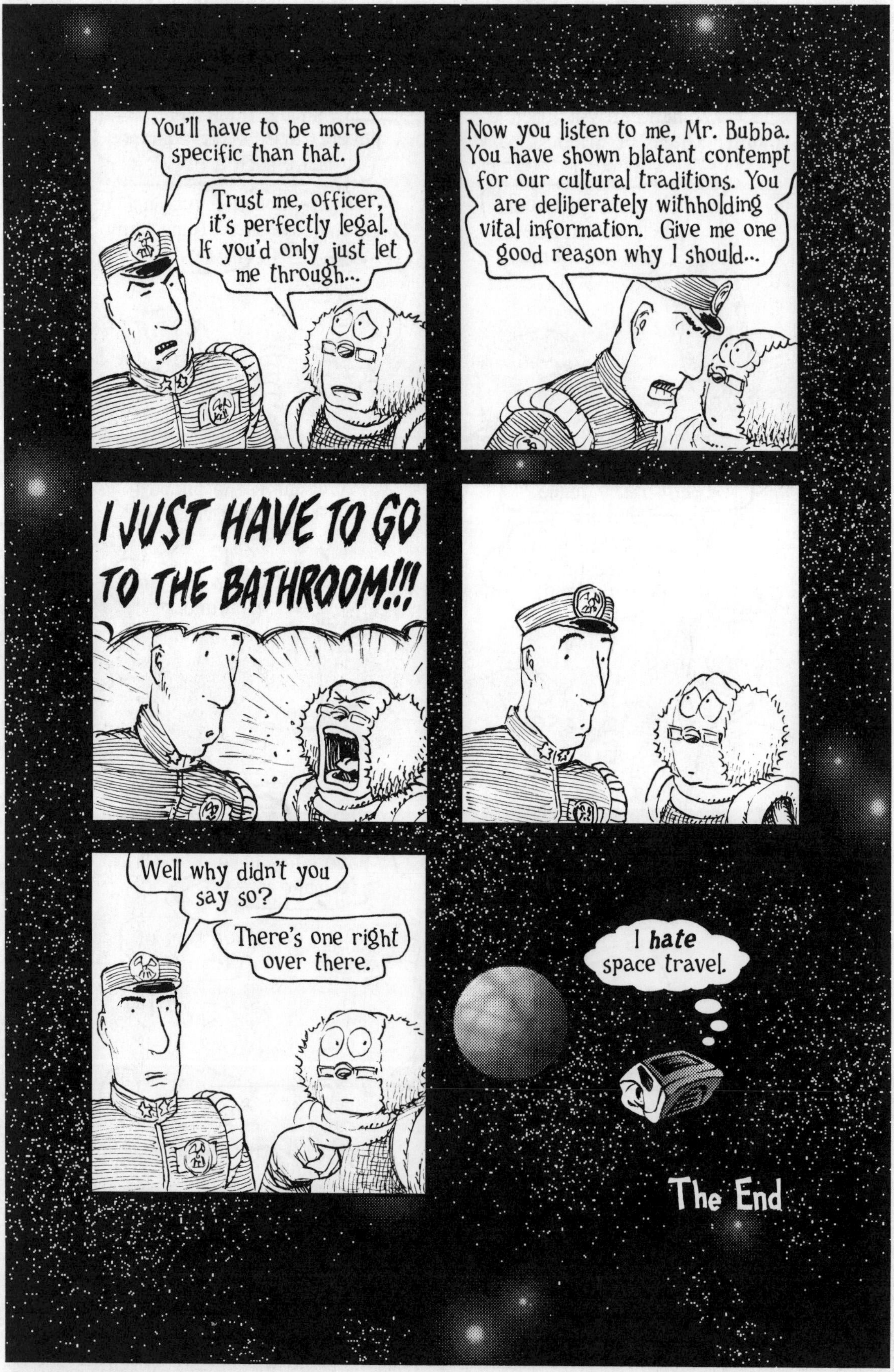

You'll have to be more specific than that.
Trust me, officer, it's perfectly legal. If you'd only just let me through...
Now you listen to me, Mr. Bubba. You have shown blatant contempt for our cultural traditions. You are deliberately withholding vital information. Give me one good reason why I should...
I JUST HAVE TO GO TO THE BATHROOM!!!
Well why didn't you say so?
There's one right over there.
I **hate** space travel.
The End

Mr. Beeba (& Akiko) in
"The Shape of Things To Come"

Hello there! I'd like to take a moment to extend my gratitude to you for purchasing yet another issue of "Akiko." Though many of you have written in expressing satisfaction with things just the way they are, I feel strongly that there is still a lot of room for improvement.

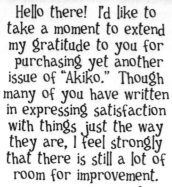

That's why you'll begin to see subtle changes in the style and substance of this comic book during the next few months. So that you won't be too alarmed when these changes occur, I'd like to preview a few of them for you right now.

First, let's have a look at the cover art. The fellow we've been using up until now has been reliable for the most part, and on occasion has even managed to produce aesthetically pleasing work.

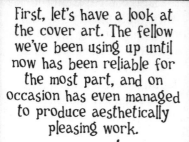

But let's face it, the "cartoony" approach is giving the book a very undesirable reputation and is no doubt practically *chasing* potential buyers away.

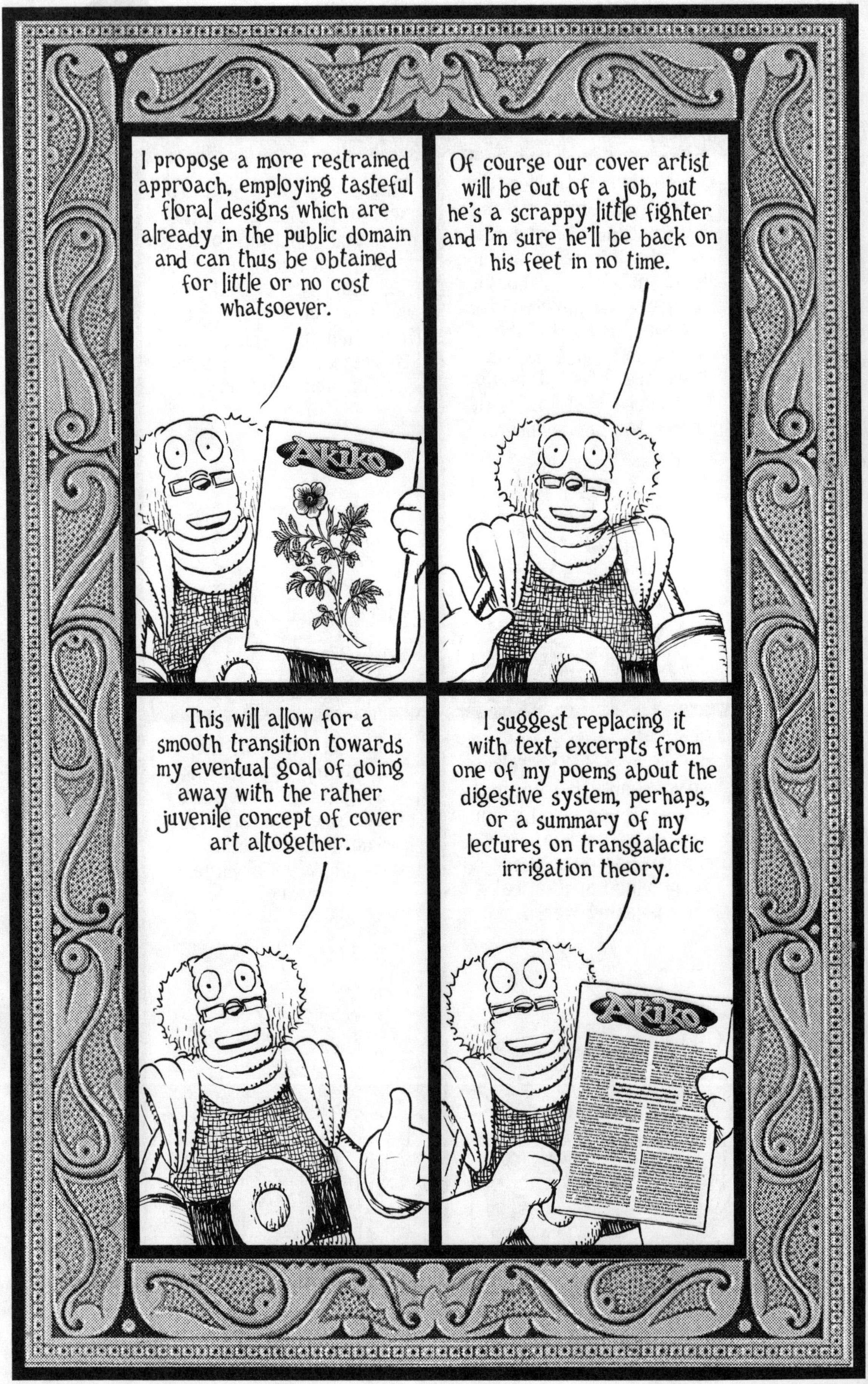

I propose a more restrained approach, employing tasteful floral designs which are already in the public domain and can thus be obtained for little or no cost whatsoever.
Akiko
Of course our cover artist will be out of a job, but he's a scrappy little fighter and I'm sure he'll be back on his feet in no time.
This will allow for a smooth transition towards my eventual goal of doing away with the rather juvenile concept of cover art altogether.
I suggest replacing it with text, excerpts from one of my poems about the digestive system, perhaps, or a summary of my lectures on transgalactic irrigation theory.
Akiko

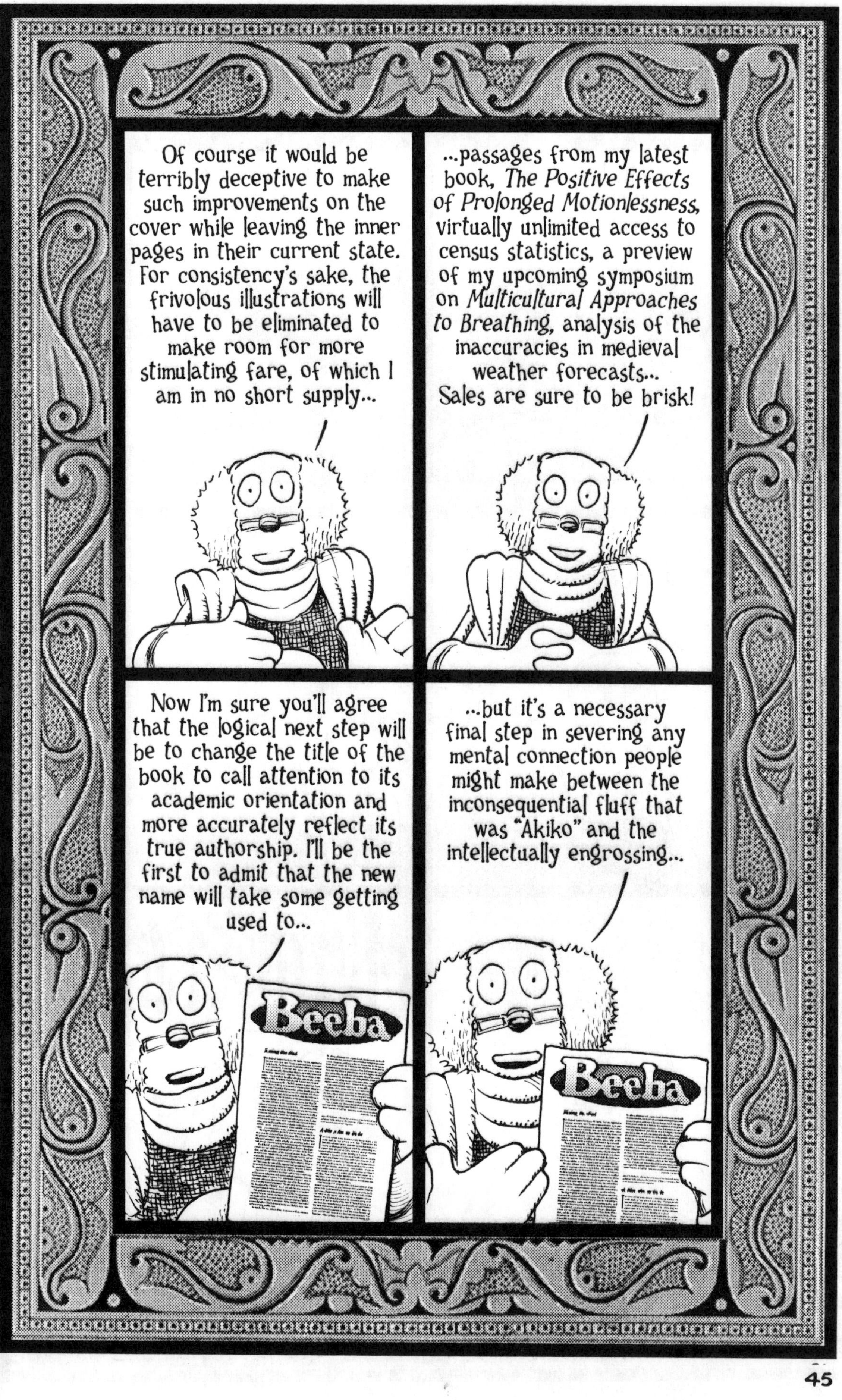
Of course it would be terribly deceptive to make such improvements on the cover while leaving the inner pages in their current state. For consistency's sake, the frivolous illustrations will have to be eliminated to make room for more stimulating fare, of which I am in no short supply...
...passages from my latest book, *The Positive Effects of Prolonged Motionlessness*, virtually unlimited access to census statistics, a preview of my upcoming symposium on *Multicultural Approaches to Breathing*, analysis of the inaccuracies in medieval weather forecasts... Sales are sure to be brisk!
Now I'm sure you'll agree that the logical next step will be to change the title of the book to call attention to its academic orientation and more accurately reflect its true authorship. I'll be the first to admit that the new name will take some getting used to...
Beeba
...but it's a necessary final step in severing any mental connection people might make between the inconsequential fluff that was "Akiko" and the intellectually engrossing...
Beeba

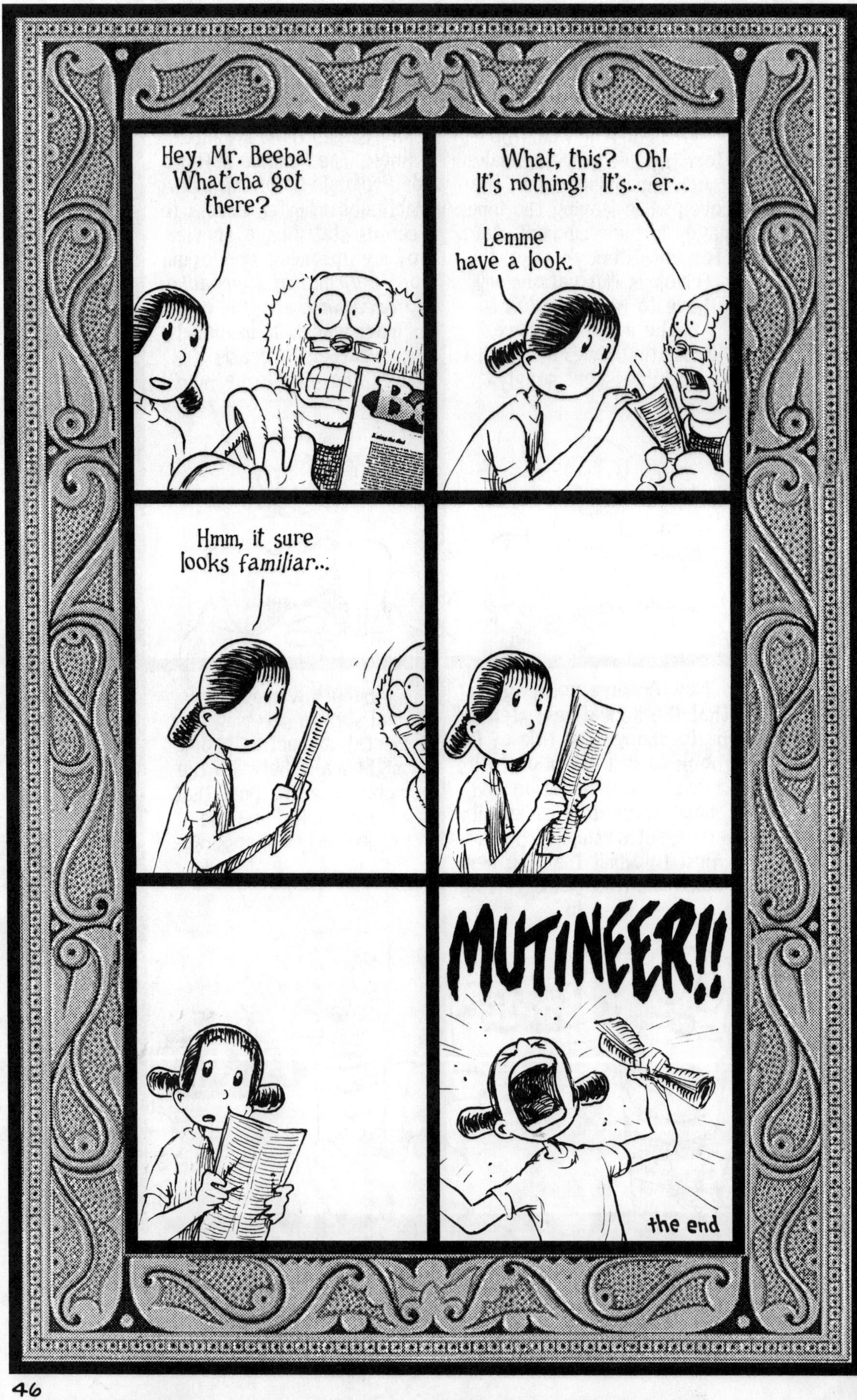
Hey, Mr. Beeba! What'cha got there?
What, this? Oh! It's nothing! It's... er...
Lemme have a look.
Hmm, it sure looks familiar...
MUTINEER!!
the end

Thirty Six Ways

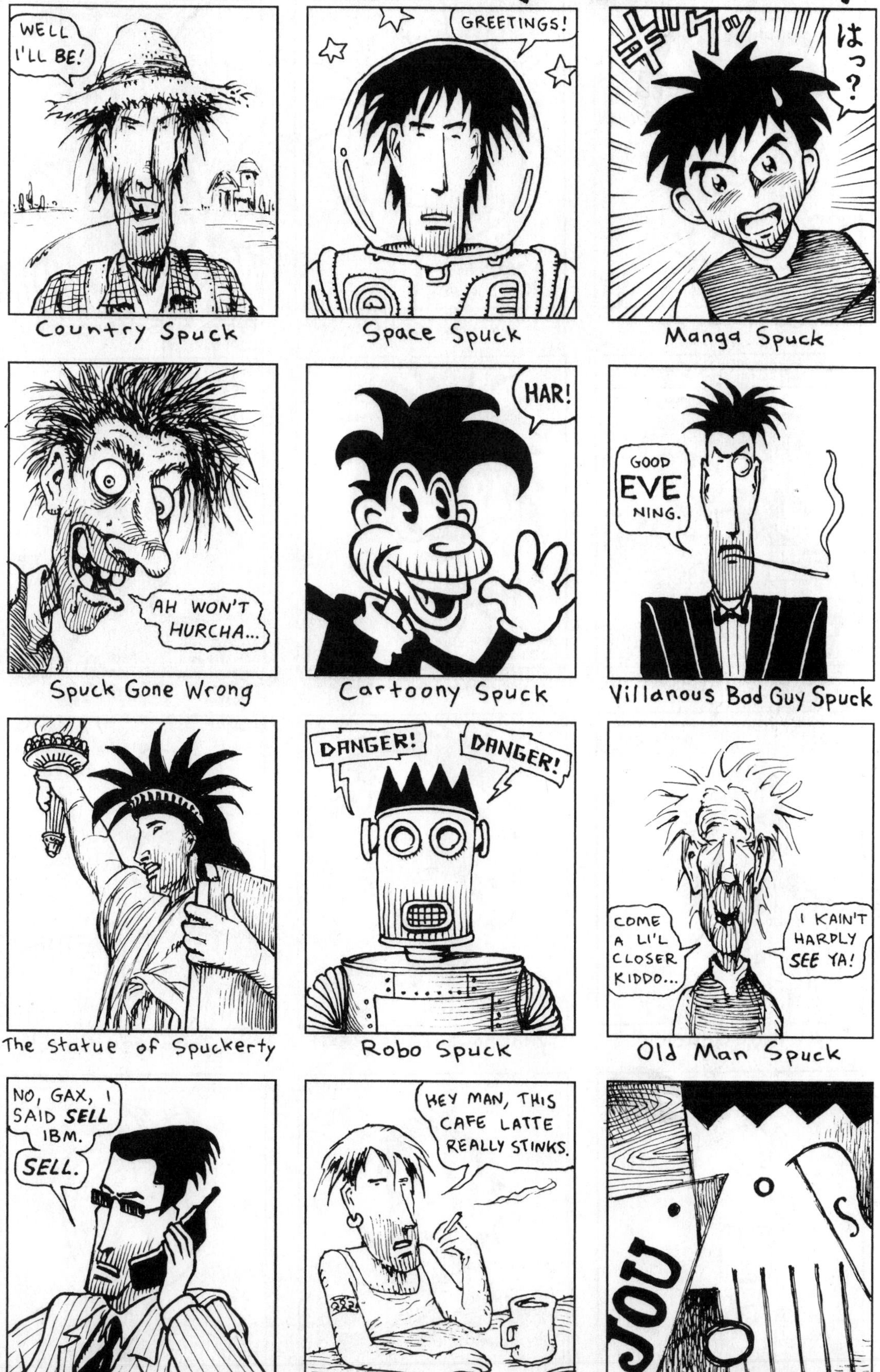

WELL I'LL BE!
Country Spuck
GREETINGS!
Space Spuck
はっ？
Manga Spuck
AH WON'T HURCHA...
Spuck Gone Wrong
HAR!
Cartoony Spuck
GOOD EVE NING.
Villanous Bad Guy Spuck
The Statue of Spuckerty
DANGER!
DANGER!
Robo Spuck
COME A LI'L CLOSER KIDDO...
I KAIN'T HARDLY SEE YA!
Old Man Spuck
NO, GAX, I SAID SELL IBM.
SELL.
Hot Shot Spuck
HEY MAN, THIS CAFE LATTE REALLY STINKS.
Slacker Spuck
Cubist Spuck

to Draw Spuckler

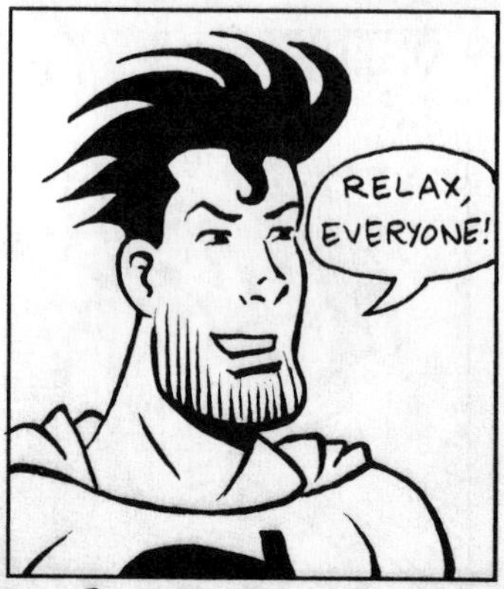
RELAX, EVERYONE!
Super Spuck

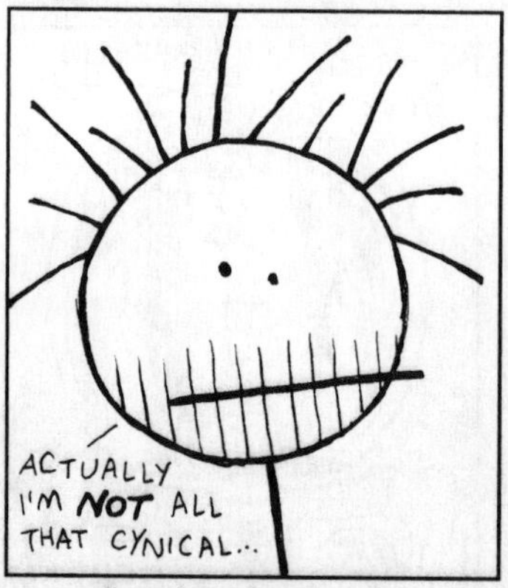
ACTUALLY I'M NOT ALL THAT CYNICAL...
Cynicalspuck

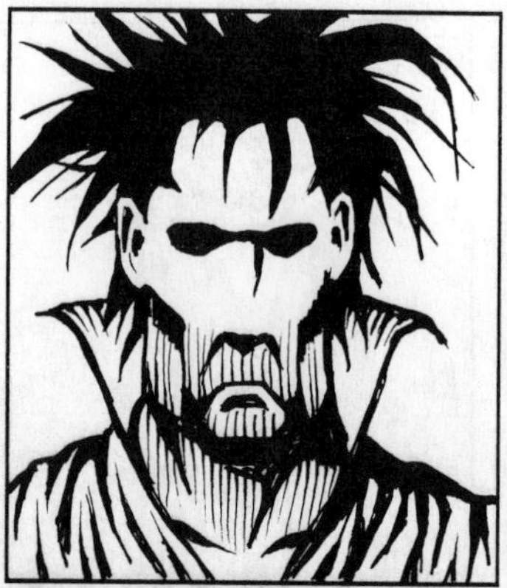
Grim'N'Gritty Spuck

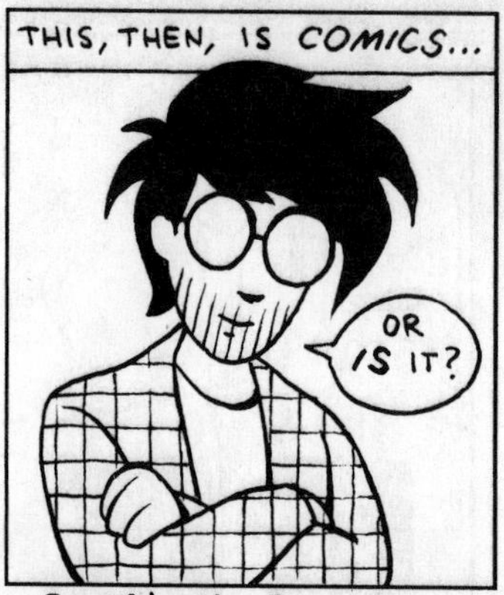
THIS, THEN, IS COMICS...
OR IS IT?
Scott McSpuck

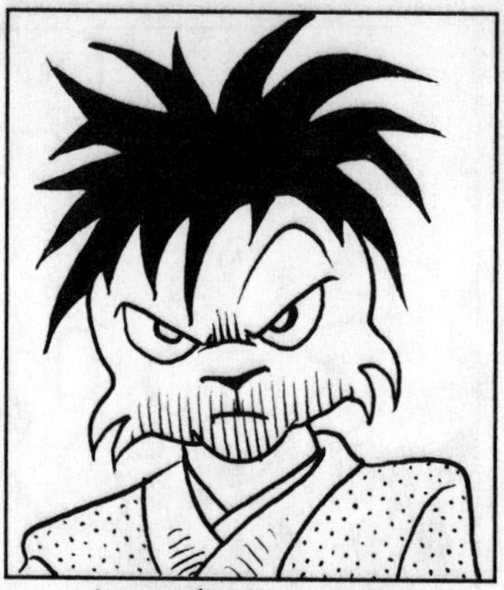
Usagi Yospucko

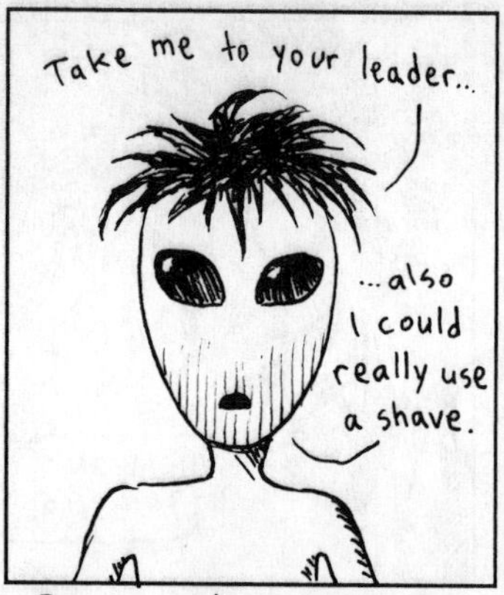
Take me to your leader..
...also I could really use a shave.
Space Alien Spuck

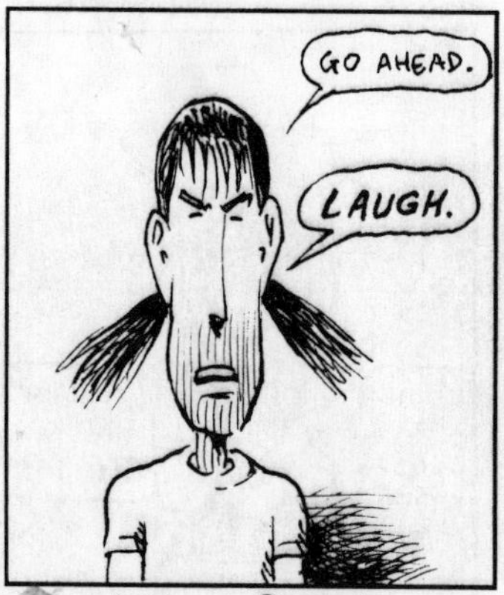
GO AHEAD.
LAUGH.
Akiko Spuck

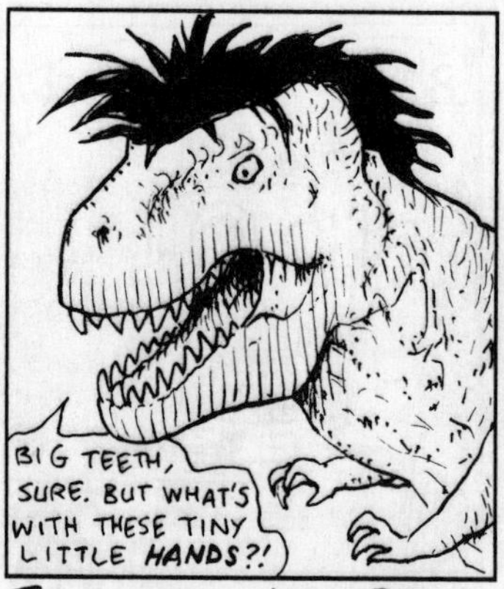
BIG TEETH, SURE. BUT WHAT'S WITH THESE TINY LITTLE HANDS?!
Tyrannospuckus Rex

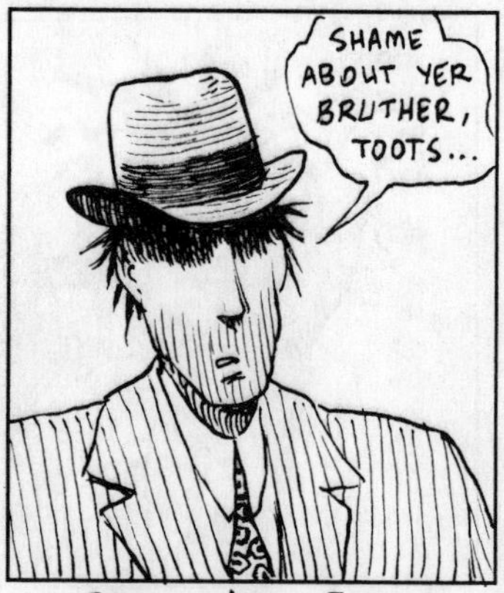
SHAME ABOUT YER BRUTHER, TOOTS...
Gangster Spuck

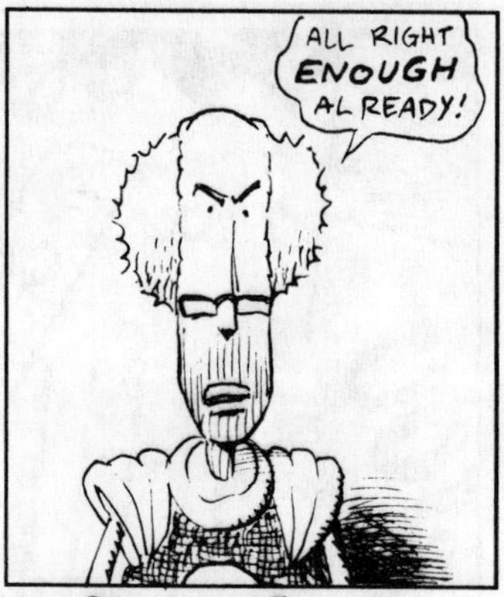
ALL RIGHT ENOUGH ALREADY!
Beeba Spuck

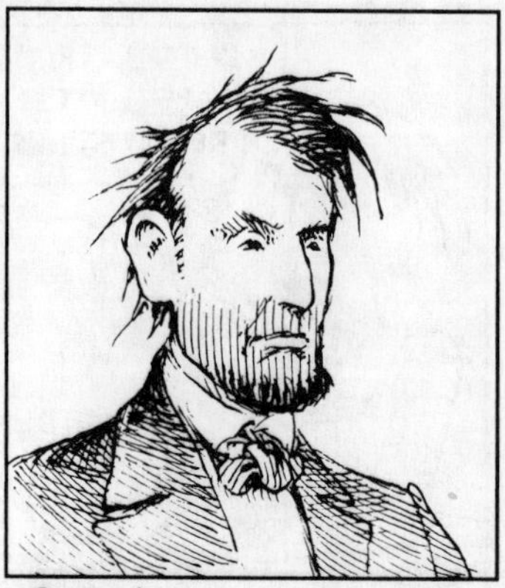
Spuckraham Lincoln

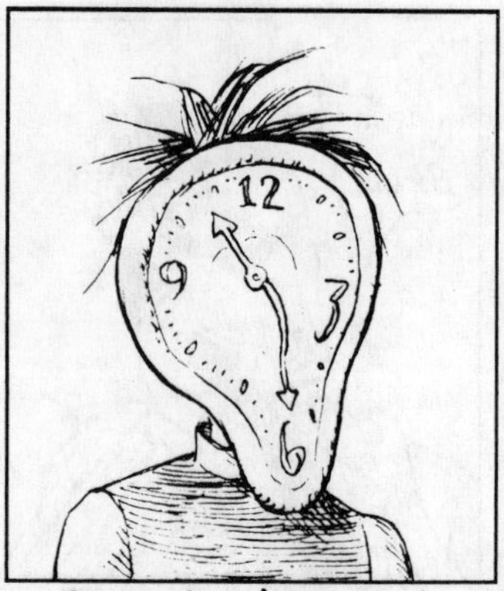
Spuckador Dali

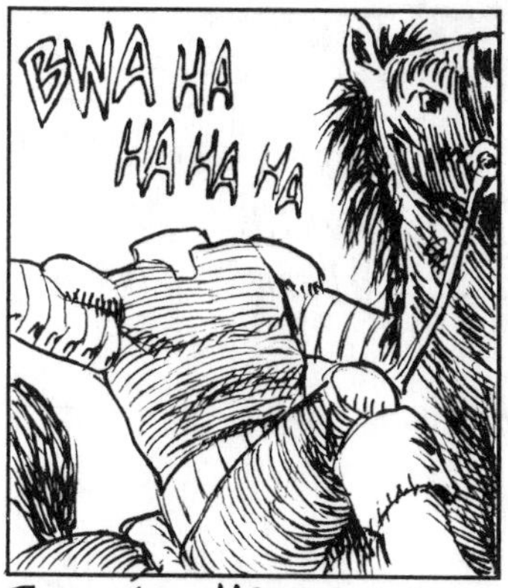
BWA HA
HA HA HA
The Headless Spuckman

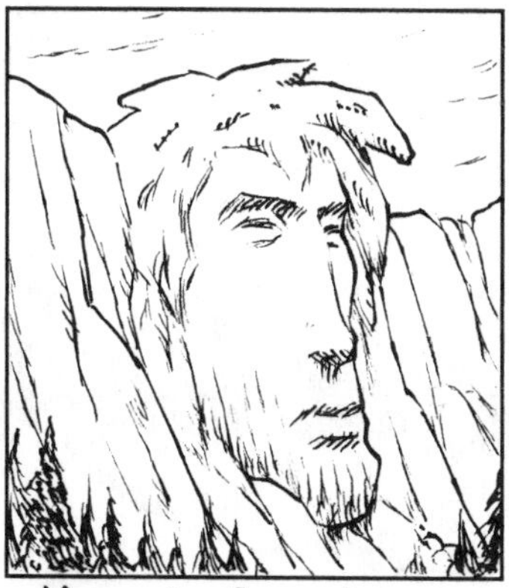
Mount Spuckmore

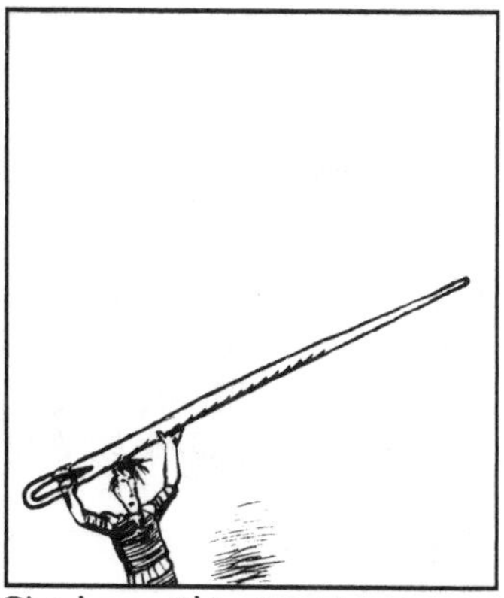
The Incredible Shrinking Spuck

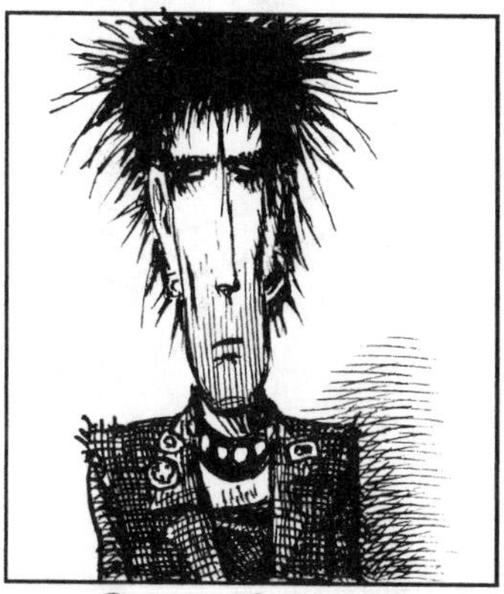
Goth Spuck

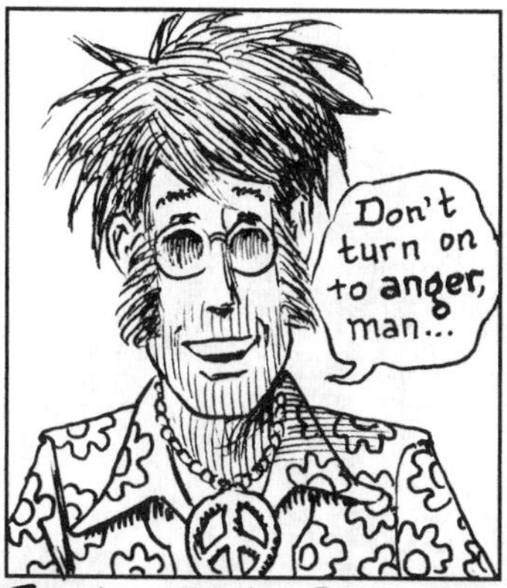
Don't turn on to anger, man...
Early 70's Spuck

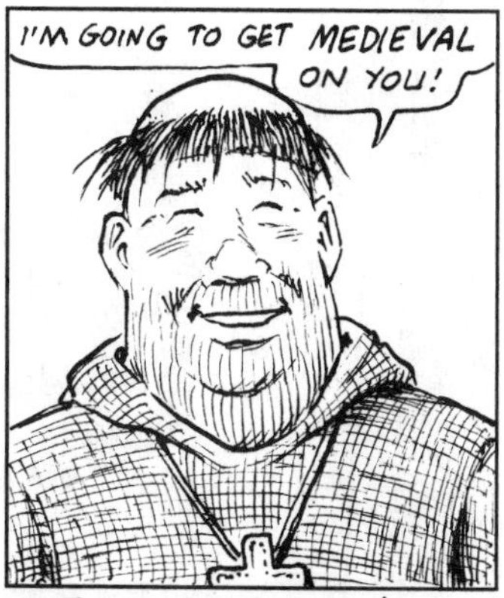
I'M GOING TO GET MEDIEVAL ON YOU!
Friar Spuck

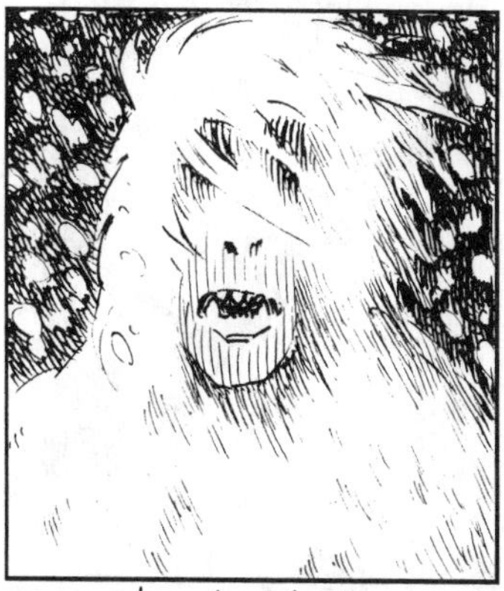
The Abominable Spuckman

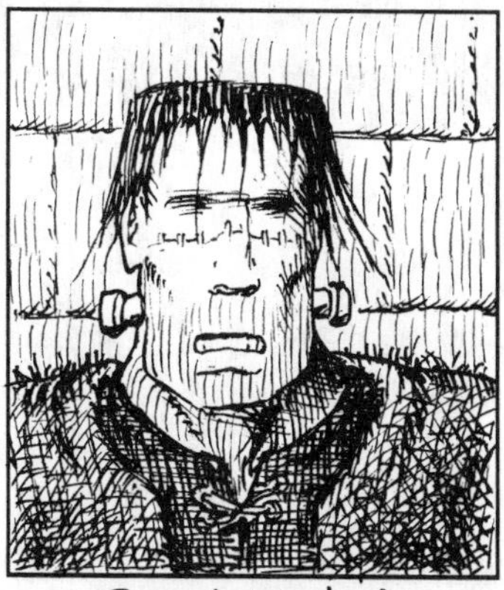
Spuckenstein

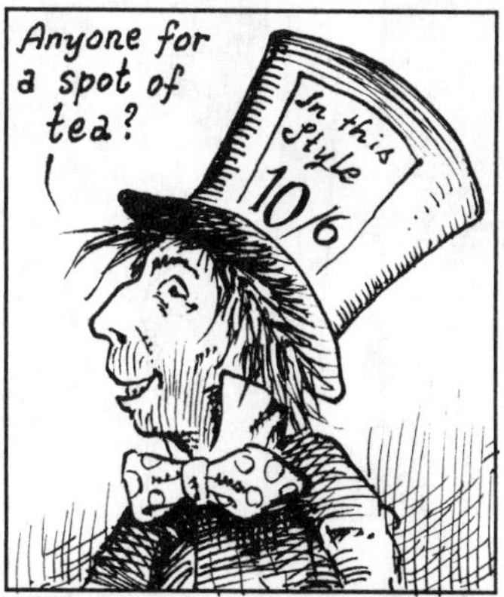
Anyone for a spot of tea?
In this Style 10/6
The Mad Spucker

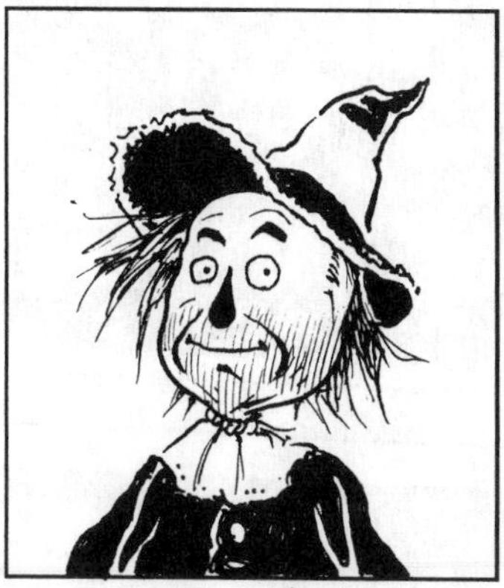
the Spuckcrow

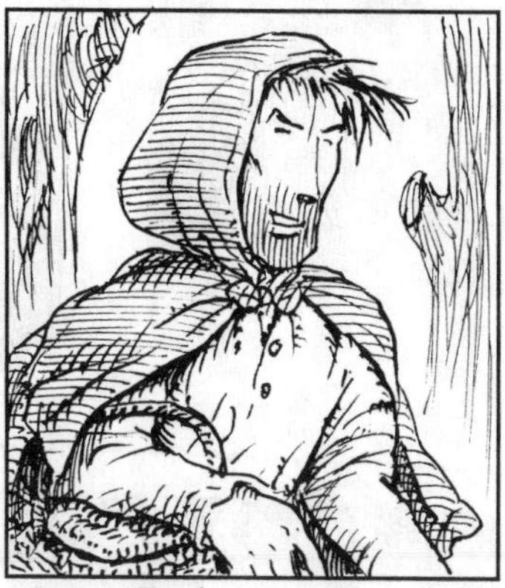
Litte Red Spuckinghood

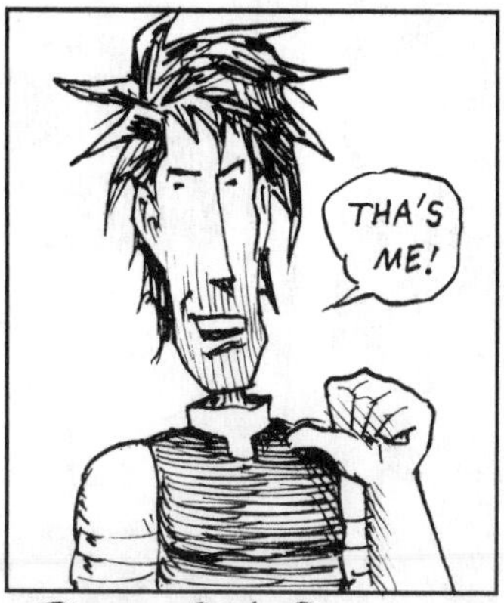
THA'S ME!
Plain Old Spuck

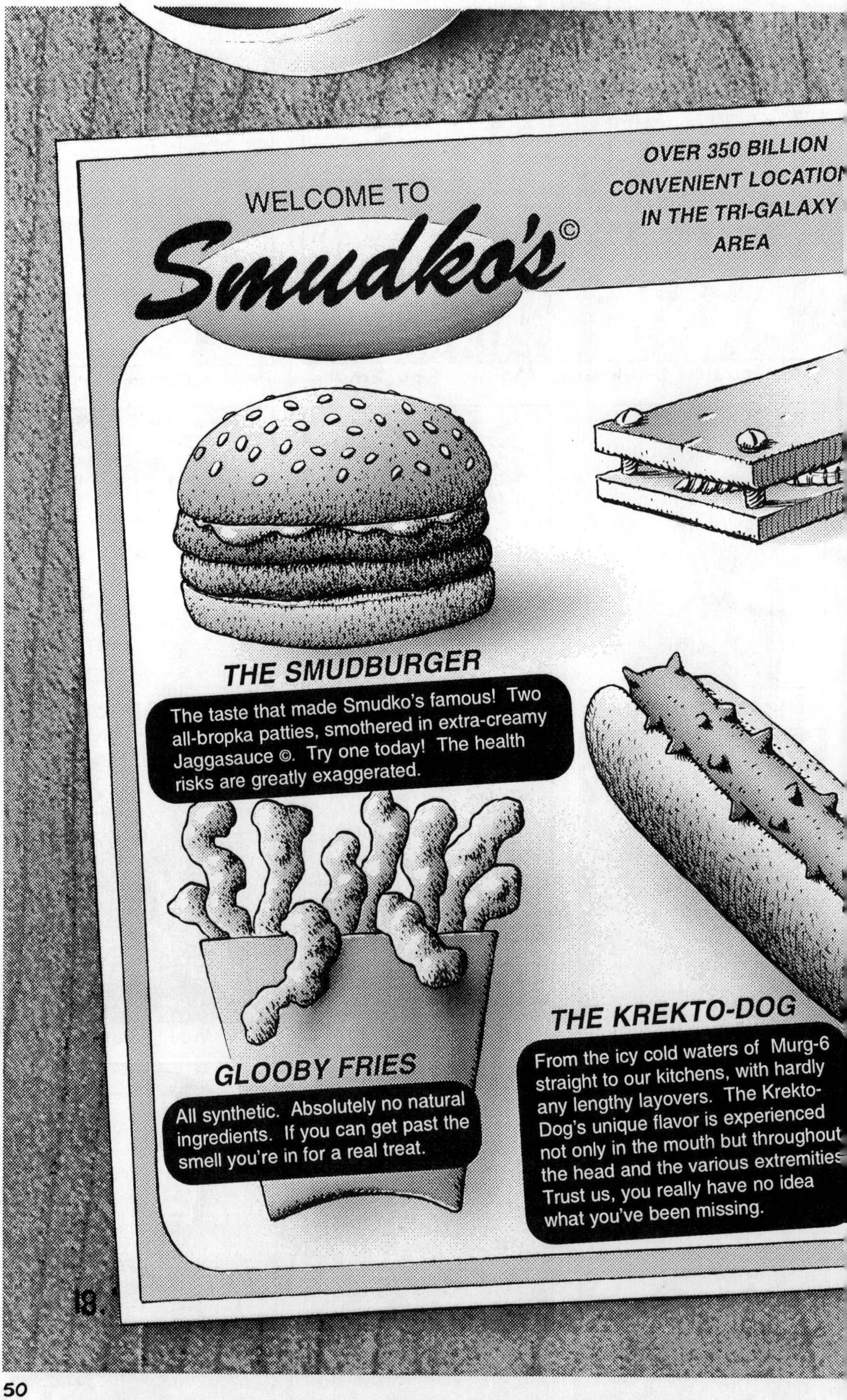
WELCOME TO
Smudko's©
OVER 350 BILLION CONVENIENT LOCATIO IN THE TRI-GALAXY AREA
THE SMUDBURGER
The taste that made Smudko's famous! Two all-bropka patties, smothered in extra-creamy Jaggasauce ©. Try one today! The health risks are greatly exaggerated.
GLOOBY FRIES
All synthetic. Absolutely no natural ingredients. If you can get past the smell you're in for a real treat.
THE KREKTO-DOG
From the icy cold waters of Murg-6 straight to our kitchens, with hardly any lengthy layovers. The Krekto-Dog's unique flavor is experienced not only in the mouth but throughout the head and the various extremities Trust us, you really have no idea what you've been missing.
18.

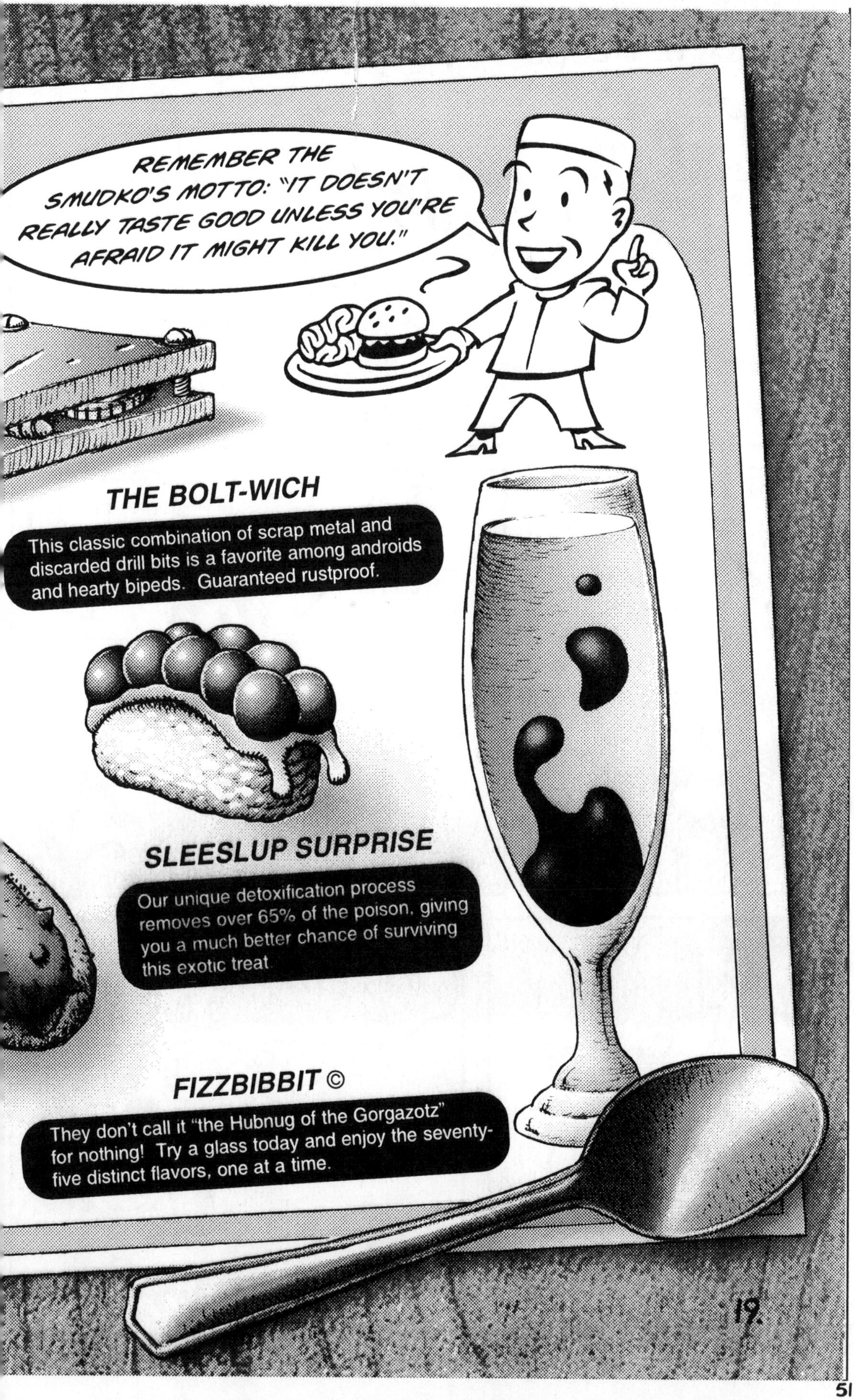
REMEMBER THE SMUDKO'S MOTTO: "IT DOESN'T REALLY TASTE GOOD UNLESS YOU'RE AFRAID IT MIGHT KILL YOU."
THE BOLT-WICH
This classic combination of scrap metal and discarded drill bits is a favorite among androids and hearty bipeds. Guaranteed rustproof.
SLEESLUP SURPRISE
Our unique detoxification process removes over 65% of the poison, giving you a much better chance of surviving this exotic treat.
FIZZBIBBIT ©
They don't call it "the Hubnug of the Gorgazotz" for nothing! Try a glass today and enjoy the seventy-five distinct flavors, one at a time.
19

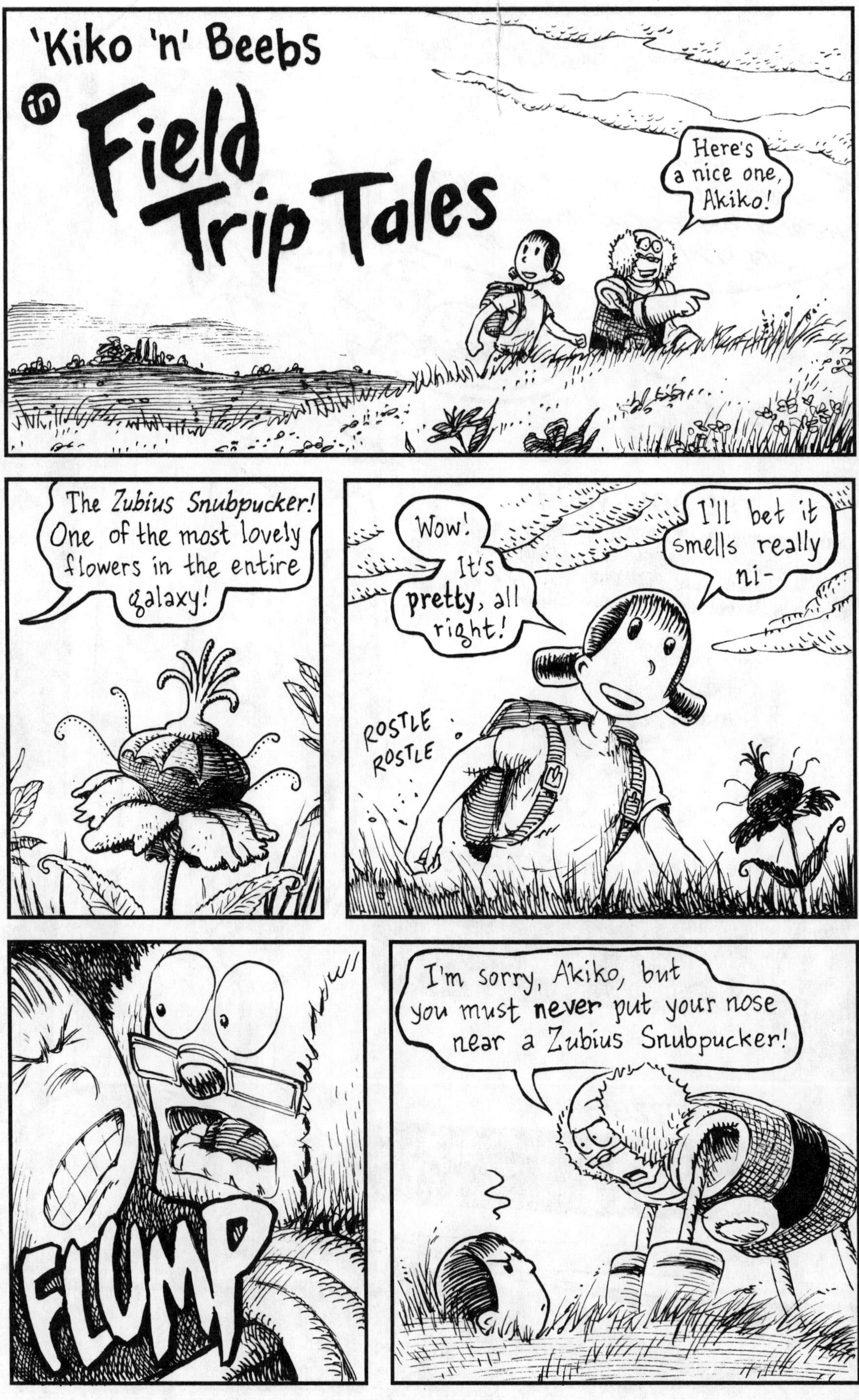
'Kiko 'n' Beebs
in
Field Trip Tales
Here's a nice one, Akiko!
The *Zubius Snubpucker!* One of the most lovely flowers in the entire galaxy!
Wow! It's **pretty**, all right!
I'll bet it smells really ni-
ROSTLE ROSTLE
FLUMP
I'm sorry, Akiko, but you must **never** put your nose near a Zubius Snubpucker!

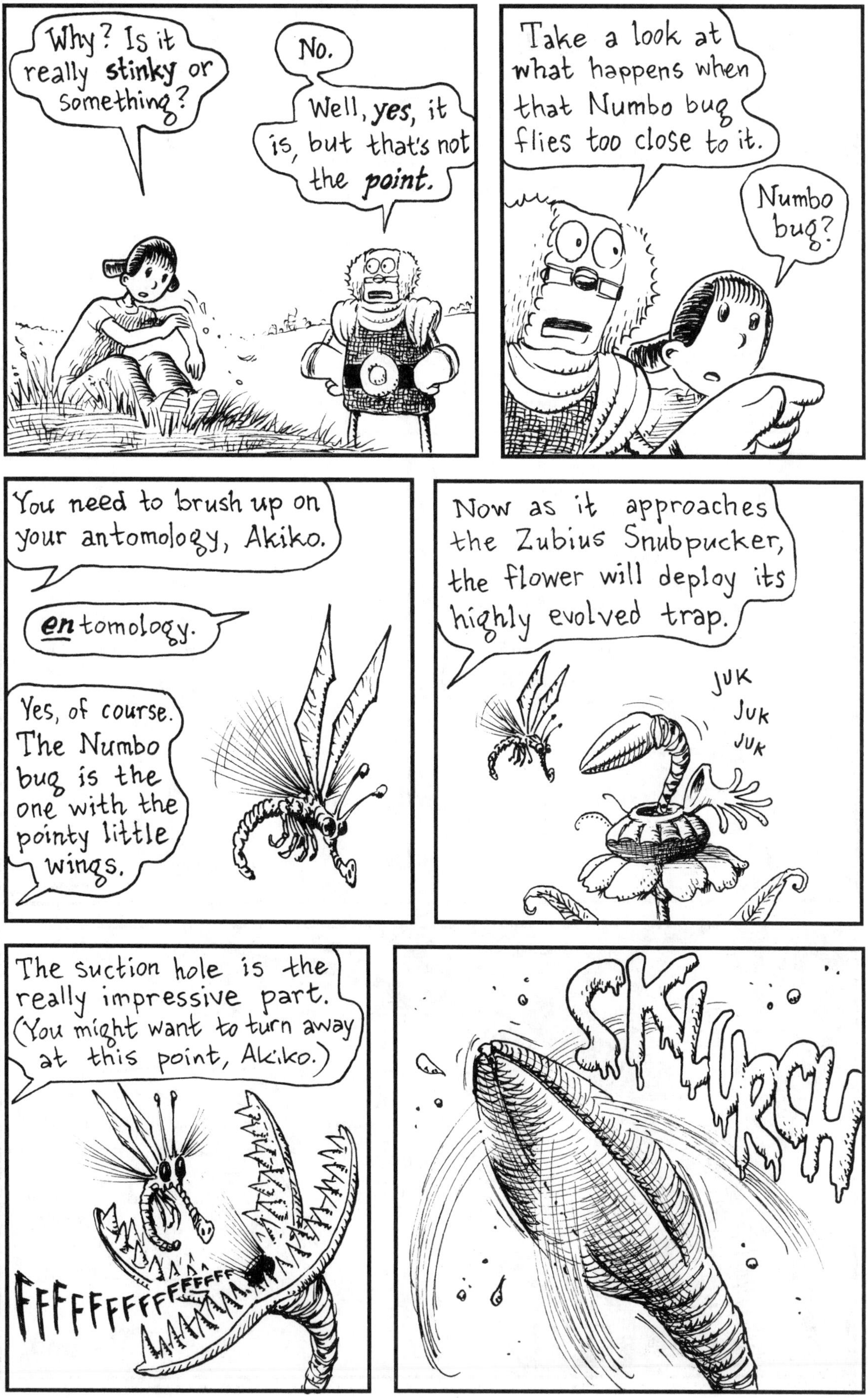
Why? Is it really stinky or something?
No.
Well, yes, it is, but that's not the point.
Take a look at what happens when that Numbo bug flies too close to it.
Numbo bug?
You need to brush up on your antomology, Akiko.
entomology.
Yes, of course. The Numbo bug is the one with the pointy little wings.
Now as it approaches the Zubius Snubpucker, the flower will deploy its highly evolved trap.
JUK
JUK
JUK
The suction hole is the really impressive part. (You might want to turn away at this point, Akiko.)
FFFFFFFFFFFFFFF
SKLURCH

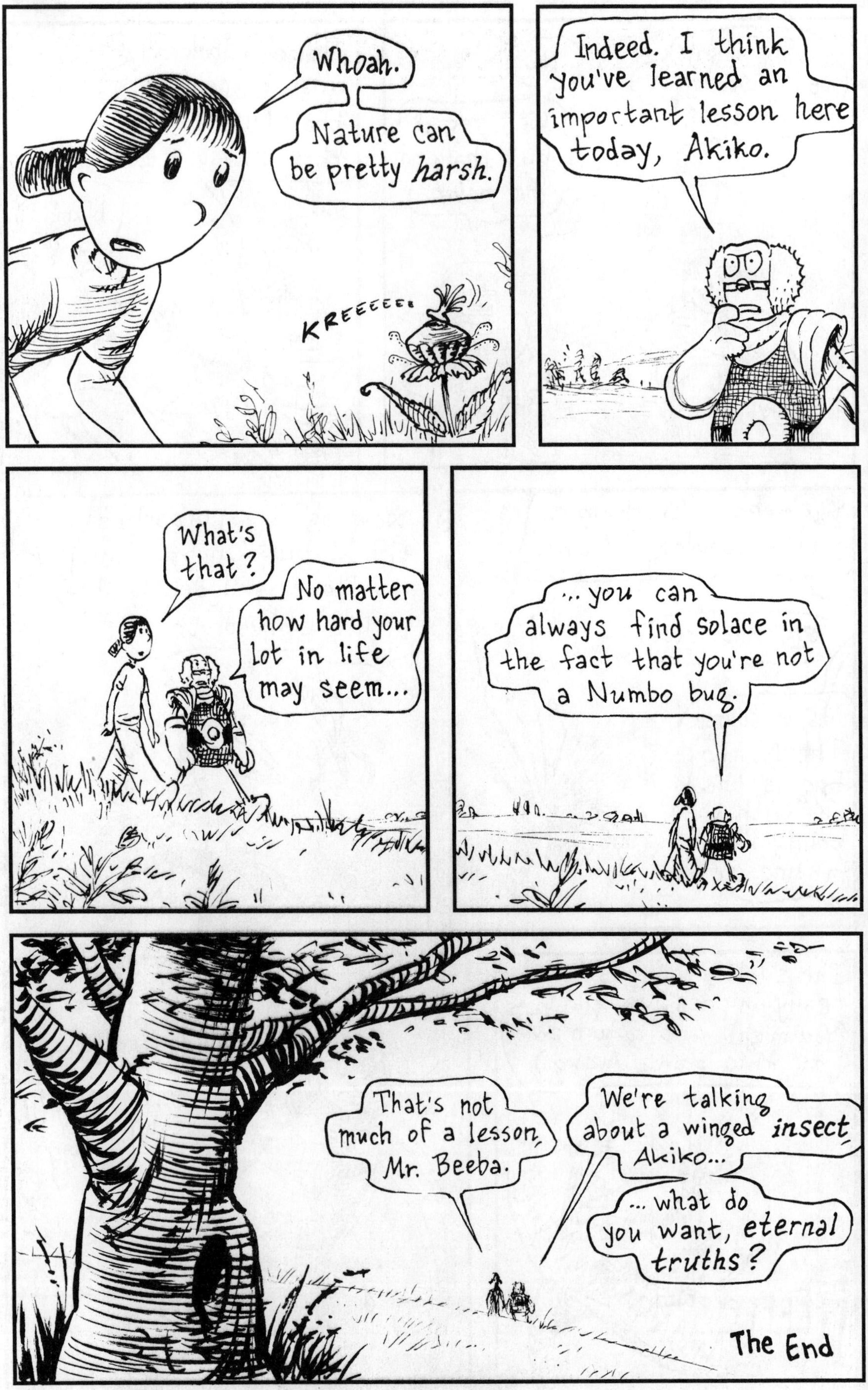
Whoah.
Nature can be pretty *harsh*.
KREEEEEE
Indeed. I think you've learned an important lesson here today, Akiko.
What's that?
No matter how hard your lot in life may seem...
... you can always find solace in the fact that you're not a Numbo bug.
That's not much of a lesson, Mr. Beeba.
We're talking about a winged *insect*, Akiko...
... what do you want, eternal *truths*?
The End

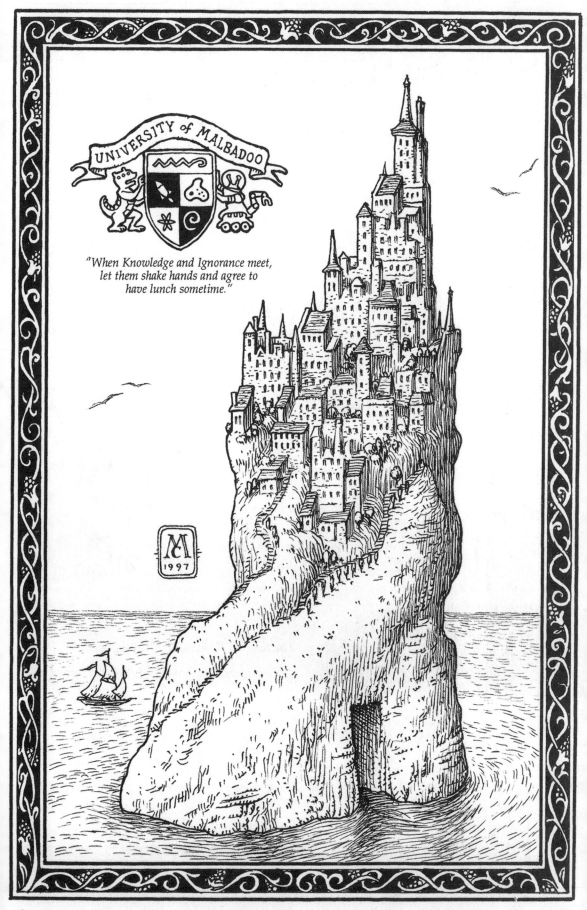

UNIVERSITY of MALBADOO

"When Knowledge and Ignorance meet,
let them shake hands and agree to
have lunch sometime."

A Very Silly Guide to Extr

The Streptidius Hern

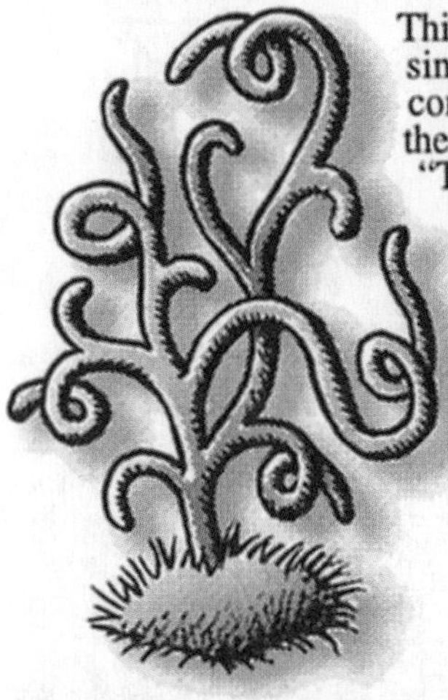

This remarkable plant has fascinated botanists since the dawn of time (or time immemorial, whichever comes first). The Streptidius Hern, commonly known as the "Little Hern," and known more commonly still as "That Little Plant with the Curly Things," requires neither sunlight nor water for its survival, and is thus free to grow wherever it chooses, so long as it respects zoning laws. The Streptidius Hern was named after the famous botanist, Leopold Streptidius-Hern, not because he was the first to discover the plant (as it is commonly believed), but because it was the end of the week, they were running short of names, and his had a pretty nice ring to it.

The Three-Eyed Bloy Bloy

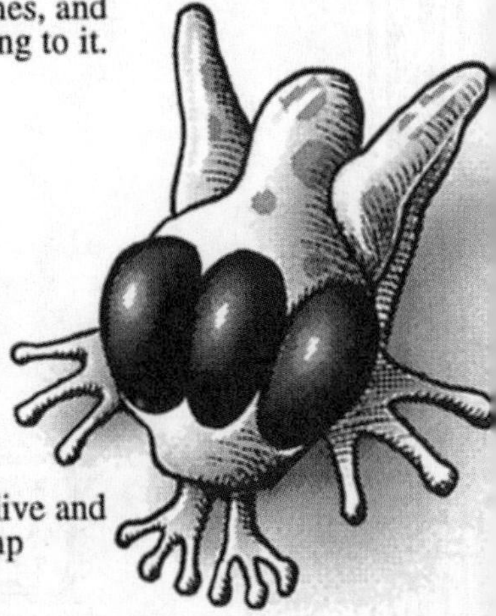

Once a common sight along the shores of Whumpucket Swamp, the Three-Eyed Bloy Bloy has very nearly been driven into extinction by the poor quality of popular music in recent years. Thanks to a team of carefully trained conservationists (and a smaller number of conversationalists), the last few Bloy Bloys are alive and well, and are considering moving to a nicer swamp in a more convenient location.

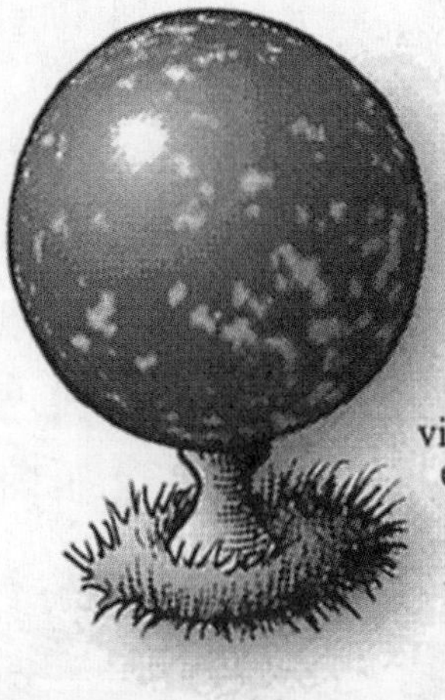

The Spotted Habnibbet-Flumoggadiller

At first glance you might mistake this rare plant for some sort of exotic mushroom. And you'd be right. That is to say, you'd be right to make the mistake. It's *not* a mushroom. But how were you to know? In actual fact it is a rare flower known as the Spotted Habnibbet-Flumoggadiller (which is virtually identical to the *Hab*nibbet-Flumoggadiller, except for the spots). Experts theorize that the spots evolved over millions of years for no particular reason, other than to give experts something to theorize about.

errestrial Flora & Fauna

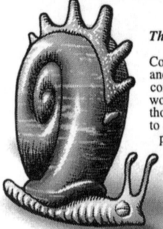

The Horned Riggbeau

Common throughout the mountains of Upper and Lower Yuzonia, the Horned Riggbeau is completely blind and thus makes its way through the world by means of a highly-refined sense of smell, though on occasion even this is insufficient, forcing it to stop and ask for directions. Once thought to possess magical properties, the shell of the Horned Riggbeau was for many years traded among Yuzonian tribesmen and witch doctors as a sort of currency; a well-crafted spear could be had for just 30 *riggbeaus*, whereas upwards of 20,000 *riggbeaus* were required for the purchase of a small motor car.

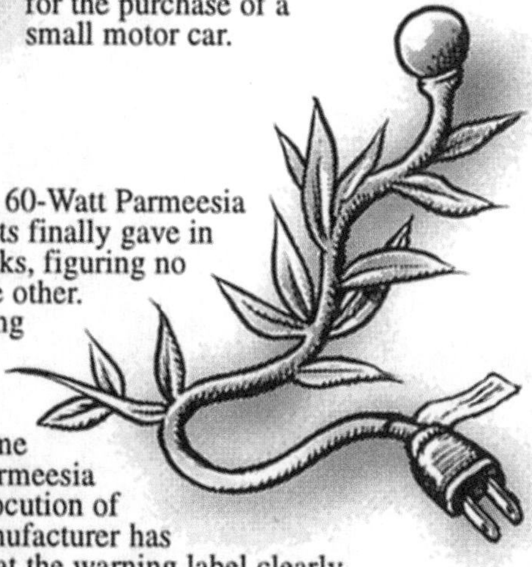

The 60-Watt Parmeesia

Although technically not a plant, the 60-Watt Parmeesia *looks* so much like a plant that experts finally gave in and began including it in botany books, figuring no one would really care one way or the other. Largely confined to cities and outlying suburbs, the 60-Watt Parmeesia can only rarely be found growing in the wild, and then only with the help of incredibly long extension cords. Some have called for an outright ban of Parmeesia plants, following the death by electrocution of a gardener earlier this year. The manufacturer has defended its product, pointing out that the warning label clearly advises against overwatering.

The Nublit Worm

The Nublit Worm caused a sensation several years ago when it decided to locate its head in the middle of its body, in open defiance of the "one end or the other" policy which had become the animal kingdom standard. This novel approach was then copied by many other animals with varying degrees of success (and in a number of cases some very badly bruised shins). Most agree that it hasn't really helped the Nublit species as a whole, apart from the increased publicity, and that the effort would have been better spent on aquiring arms and legs, or even just a bit of body hair.

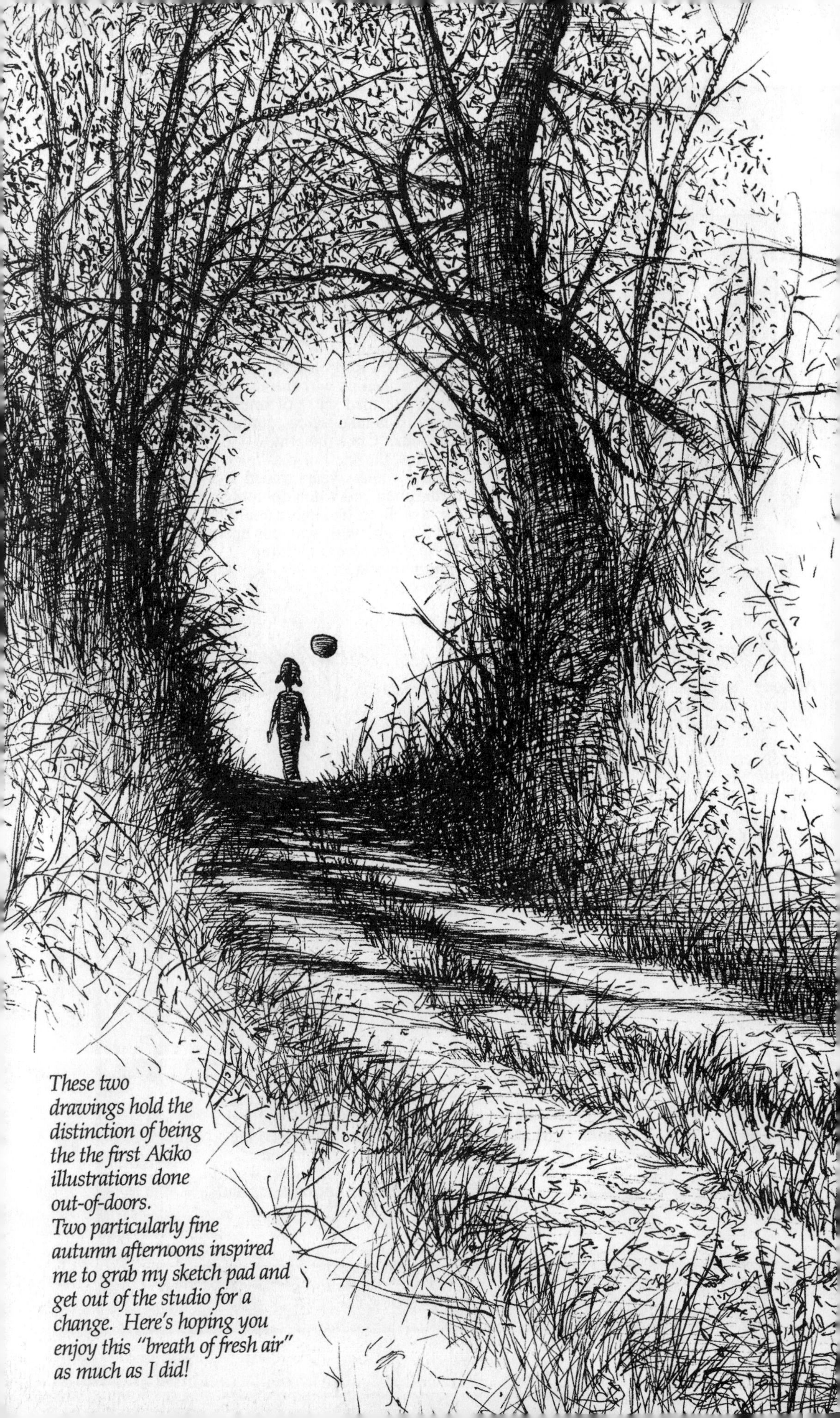

These two drawings hold the distinction of being the the first Akiko illustrations done out-of-doors. Two particularly fine autumn afternoons inspired me to grab my sketch pad and get out of the studio for a change. Here's hoping you enjoy this "breath of fresh air" as much as I did!

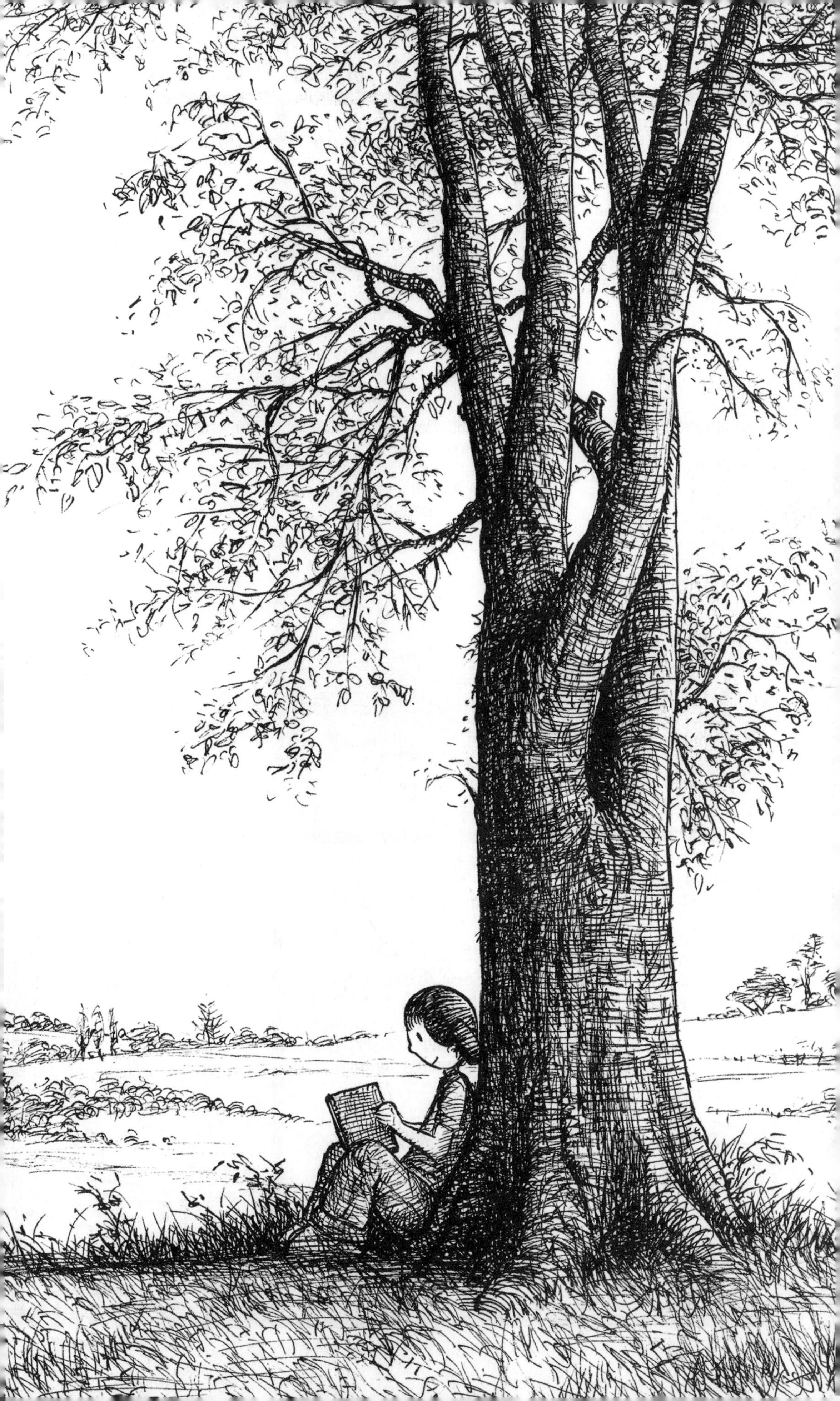

'KiKO 'n' GAX in "Man vs. Machine"

It must be pretty cool to be a robot, Gax. I mean, you never have to worry about getting sick or anything like that, do you?
NO MA'AM, ALTHOUGH I COULD BE PROGRAMMED TO GET SICK...
I wouldn't recommend it, Gax. Unless there's a test or something you need to get out of.
I SUPPOSE THE CLOSEST I GET TO ILLNESS IS WHEN I HAVE ONE OF MY PERIODIC BREAKDOWNS.
What's that like?
MOST UNPLEASANT, MA'AM. A BIT LIKE HAVING YOUR BRAIN MELT.
Eeew. That doesn't sound cool at all.
THERE'S NOTHING LIKE THAT FEELING WHEN THEY GET YOU UP AND RUNNING AGAIN, THOUGH.
Pretty nice, huh?
EXHILARATING, MA'AM. ESPECIALLY AFTER A GOOD OIL CHANGE: THAT REALLY GETS THE OLD PISTONS MOVING...
I guess I'll have to take your word for it.
IF YOU DON'T MIND ME ASKING, MA'AM, WHAT IS IT LIKE TO BE HUMAN?
Oh, it's mostly really cool, so long as you're still a kid. Adult humans have it pretty rough...
...at least they make it look that way. Always running around making phonecalls and worrying about stuff.
Some grownups look so busy half the time it's as if there's a great, big monster chasing them around all day.
IT SOUNDS LIKE I'M BETTER OFF AS A ROBOT, MA'AM.
Yeah, Gax. You probably are...
The End

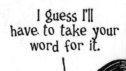

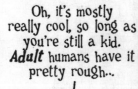

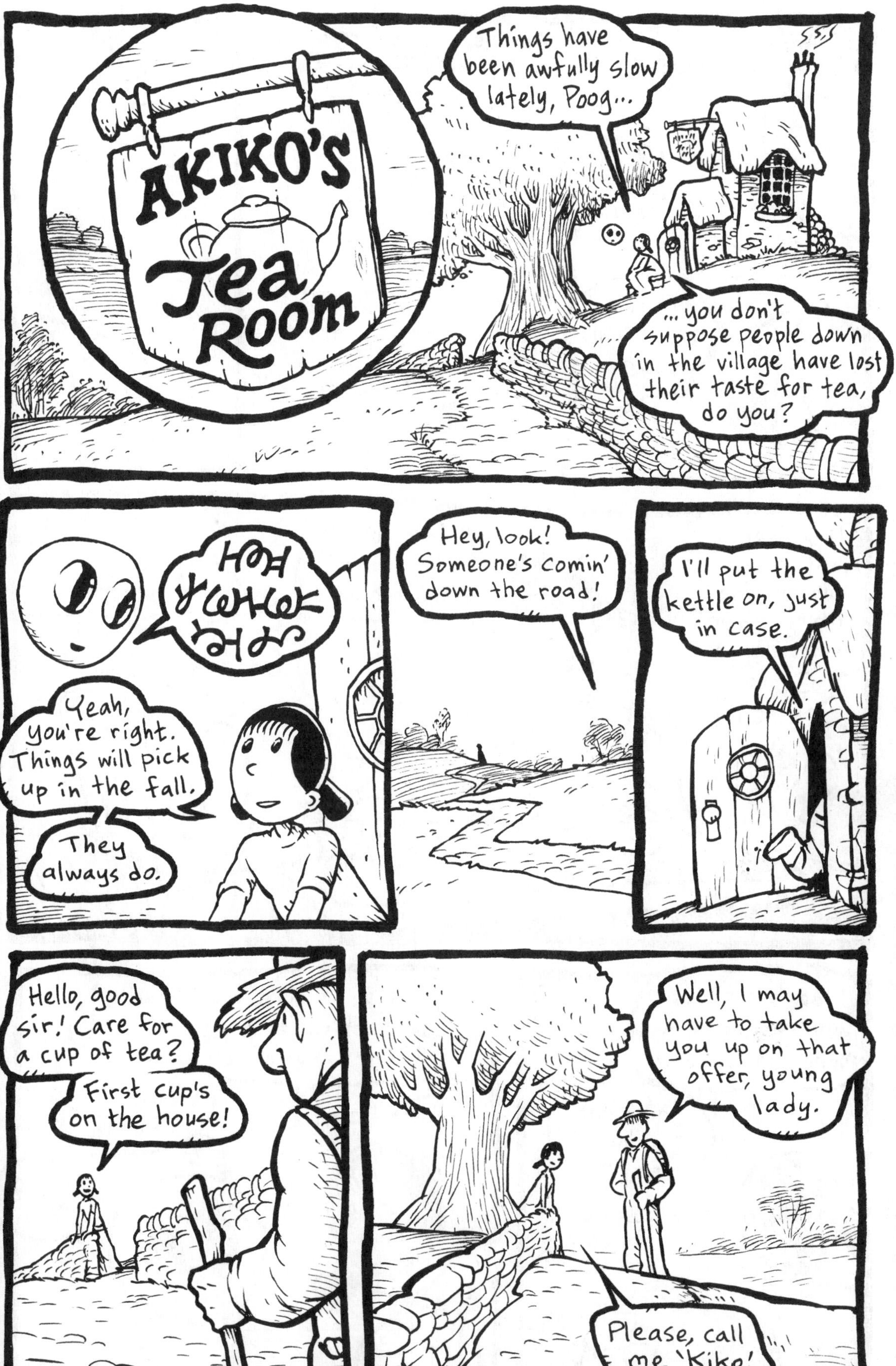
AKIKO'S Tea Room
Things have been awfully slow lately, Poog...
...you don't suppose people down in the village have lost their taste for tea, do you?
Yeah, you're right. Things will pick up in the fall.
They always do.
Hey, look! Someone's comin' down the road!
I'll put the kettle on, just in case.
Hello, good sir! Care for a cup of tea?
First cup's on the house!
Well, I may have to take you up on that offer, young lady.
Please, call me 'Kiko!

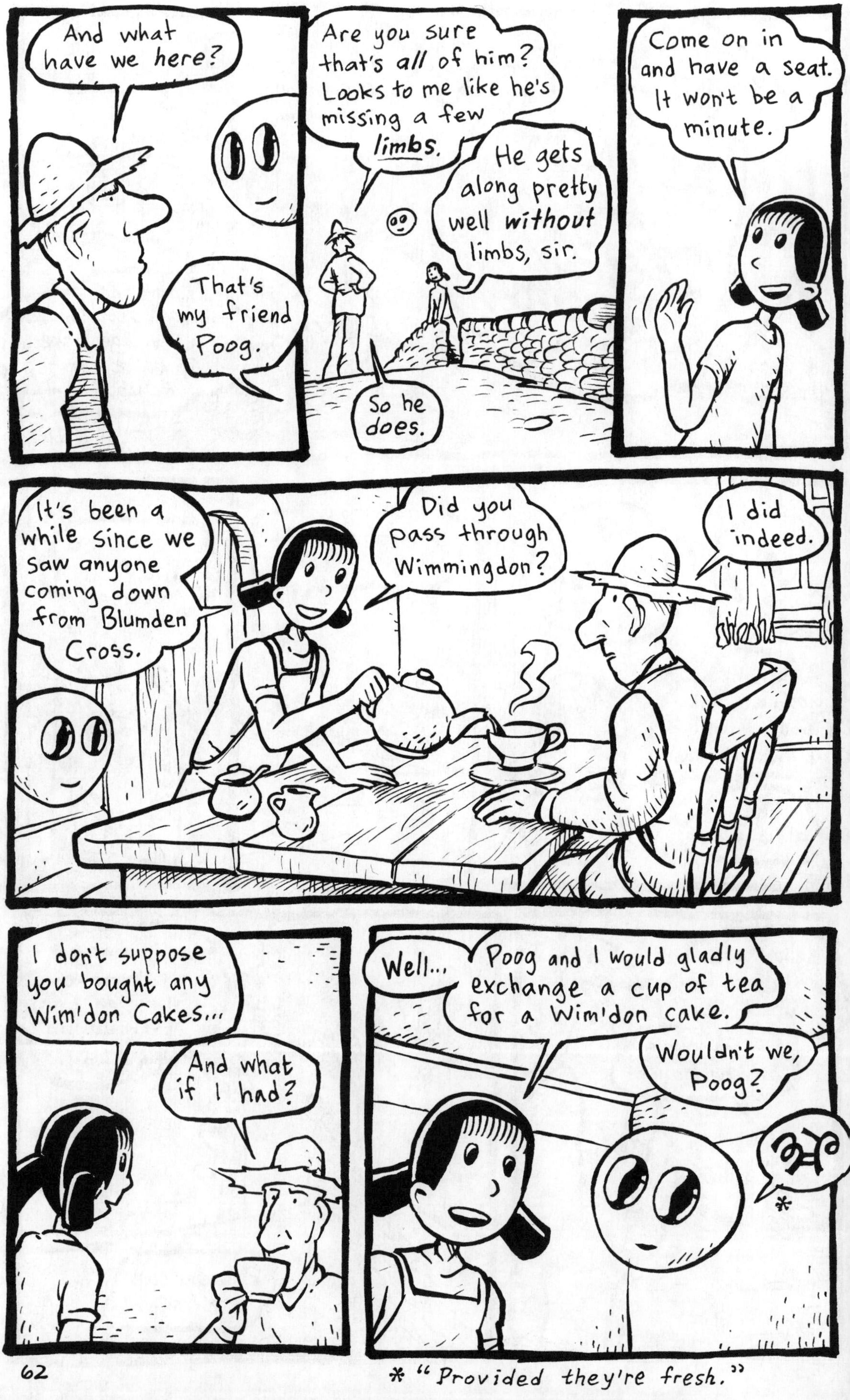
And what have we here?
That's my friend Poog.
Are you sure that's all of him? Looks to me like he's missing a few limbs.
He gets along pretty well without limbs, sir.
So he does.
Come on in and have a seat. It won't be a minute.
It's been a while since we saw anyone coming down from Blumden Cross.
Did you pass through Wimmingdon?
I did indeed.
I don't suppose you bought any Wim'don Cakes...
And what if I had?
Well...
Poog and I would gladly exchange a cup of tea for a Wim'don cake.
Wouldn't we, Poog?
*

* "Provided they're fresh."

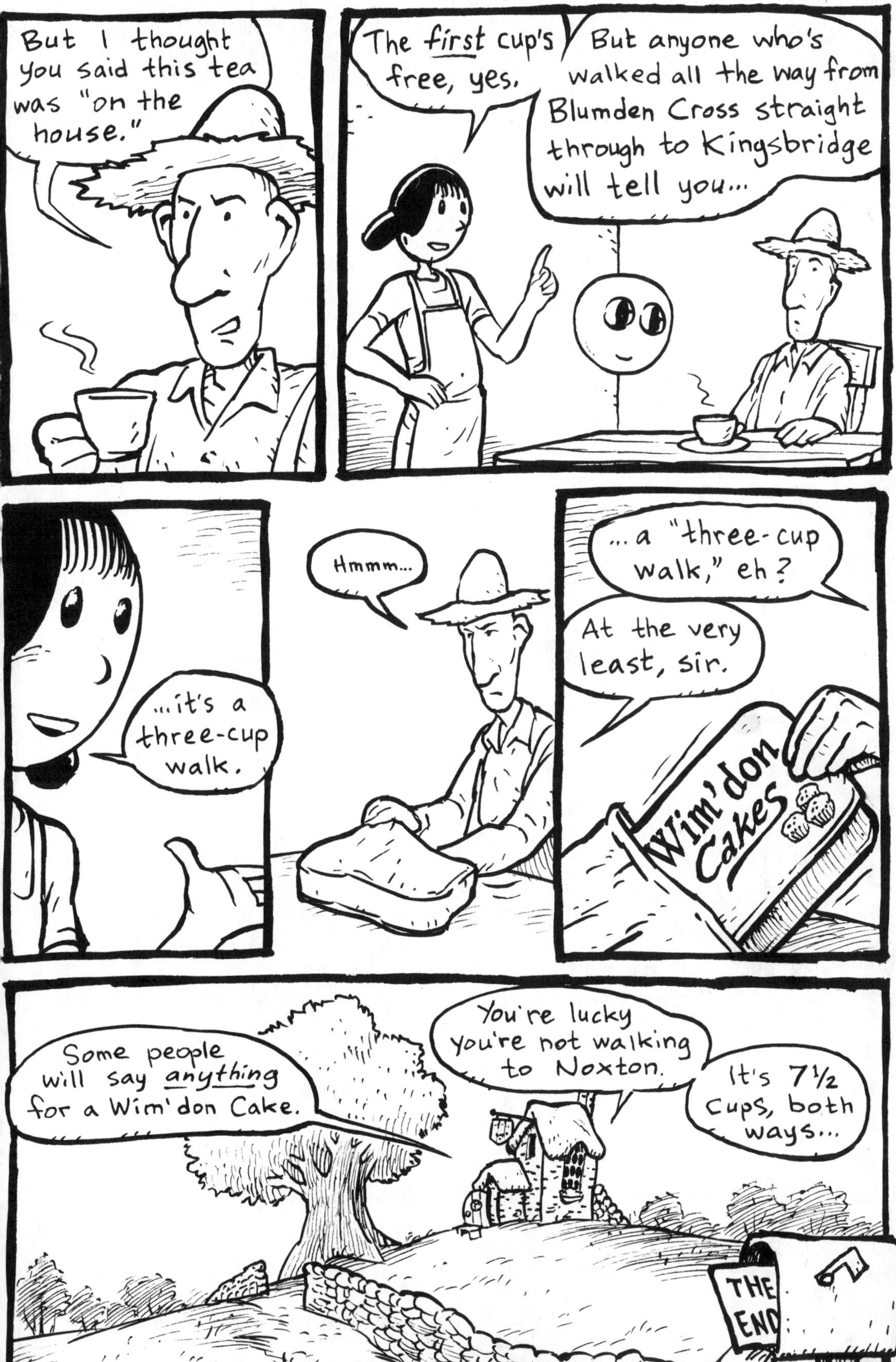

But I thought you said this tea was "on the house."
The first cup's free, yes.
But anyone who's walked all the way from Blumden Cross straight through to Kingsbridge will tell you...
...it's a three-cup walk.
Hmmm...
...a "three-cup walk," eh?
At the very least, sir.
Wim'don Cakes
Some people will say anything for a Wim'don Cake.
You're lucky you're not walking to Noxton.
It's 7½ cups, both ways...
THE END

Okay, you've seen these guys in action, but do you really *know* these robots? Sharpen your pencils and take some notes, friends. It's time to review...

The Crew: An Introduction

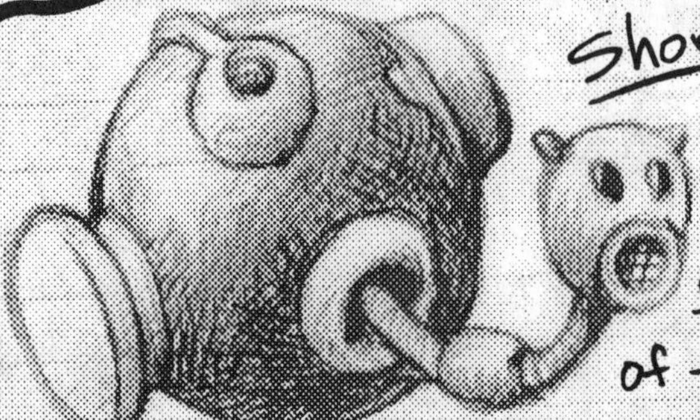

Shorpy

Sassy, sharp-tongued, & self-assured, Shorpy is a street-smart 'bot from the lower east side of the Andromeda Galaxy. He's capable of understanding seventeen different languages, and of making flippant remarks in each and every one of them.

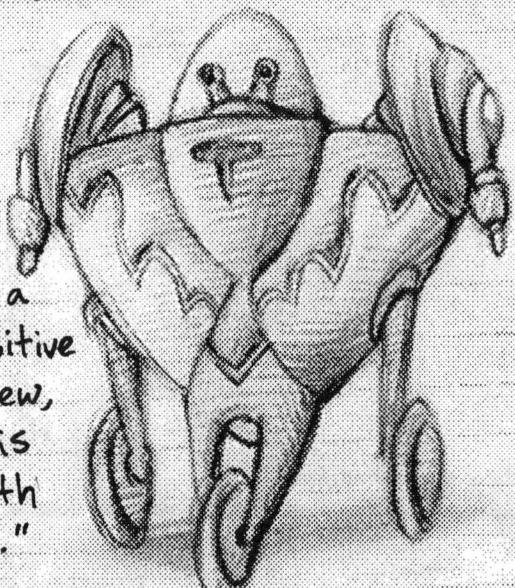

Captain Tupp

Beneath Tupp's pink-and-green exterior lies a heart of gold. Ever sensitive to the needs of his crew, Tupp's code of ethics is gravely out of step with Gothtek's "bottom line."

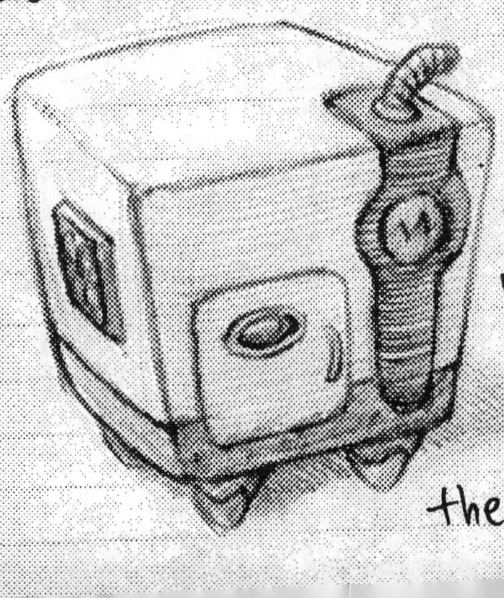

Nonk

Incapable of speech, Nonk is anything but dumb. Within his databank lies the blueprint of the entire Fognon-6, knowledge that may prove crucial to the survival of the crew.

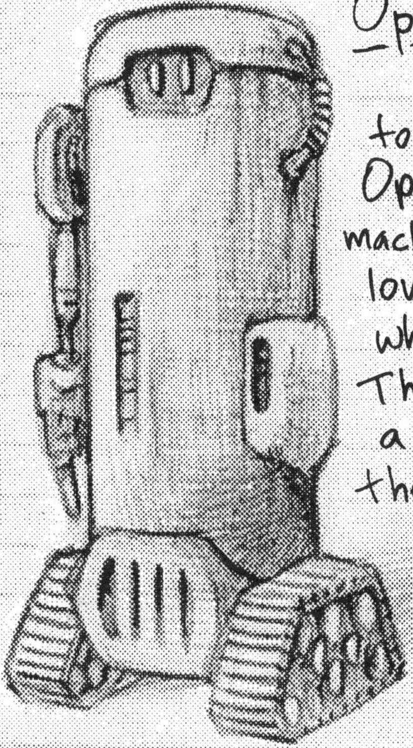

Op-Wud

A low-cost alternative to the newer welding 'bots, Op-Wud is the sort of machine the Gothtek Corporation loves: an obedient workhorse who never questions authority. The last surviving member of a set of six, Op-Wud is on the verge of breaking down for good.

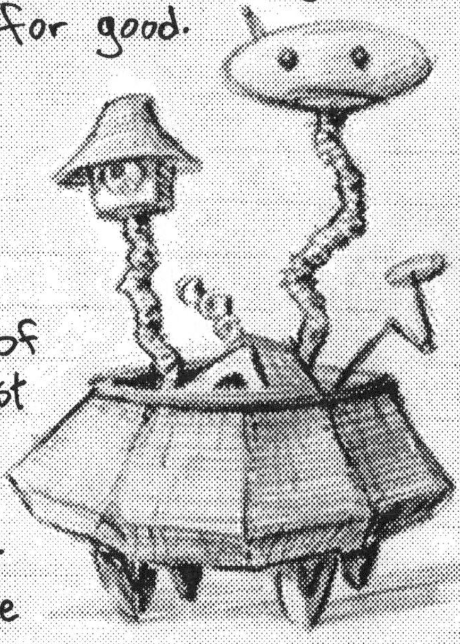

Gricks

The oldest member of the crew is also the most ill-suited for the rigors of the Fognon-6. Gricks would suffer from a split personality if not for the fact that his second head is usually half-asleep.

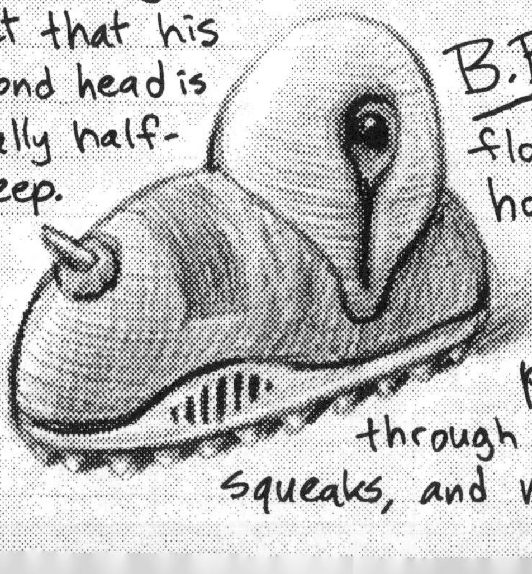

B.B.

Built for cleaning floors and exterminating household pests, B.B. is a tough little 'bot who never cracks under pressure. He converses through an odd dialect of pips, squeaks, and muffled thumps.

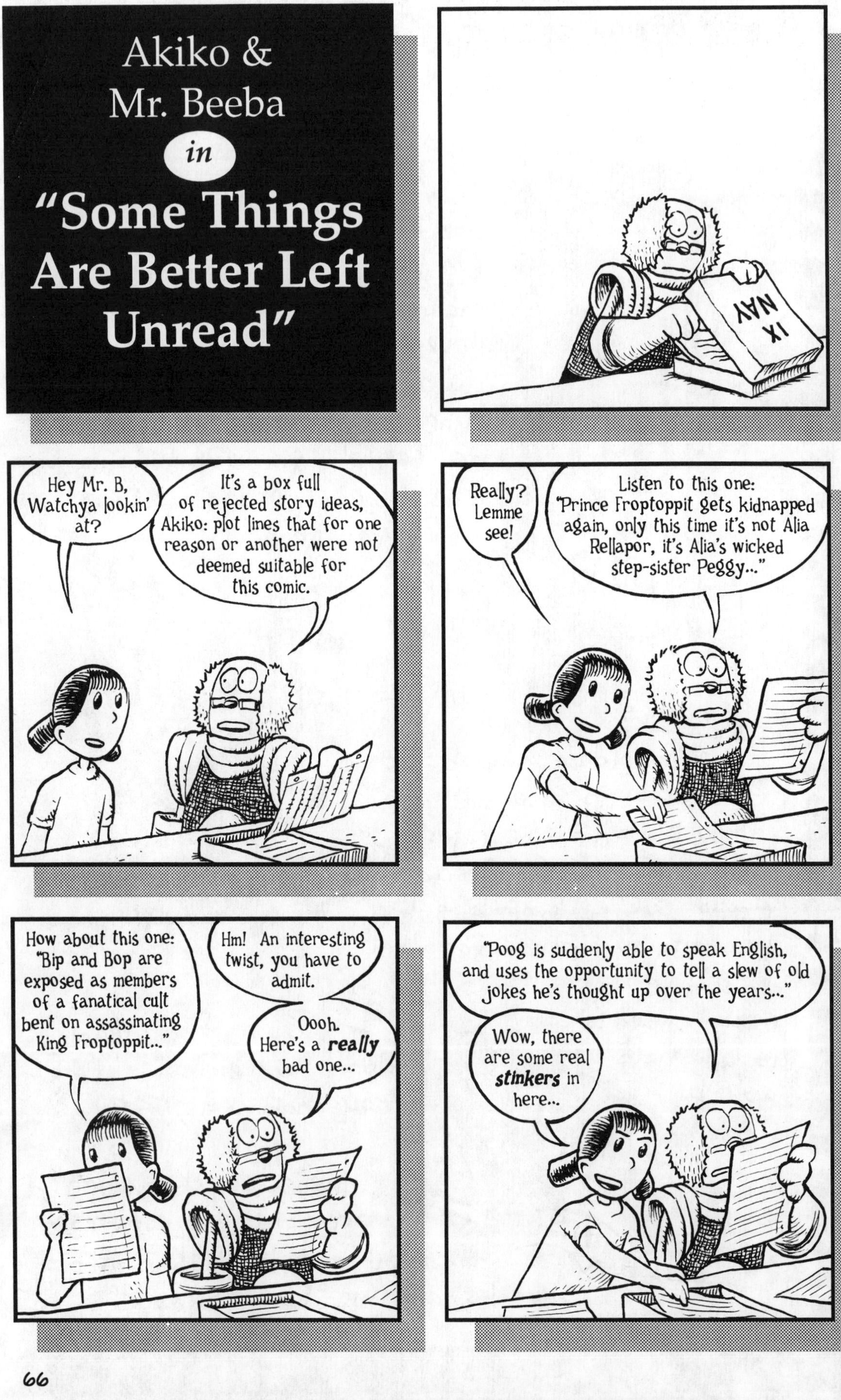
Akiko & Mr. Beeba
in
"Some Things Are Better Left Unread"
IX NAY
Hey Mr. B, Watchya lookin' at?
It's a box full of rejected story ideas, Akiko: plot lines that for one reason or another were not deemed suitable for this comic.
Really? Lemme see!
Listen to this one: "Prince Froptoppit gets kidnapped again, only this time it's not Alia Rellapor, it's Alia's wicked step-sister Peggy..."
How about this one: "Bip and Bop are exposed as members of a fanatical cult bent on assassinating King Froptoppit..."
Hm! An interesting twist, you have to admit.
Oooh. Here's a **really** bad one...
"Poog is suddenly able to speak English, and uses the opportunity to tell a slew of old jokes he's thought up over the years..."
Wow, there are some real ***stinkers*** in here...

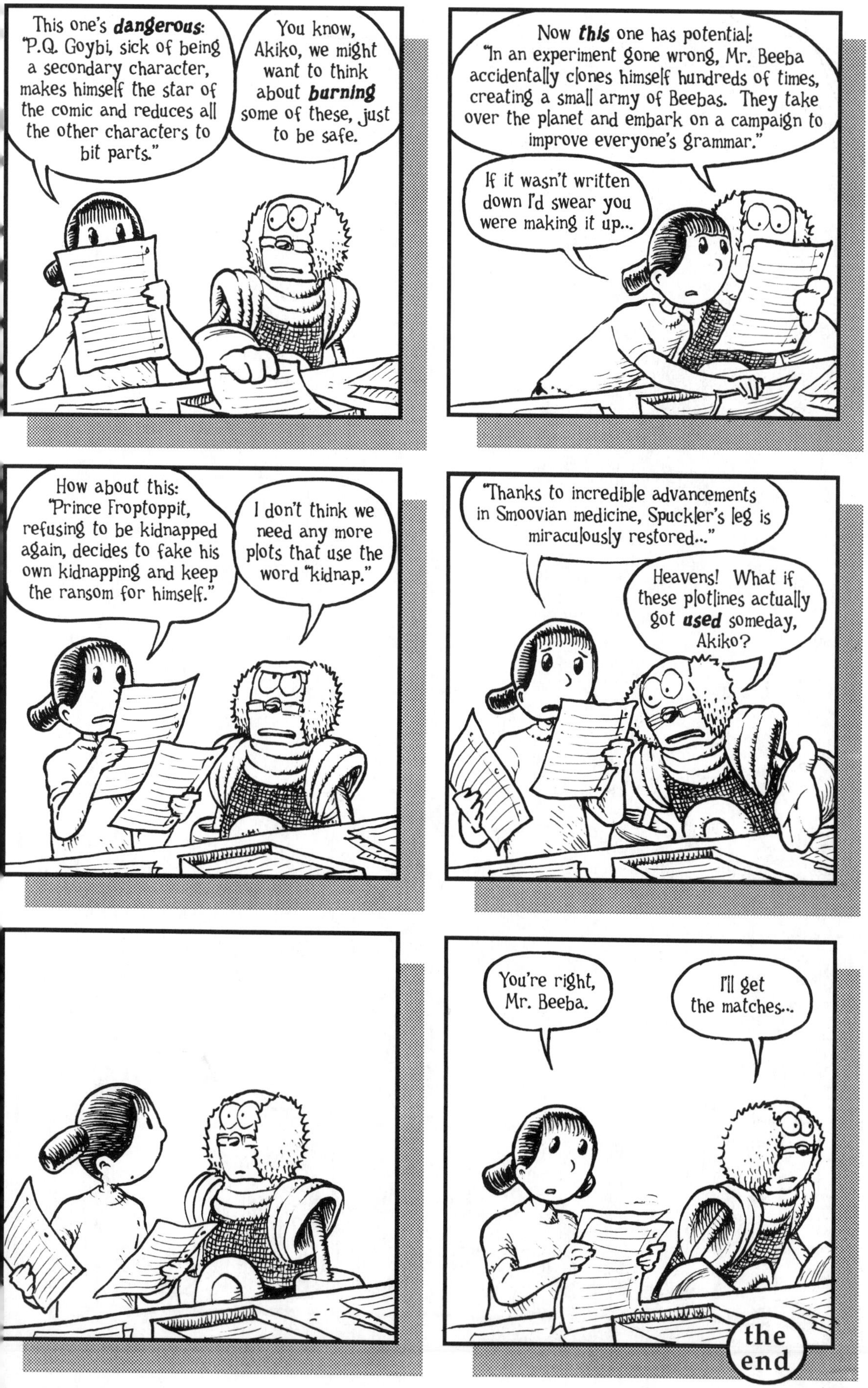

This one's **dangerous**: "P.Q. Goybi, sick of being a secondary character, makes himself the star of the comic and reduces all the other characters to bit parts."
You know, Akiko, we might want to think about **burning** some of these, just to be safe.
Now **this** one has potential: "In an experiment gone wrong, Mr. Beeba accidentally clones himself hundreds of times, creating a small army of Beebas. They take over the planet and embark on a campaign to improve everyone's grammar."
If it wasn't written down I'd swear you were making it up...
How about this: "Prince Froptoppit, refusing to be kidnapped again, decides to fake his own kidnapping and keep the ransom for himself."
I don't think we need any more plots that use the word "kidnap."
"Thanks to incredible advancements in Smoovian medicine, Spuckler's leg is miraculously restored..."
Heavens! What if these plotlines actually got **used** someday, Akiko?
You're right, Mr. Beeba.
I'll get the matches...
the end

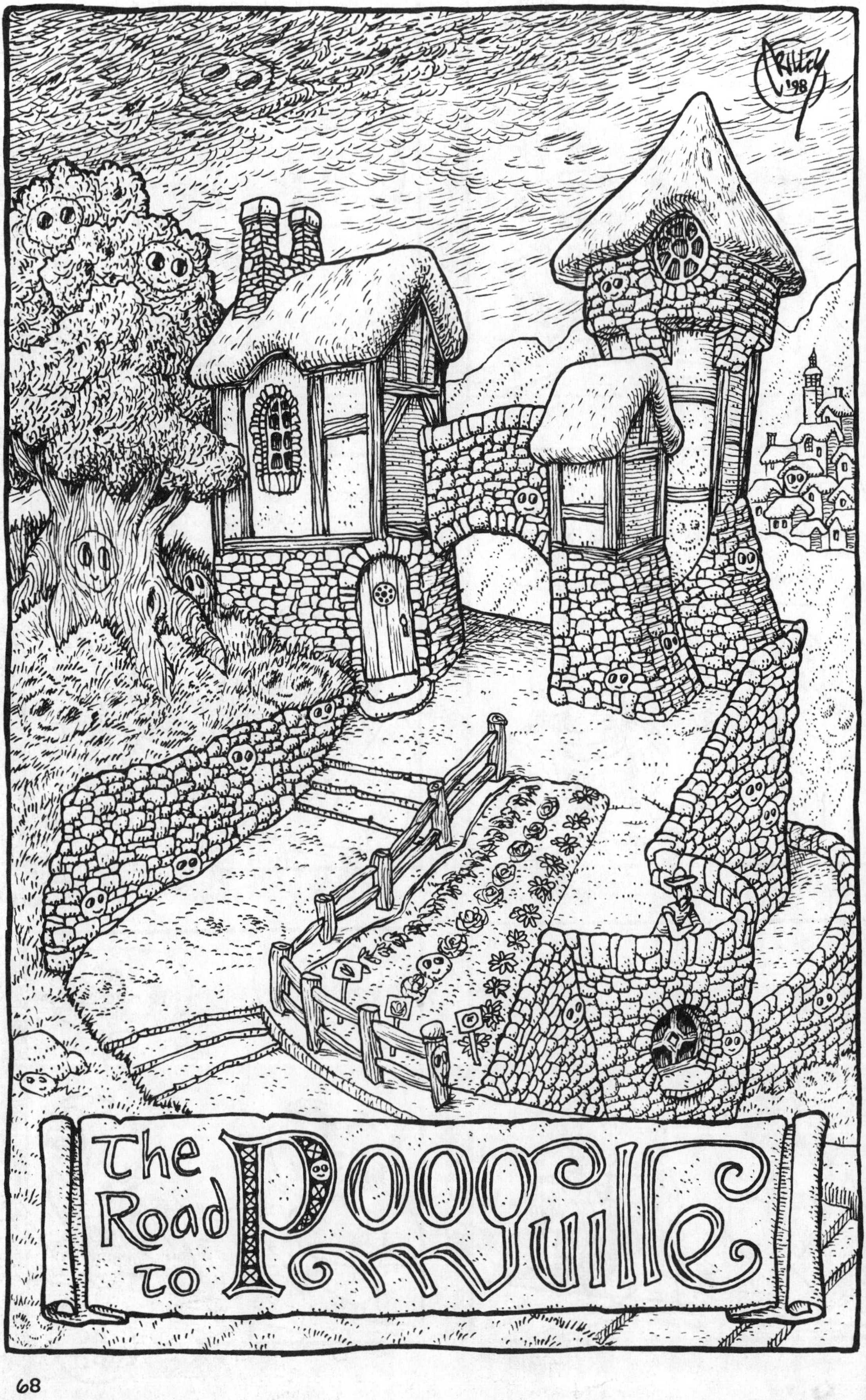
The Road to Pooguille

Akiko's Guide to Earth
For People Who've Never Been There

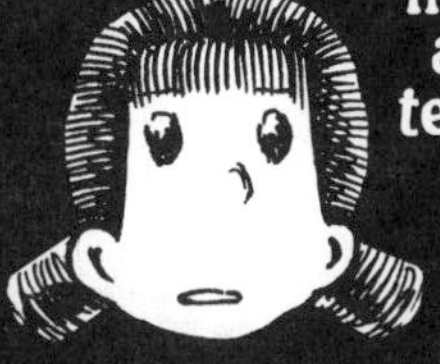

Hi. Um, they asked me to tell you a little about my home planet, Earth. Not like I'm some big expert on the place, but I can tell you a *few* things, anyway. Here goes...

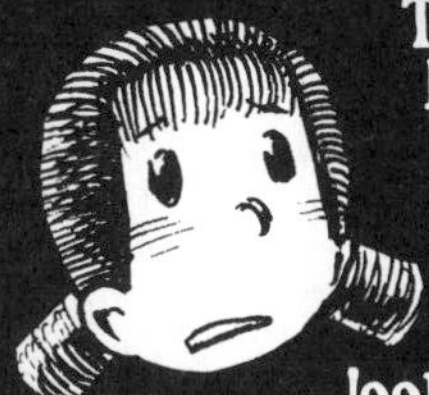

This is what Earth looks like from a distance. It's bigger than it looks, actually. Depending on what part you land on, it'll either be really, really hot, or really cold, or else somewhere in between. Uh, maybe we'd better move on to the next slide.

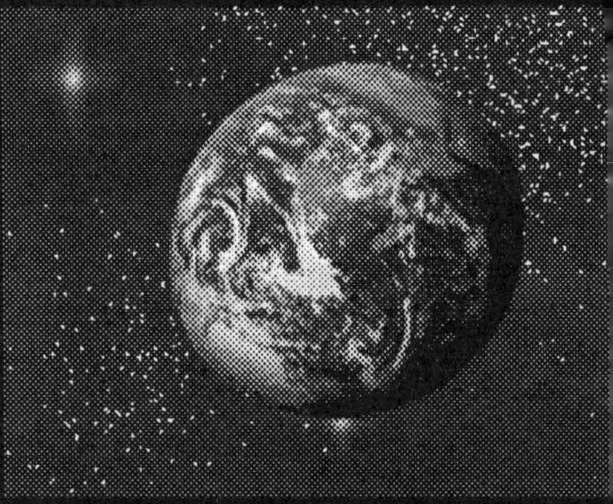

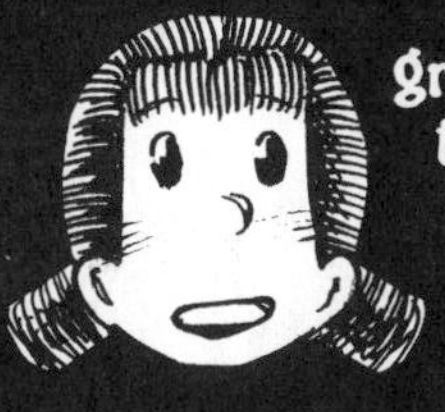

Oh right, gravity. Well, there's a lot of stuff on Earth, and most of it's stuck there because of gravity. There must be some sort of an exception for balloons, though, because you let go of them and they're pretty much *gone.*

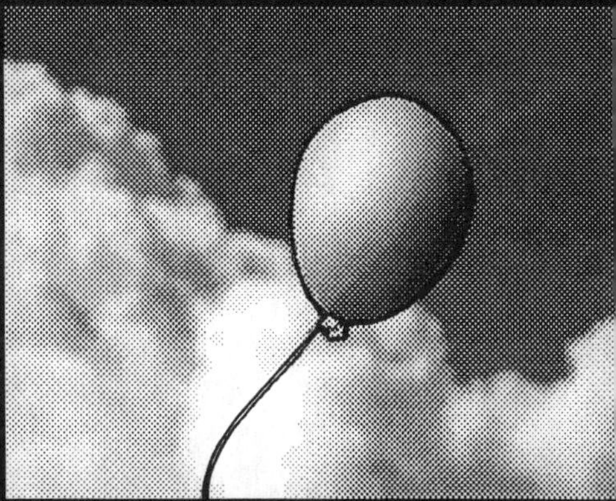

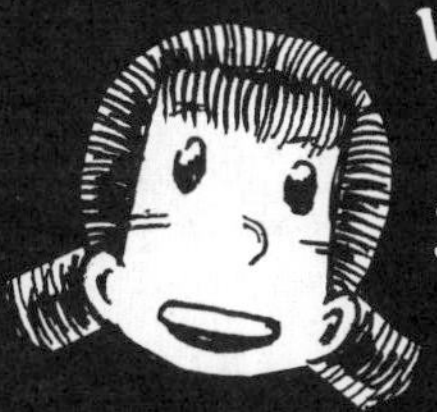

When you get to Earth the first thing you'll want to do is try the donuts. I don't even know what they're made of, but it doesn't really matter: *they're all good.* You're just going to have to trust me on this one.

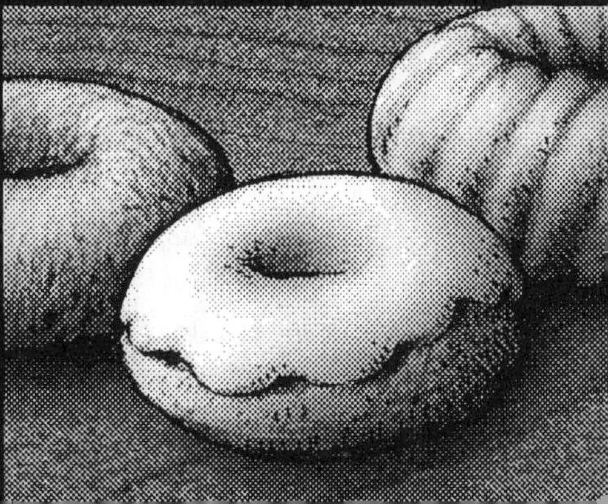

Pretty much anywhere you go on earth you'll run into human beings. They're mostly pretty cool, especially if they're your friends. Being a human is pretty simple: you start out young and then you slowly get old.

Humans generally have two eyes, with eyebrows that go up or down depending on what mood you're in. I think it's a pretty good arrangement, but I have to admit I'm a little biased.

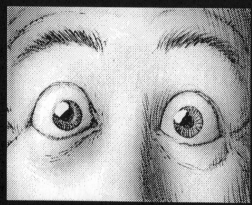

One of the coolest things that humans are able to do is fall in love. You can tell when people are in love because they try to be nice to each other all the time. Well, that's the way it works in *theory*, anyway.

One of the first things you have to do on earth is learn how to read, because if you don't you'll get into a lot of trouble. It's not easy, though. Even *smart* people take a few years to get the hang of it.

WET PAINT

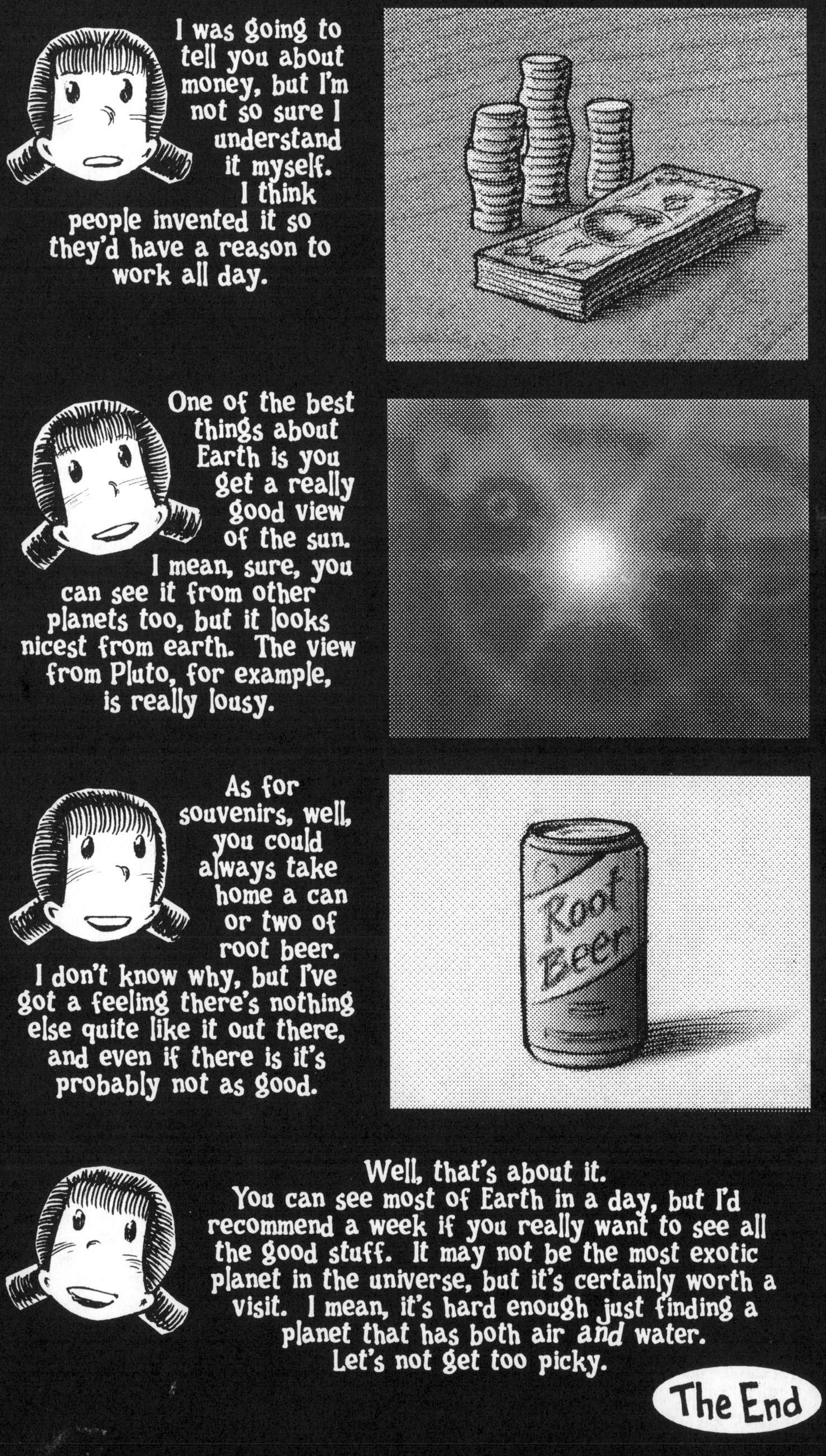
I was going to tell you about money, but I'm not so sure I understand it myself. I think people invented it so they'd have a reason to work all day.
One of the best things about Earth is you get a really good view of the sun. I mean, sure, you can see it from other planets too, but it looks nicest from earth. The view from Pluto, for example, is really lousy.
As for souvenirs, well, you could always take home a can or two of root beer. I don't know why, but I've got a feeling there's nothing else quite like it out there, and even if there is it's probably not as good.
Root Beer
Well, that's about it. You can see most of Earth in a day, but I'd recommend a week if you really want to see all the good stuff. It may not be the most exotic planet in the universe, but it's certainly worth a visit. I mean, it's hard enough just finding a planet that has both air *and* water. Let's not get too picky.
The End

Once upon a very long time ago...

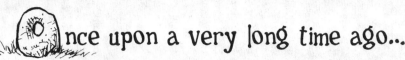

...there lived a humble merchant by the name of Beeba. He made a meager living selling books and paintings and pieces of wood, and lived by a simple motto: "Mind your own business, or your business will own your mind." He wasn't exactly sure what it meant, but he thought it had a pretty nice ring to it, and was about as good a motto as a humble merchant like himself could wish for.

One day, when he was just settling down to make his way through a stack of old dictionaries and encyclopedias, he was interrupted by a visit from his old friend, Spuckler. Now Spuckler was a reckless fellow, who lived without regard for books or paintings, and had long forgotten his motto, if indeed he'd ever had one. But Beeba felt is was important to forgive a fellow for his lack of education, or at least to refrain from making fun of it to his face, so he'd resolved not to let Spuckler's inferiority of intellect get in the way of them being friends.

"Hey, Beebs," bellowed Spuckler as he pounded on the door, "Get off your duff and give me a hand! I'm makin' a present for Akiko."

"Hold on Spuckler, I'll be there at once!" called out Beeba, hoping to get there before Spuckler could do his door any further damage. A moment later he was on his front porch, staring in amazement at the giant boulder that Spuckler had somehow dragged to his doorstep.

"What on earth..." began Beeba.

"Now hang on, Beebs. It ain't finished yet. That's why I came here t' get your help."

"But what is it supposed to be?"

"It's a birdbath. For 'Kiko's garden." As Spuckler mopped the sweat from his forehead, Beeba tried his best to imagine how the massive piece of rock could be transformed into anything resembling a birdbath,

"Now Spuckler, my dear fellow, didn't it occur to you that we'd have been better off starting with a smaller piece of stone?"

"Well, I sorta figured that the bigger the bath, the more birds you're gonna get," replied Spuckler, handing Beeba a hammer and chisel. "Now, enough of the chit-chat, Beebs, let's get to work."

And so it was that Beeba was forced to abandon the comfort of his books in order to hammer away at a rock in the hot afternoon sun. Before they'd made very much progress, Spuckler's robot Gax came squeaking and wobbling down the road, pulling behind him a small cart covered with a blanket.

"Good day, Mr. Beeba," said the robot, who was a good bit more refined than his roughneck master, "I thought the two of you would enjoy a few refreshments." There in his cart was a kettle of tea and a plateful of biscuits. It seemed that Spuckler's little visit might not turn out to be such a bad thing after all!

"Well, now, Gax, that was mighty thoughtful of ya," said Spuckler as he tossed his mallet into the weeds, "I reckon it ***is*** about time for a little break." And so they enjoyed the tea and biscuits in the shade of a nearby tree, and considered the fate of their giant birdbath.

Meanwhile, Akiko was working in her garden, having a little chat with Poog. I say a *little* chat, mind you, because Poog hardly ever said a word. But Akiko had learned long ago not to question Poog's silences, and had even come to enjoy them over time.

"This ought to be a good year for roses, Poog, what with all the rain we've had lately." Poog nodded in agreement.

"I do need to keep after the weeds, though. They sprout up every time I turn my back."

Akiko got down on her hands and knees and started digging at a particularly stubborn patch of weeds near the edge of the garden. Poog hummed a little tune to keep her company.

Looking up, Akiko saw Spuckler, Gax, and Mr. Beeba trudging along the road down below, dragging behind them a huge wheelbarrow filled with rocks. Spuckler and Mr. Beeba were in the middle of a heated argument, as usual.

"I told you to hold the chisel in one place, ya dadburned idiot!"

"You were about to hammer my thumb into oblivion, Spuckler," protested Beeba, visibly exhausted from the day's labor. "It was a matter of self-defense."

"Yeah? Well thanks to your precious little thumb, we ruined Akiko's new birdbath!"

"I didn't know I *had* a new birdbath," said Akiko, as she joined them on the road.

"That's 'cause ya don't," explained Spuckler with a sigh, "Ya *almost* did, but not no more. These rocks is all that's left of it, and we're fixin' to wheel 'em on down t' the dump."

"It's just as well," smiled Akiko, "because I don't really need a birdbath."

"But I was under the impression that you were quite *fond* of birds, Akiko," said Mr. Beeba, genuinely puzzled.

"I am. The reason I don't need a birdbath because I've already *got* one." Akiko took them around to the back of the house to an old pail of water on her window ledge.

"I left this bucket out here one night when it rained. Next thing I knew the local birds had decided this would be their birdbath," Akiko explained. "It's the perfect location, too, because I can sit at the kitchen table when I'm having tea and watch them come and go."

"But Akiko, surely you need something a bit more substantial," said Mr. Beeba.

"Something bigger," agreed Spuckler. "There ain't space in that thing but for one or two birds."

"I think it's just perfect," said Akiko with a smile, "But I can tell you one thing this garden *does* need."

"What's that?"

"A wall. A nice, little wall running along the edge, just like the one down at Mrs. McGamby's."

"I've seen that wall," said Mr. Beeba, "It's made entirely of rocks, stacked one upon the other."

"Yes," said Akiko, with a rather unconvincing look of disappointment on her face, "It's a shame you're going to wheel all those rocks down to the dump..."

Spuckler grinned as he reached into the wheelbarrow and tossed a stone to Mr. Beeba. "Come on, Beebs, let's see just how well you remember how that old wall was put together."

Akiko smiled and ran back up to the house. "I'll put the kettle on."

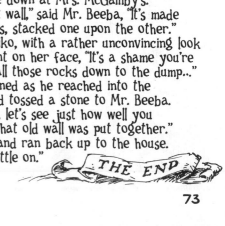

THE END

Mr. Beeba in "Doctor's Orders"

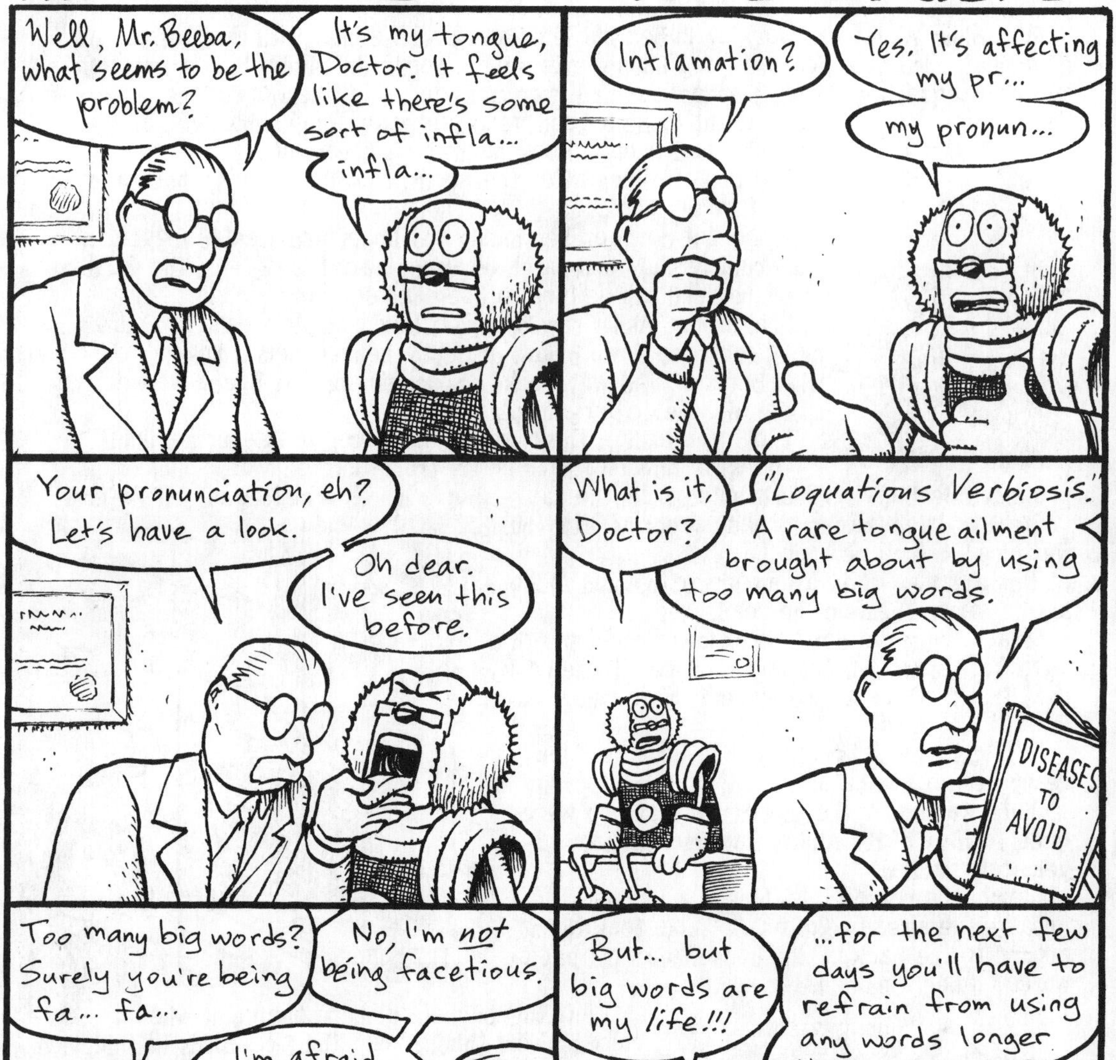
Well, Mr. Beeba, what seems to be the problem?
It's my tongue, Doctor. It feels like there's some sort of infla... infla...
Inflamation?
Yes. It's affecting my pr...
my pronun...
Your pronunciation, eh? Let's have a look.
Oh dear. I've seen this before.
What is it, Doctor?
"Loquatious Verbiosis." A rare tongue ailment brought about by using too many big words.
DISEASES TO AVOID
Too many big words? Surely you're being fa... fa...
No, I'm not being facetious.
I'm afraid you're going to have to go on a "word diet."
But... but big words are my life!!!
...for the next few days you'll have to refrain from using any words longer than one syllable.
ONE SYLLABLE?! That's im... im...
Oh dear. You can't even say a simple word like "impossible."
Then again, that's just the sort of word you need to avoid: It's two syllables over your limit.
Three.
Ah. So it is.
In any case, if you ever hope to use big words again, I urge you to heed my advice.

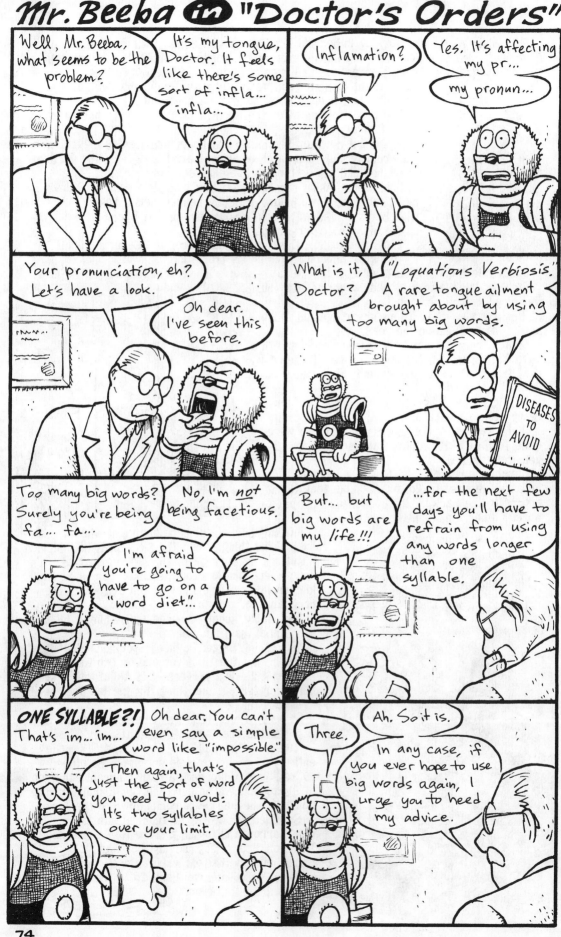

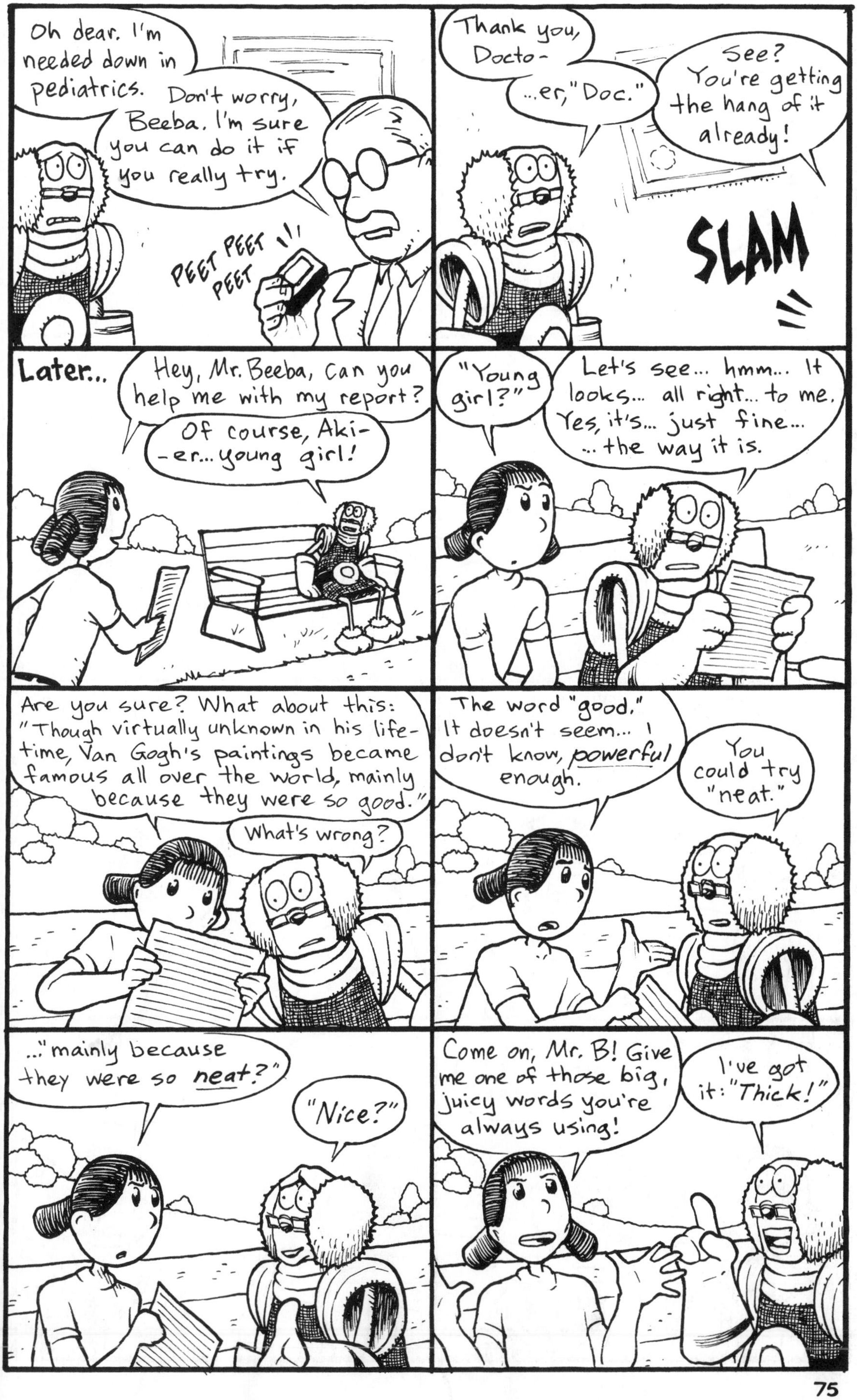

Oh dear. I'm needed down in pediatrics.
Don't worry, Beeba. I'm sure you can do it if you really try.
PEET PEET PEET
Thank you, Docto-
...er, "Doc."
See? You're getting the hang of it already!
SLAM
Later...
Hey, Mr. Beeba, can you help me with my report?
Of course, Aki- -er... young girl!
"Young girl?"
Let's see... hmm... It looks... all right... to me. Yes, it's... just fine... ...the way it is.
Are you sure? What about this: "Though virtually unknown in his life-time, Van Gogh's paintings became famous all over the world, mainly because they were so good."
What's wrong?
The word "good." It doesn't seem... I don't know, powerful enough.
You could try "neat."
..."mainly because they were so neat?"
"Nice?"
Come on, Mr. B! Give me one of those big, juicy words you're always using!
I've got it: "Thick!"

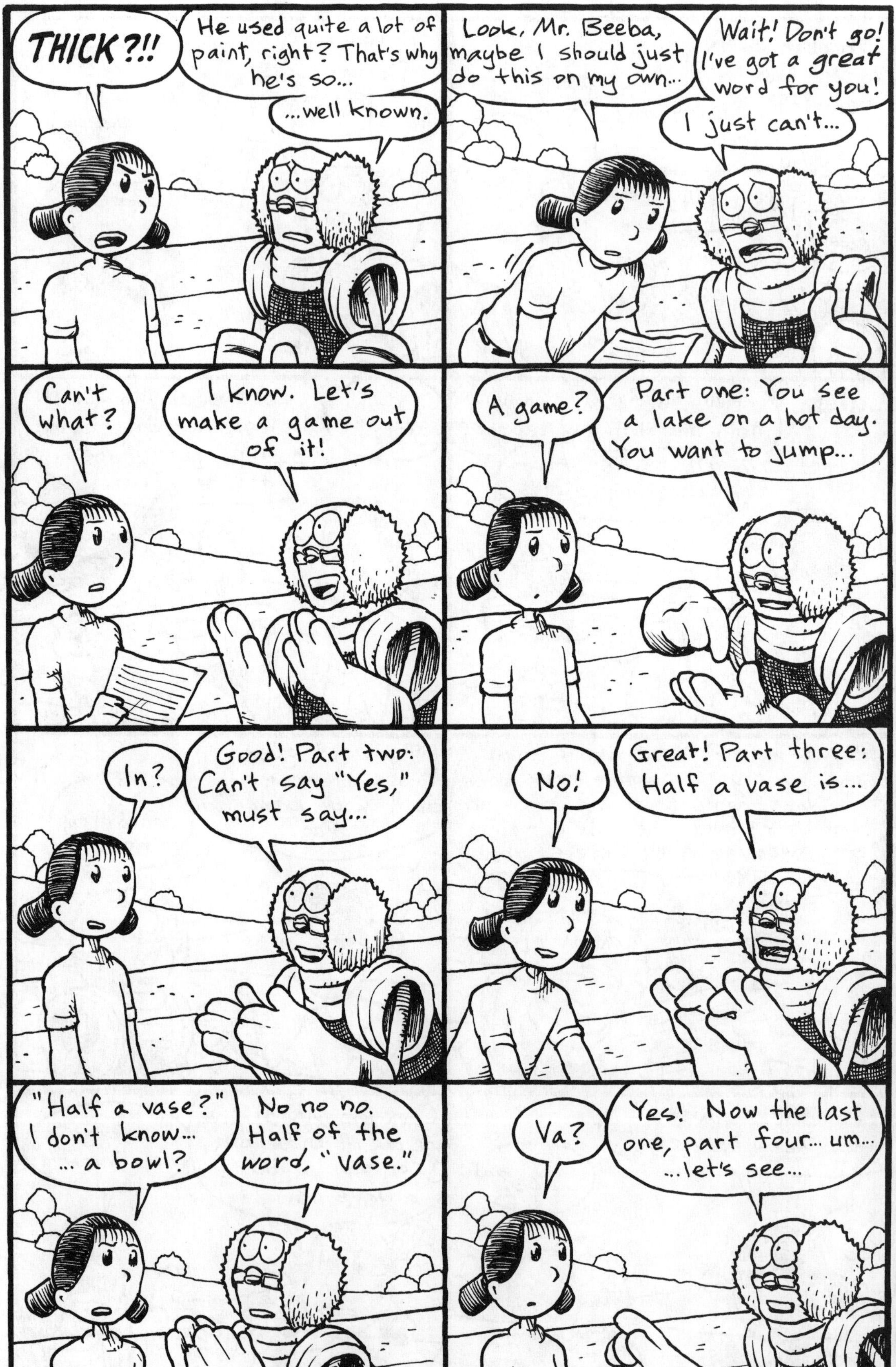
THICK?!!
He used quite a lot of paint, right? That's why he's so...
...well known.
Look, Mr. Beeba, maybe I should just do this on my own...
Wait! Don't go! I've got a great word for you!
I just can't...
Can't what?
I know. Let's make a game out of it!
A game?
Part one: You see a lake on a hot day. You want to jump...
In?
Good! Part two: Can't say "Yes," must say...
No!
Great! Part three: Half a vase is...
"Half a vase?" I don't know... ...a bowl?
No no no. Half of the word, "vase."
Va?
Yes! Now the last one, part four... um... ...let's see...

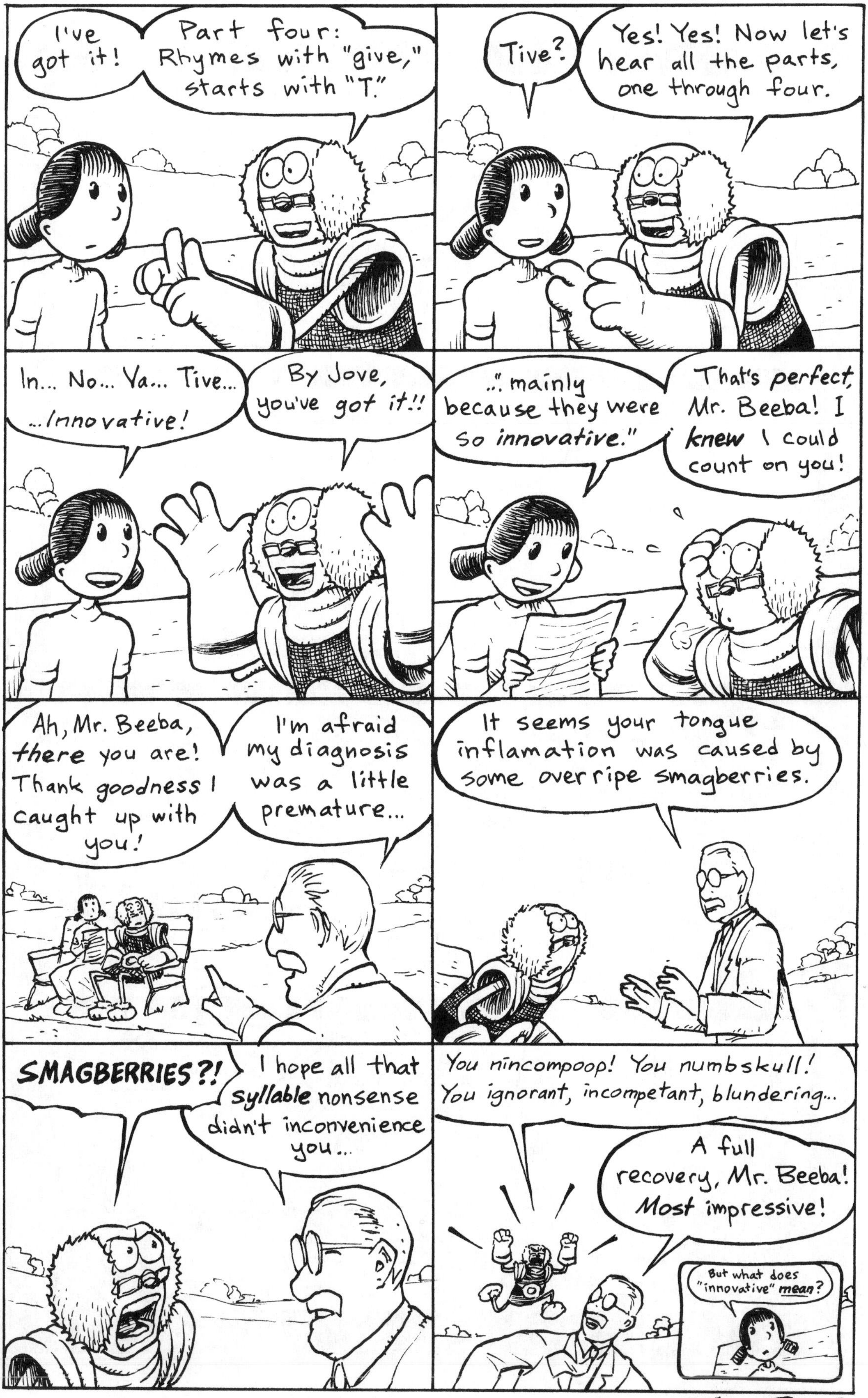

I've got it!
Part four: Rhymes with "give," starts with "T."
Tive?
Yes! Yes! Now let's hear all the parts, one through four.
In... No... Va... Tive... ...Innovative!
By Jove, you've got it!!
"... mainly because they were so innovative."
That's perfect, Mr. Beeba! I knew I could count on you!
Ah, Mr. Beeba, there you are! Thank goodness I caught up with you!
I'm afraid my diagnosis was a little premature...
It seems your tongue inflamation was caused by some overripe smagberries.
SMAGBERRIES?!
I hope all that syllable nonsense didn't inconvenience you...
You nincompoop! You numbskull! You ignorant, incompetant, blundering...
A full recovery, Mr. Beeba! Most impressive!
But what does "innovative" mean?

The End 77

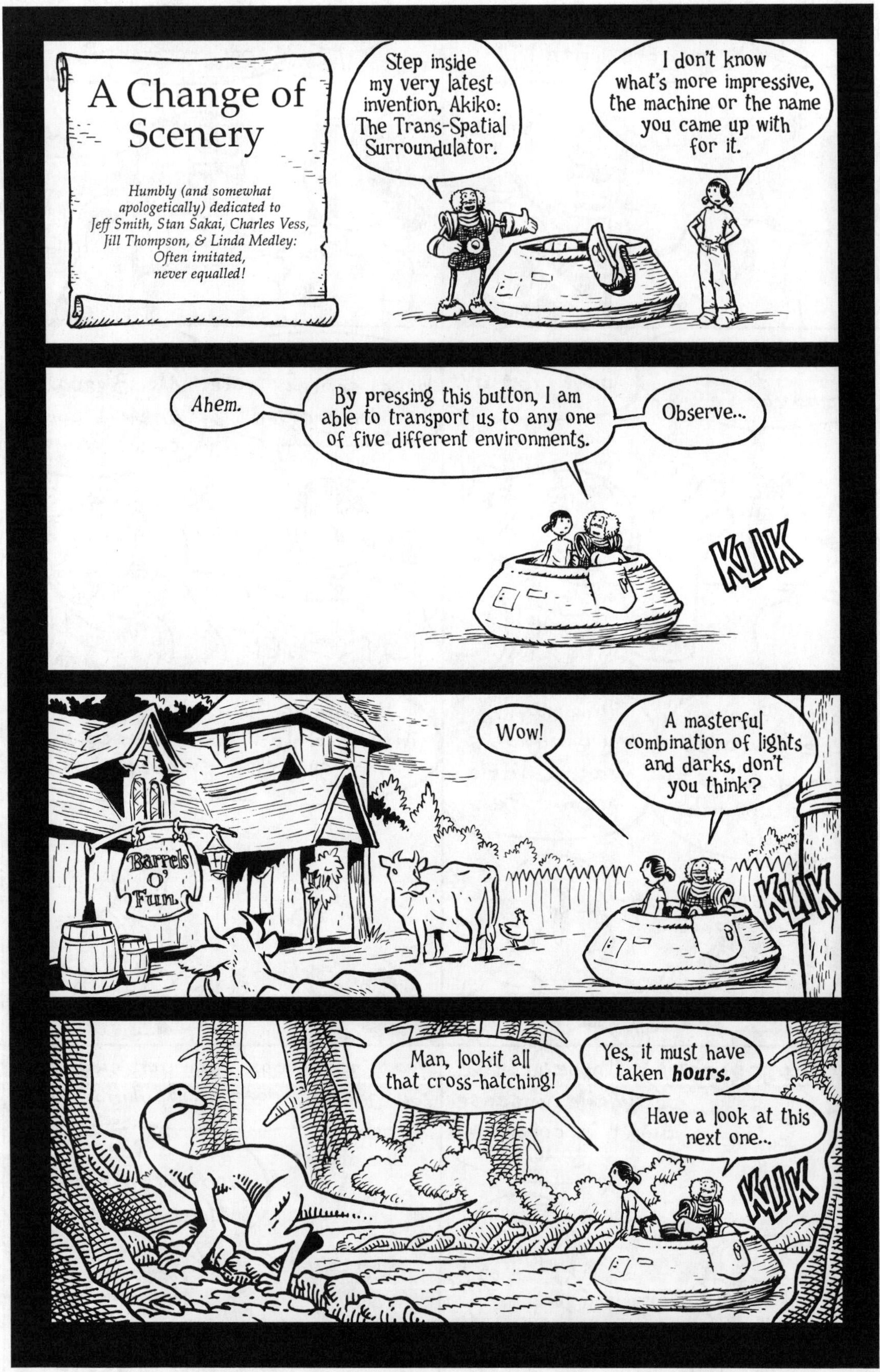

A Change of Scenery
Humbly (and somewhat apologetically) dedicated to Jeff Smith, Stan Sakai, Charles Vess, Jill Thompson, & Linda Medley: Often imitated, never equalled!
Step inside my very latest invention, Akiko: The Trans-Spatial Surroundulator.
I don't know what's more impressive, the machine or the name you came up with for it.
Ahem.
By pressing this button, I am able to transport us to any one of five different environments.
Observe..
KLIK
Barrels O' Fun
Wow!
A masterful combination of lights and darks, don't you think?
KLIK
Man, lookit all that cross-hatching!
Yes, it must have taken **hours.**
Have a look at this next one..
KLIK

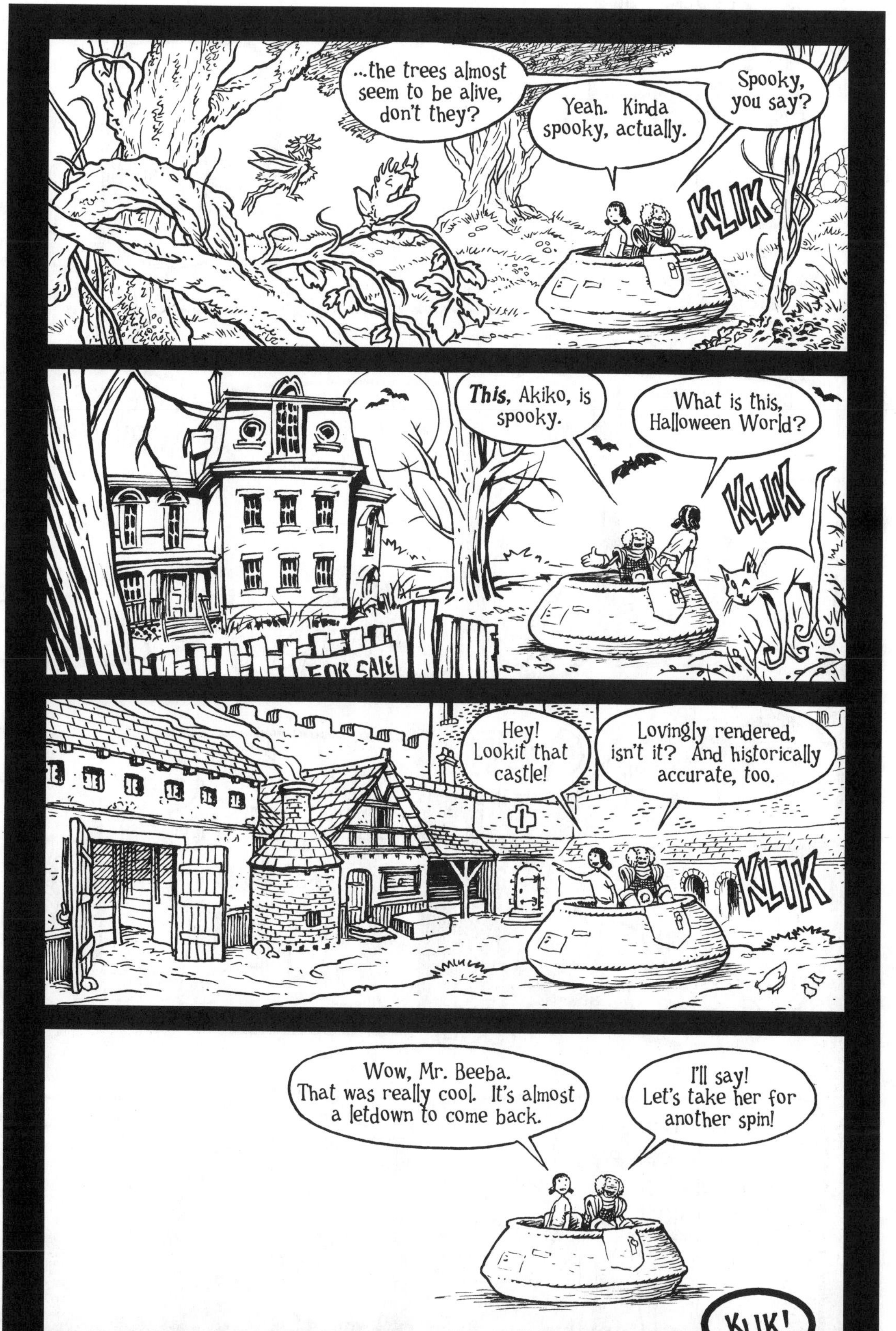
...the trees almost seem to be alive, don't they?
Yeah. Kinda spooky, actually.
Spooky, you say?
KLIK
This, Akiko, is spooky.
What is this, Halloween World?
KLIK
FOR SALE
Hey! Lookit that castle!
Lovingly rendered, isn't it? And historically accurate, too.
KLIK
Wow, Mr. Beeba. That was really cool. It's almost a letdown to come back.
I'll say! Let's take her for another spin!
KLIK!

AKIKO in "A Weird Little Story"

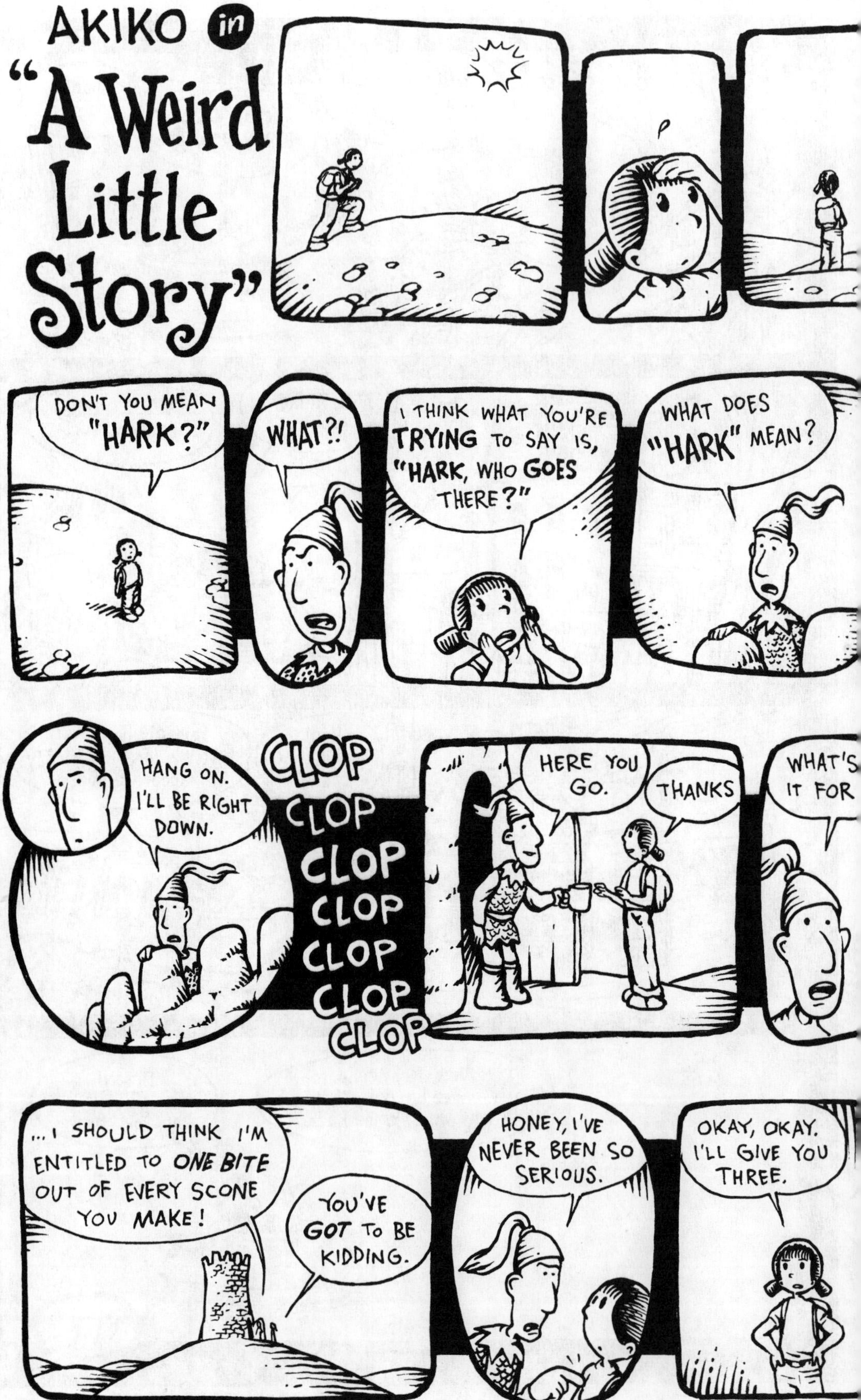

DON'T YOU MEAN "HARK?"
WHAT?!
I THINK WHAT YOU'RE TRYING TO SAY IS, "HARK, WHO GOES THERE?"
WHAT DOES "HARK" MEAN?
HANG ON. I'LL BE RIGHT DOWN.
CLOP CLOP CLOP CLOP CLOP CLOP CLOP
HERE YOU GO.
THANKS
WHAT'S IT FOR
...I SHOULD THINK I'M ENTITLED TO ONE BITE OUT OF EVERY SCONE YOU MAKE!
YOU'VE GOT TO BE KIDDING.
HONEY, I'VE NEVER BEEN SO SERIOUS.
OKAY, OKAY. I'LL GIVE YOU THREE.

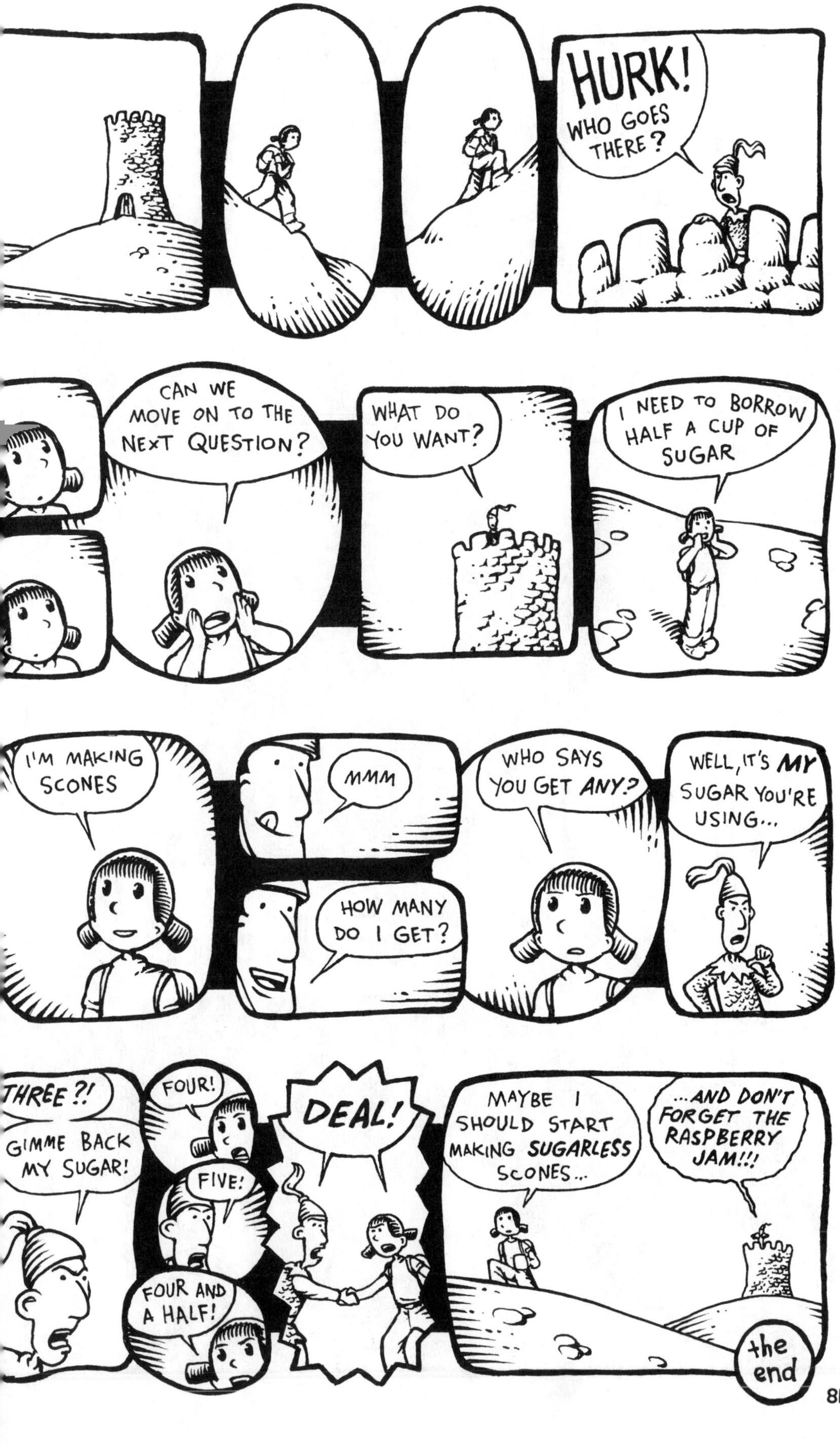
HURK!
WHO GOES THERE?
CAN WE MOVE ON TO THE NEXT QUESTION?
WHAT DO YOU WANT?
I NEED TO BORROW HALF A CUP OF SUGAR
I'M MAKING SCONES
MMM
HOW MANY DO I GET?
WHO SAYS YOU GET *ANY?*
WELL, IT'S *MY* SUGAR YOU'RE USING...
THREE?!
GIMME BACK MY SUGAR!
FOUR!
FIVE!
FOUR AND A HALF!
DEAL!
MAYBE I SHOULD START MAKING *SUGARLESS* SCONES...
...AND DON'T FORGET THE RASPBERRY JAM!!!
the end

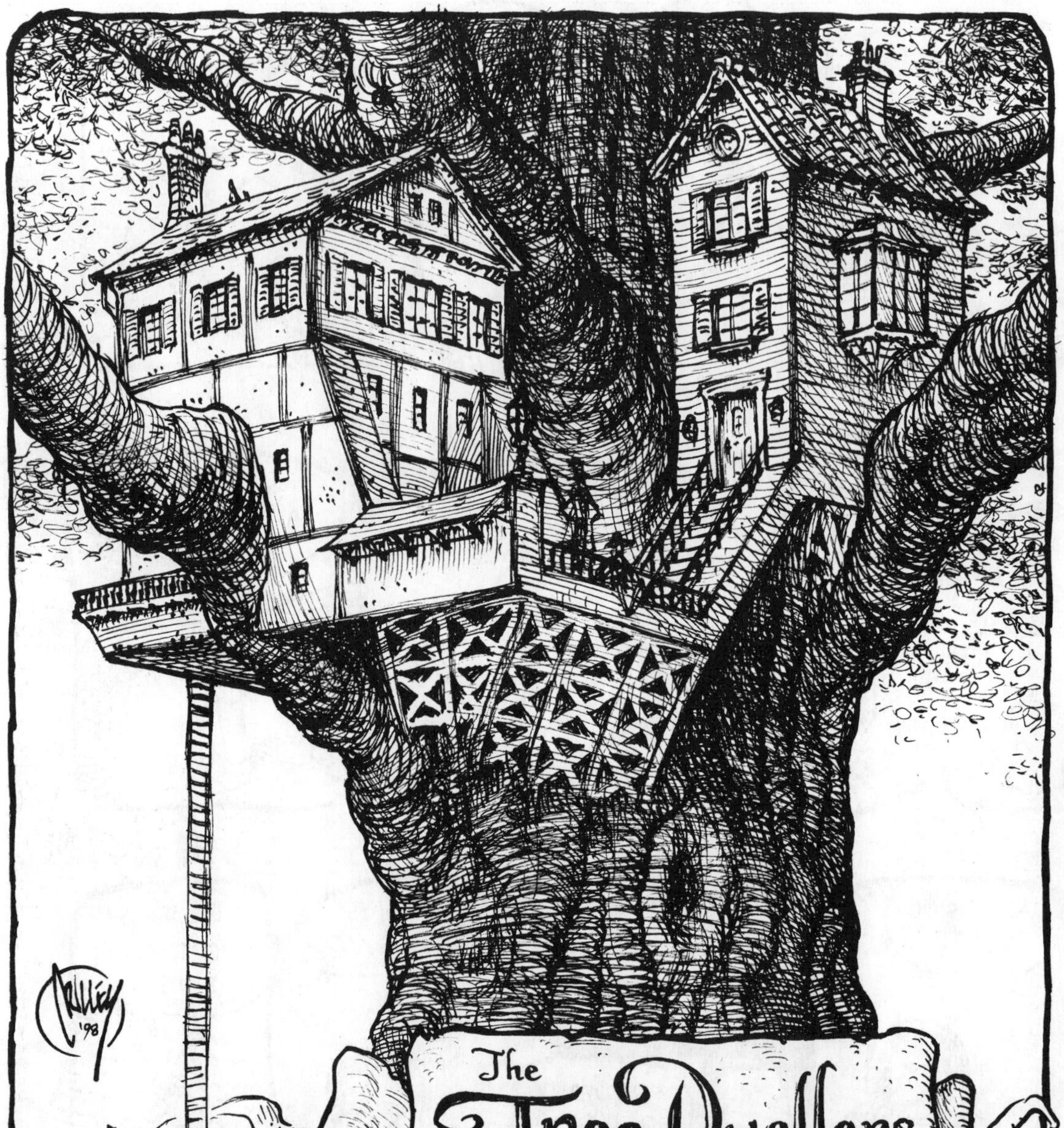
The Tree Dwellers

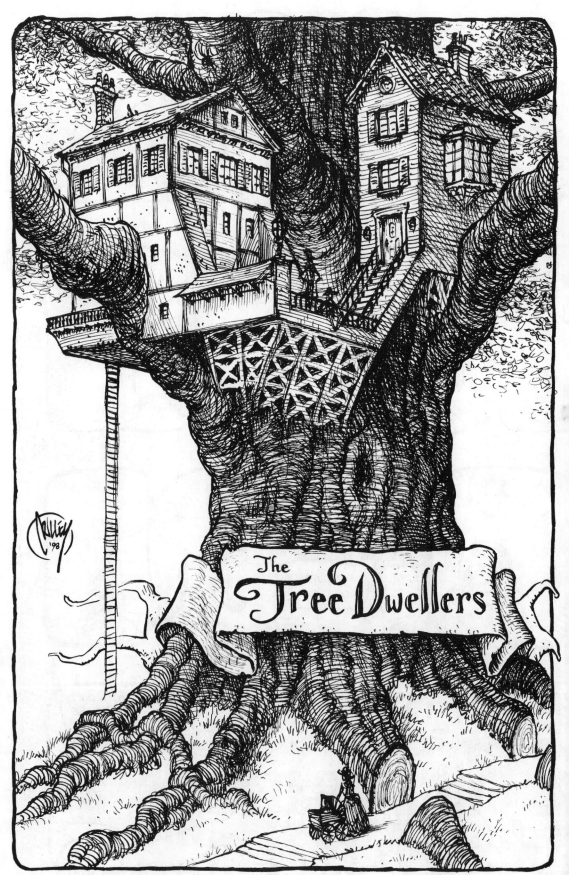

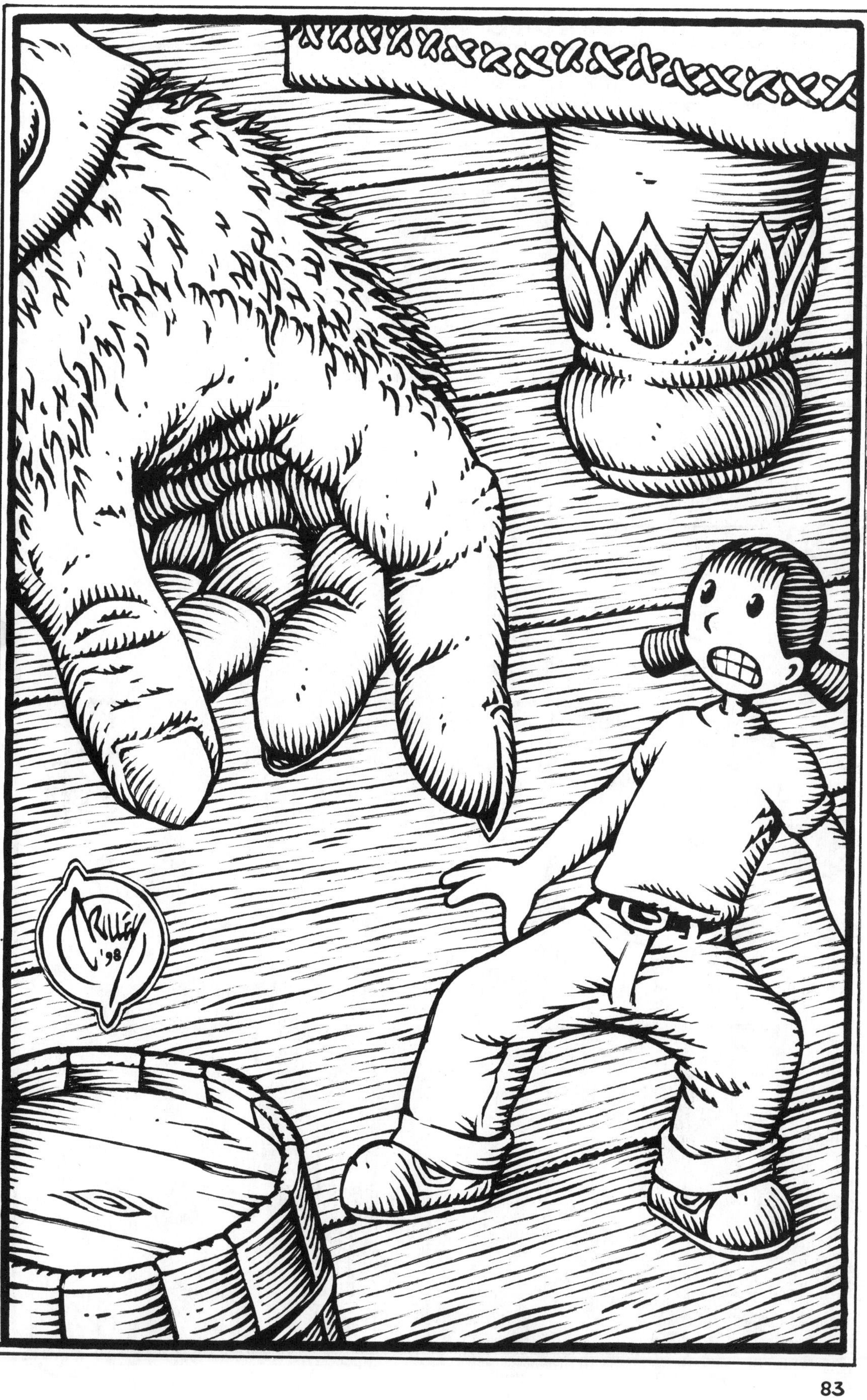
'98

AKIKO in "WRONG NUMBERS"

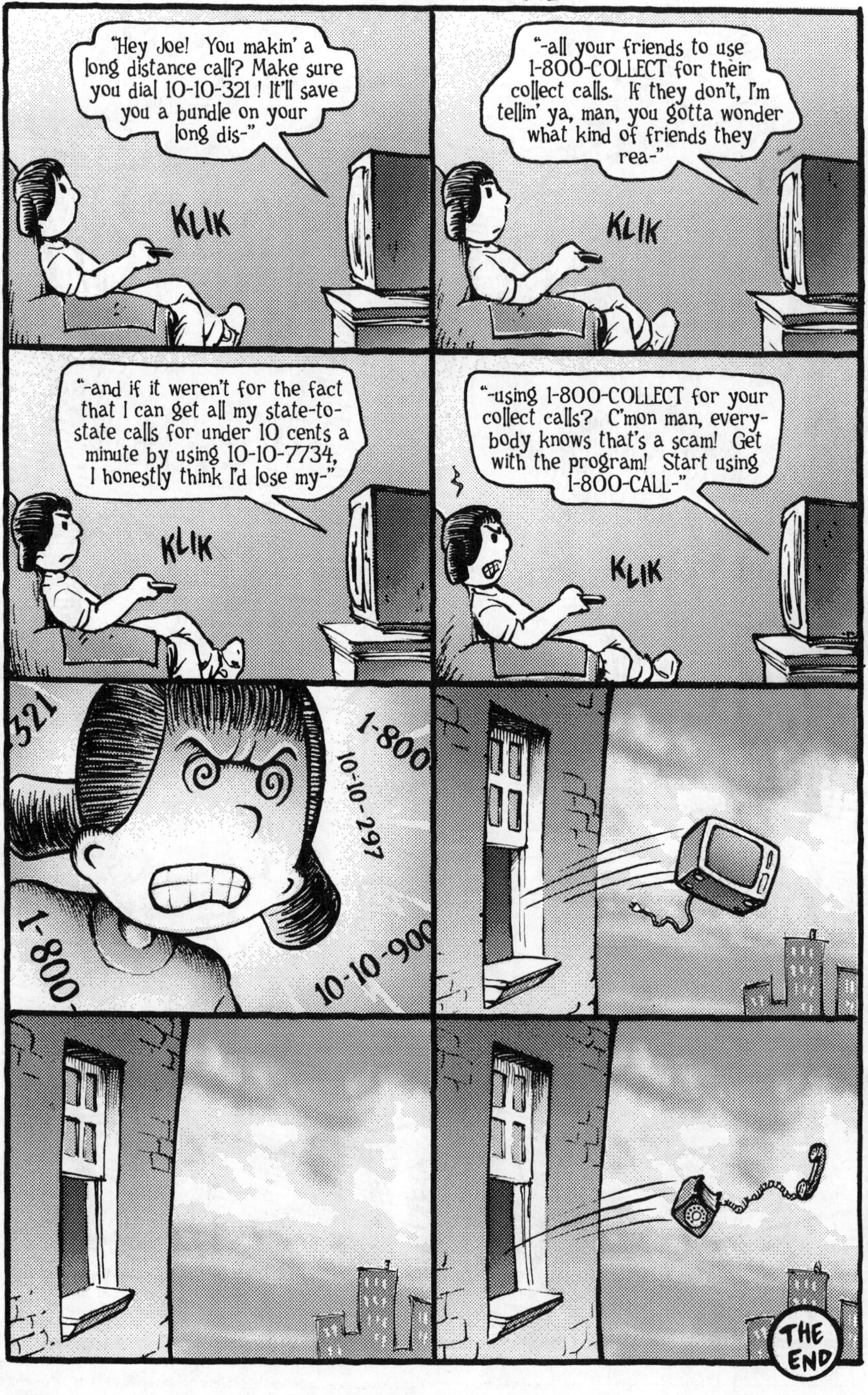

"Hey Joe! You makin' a long distance call? Make sure you dial 10-10-321 ! It'll save you a bundle on your long dis-"
KLIK
"-all your friends to use 1-800-COLLECT for their collect calls. If they don't, I'm tellin' ya, man, you gotta wonder what kind of friends they rea-"
KLIK
"-and if it weren't for the fact that I can get all my state-to-state calls for under 10 cents a minute by using 10-10-7734, I honestly think I'd lose my-"
KLIK
"-using 1-800-COLLECT for your collect calls? C'mon man, every-body knows that's a scam! Get with the program! Start using 1-800-CALL-"
KLIK
321
1-800
10-10-297
1-800
10-10-900
THE END

AKIKO in "The BiG Picture"

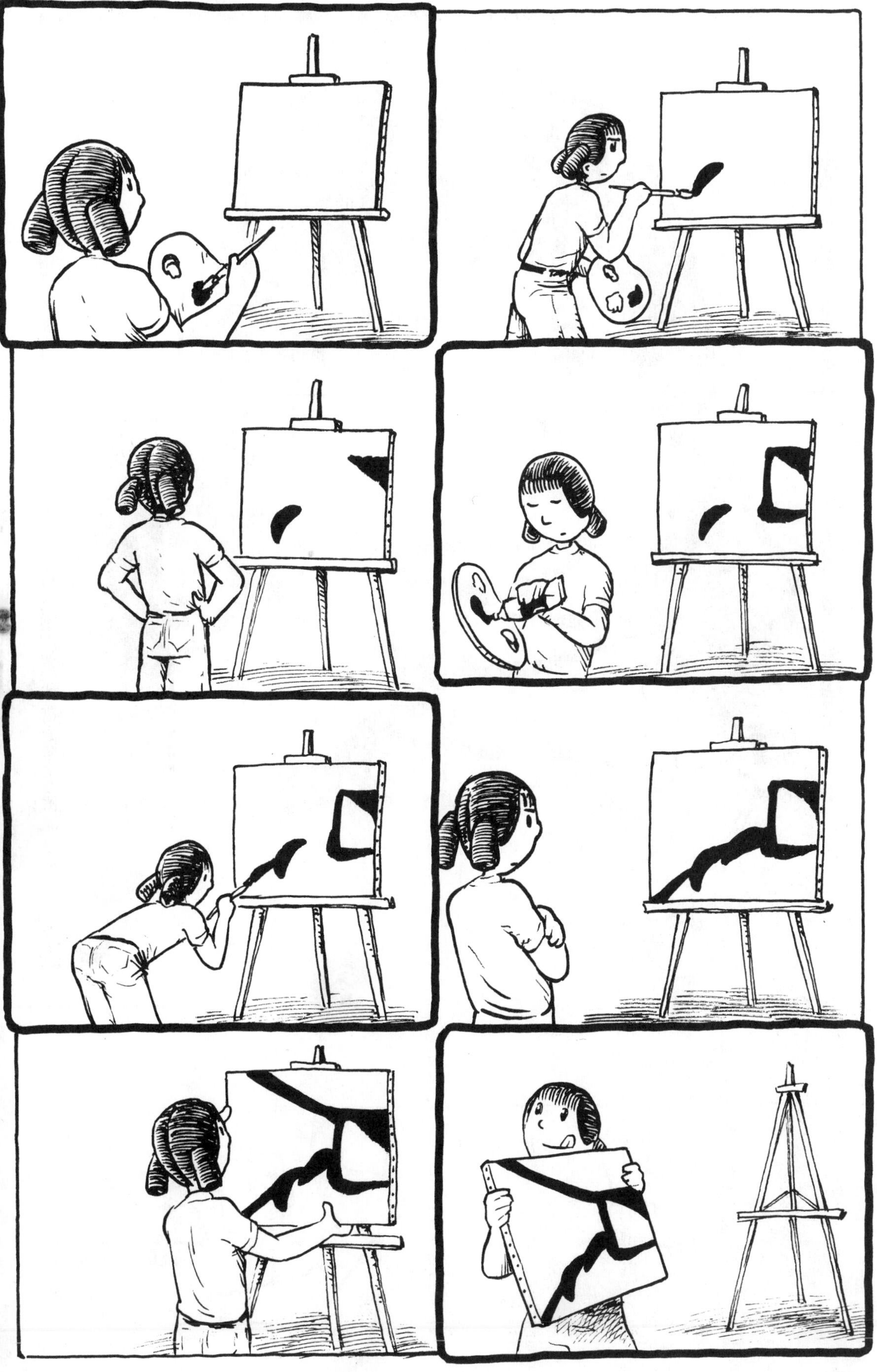

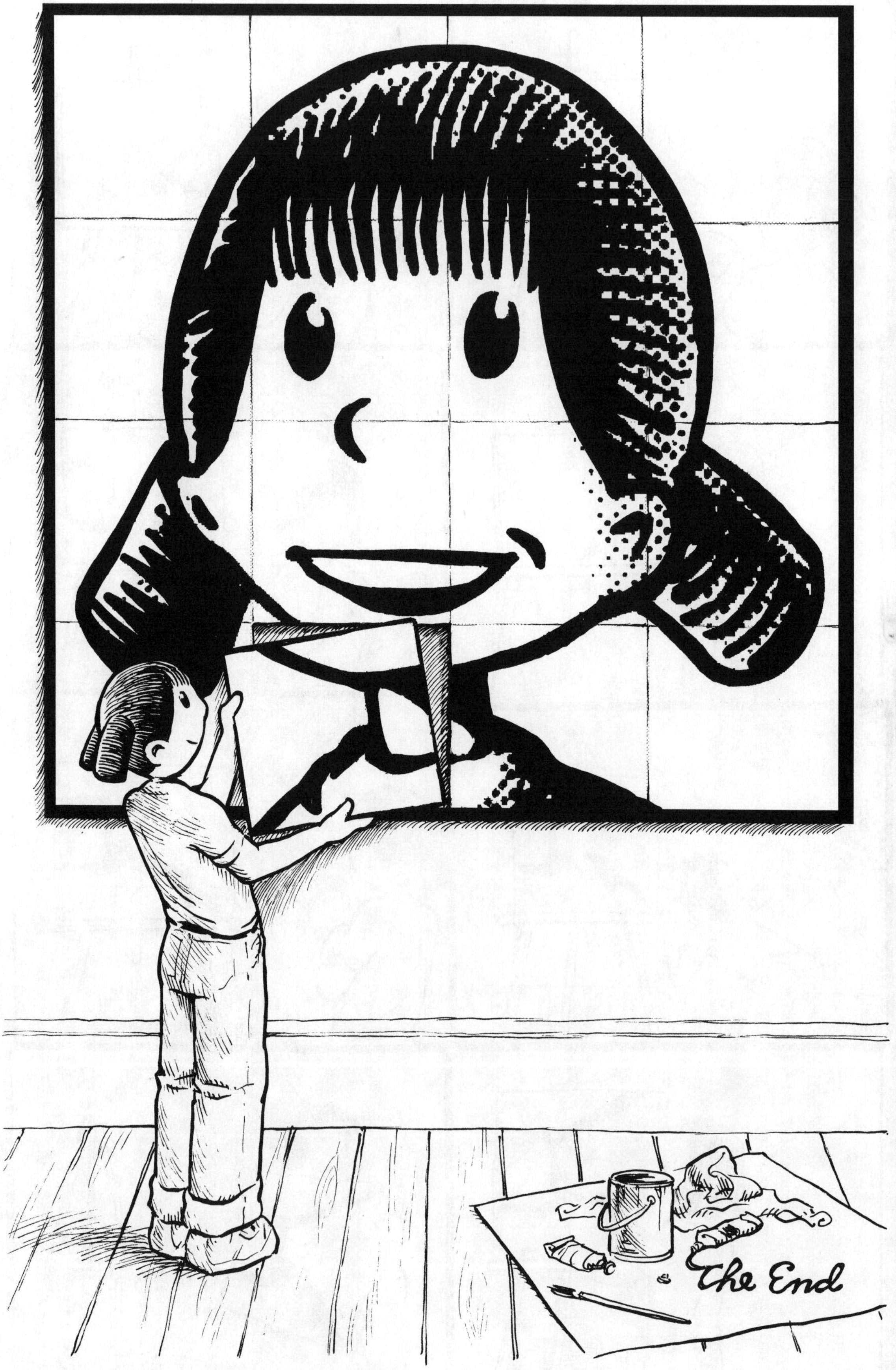
The End

planets

Planets, planets, everywhere,
Some are round, and some are square,
Some are ugly, some are nice,
Some I'd like to visit twice.

Have you heard of the Planet Thoo,
Where people's heads are filled with glue?
And every day 'bout half past four,
The King declares another war?

I much prefer the Planet Bloon,
Where every Tuesday afternoon
The Queen must practice her bassoon.
(She plays a wee bit out of tune)

Planets, planets, all around,
Some are square, and some are round,
Some are big, and some are small,
Some I do not like at all.

You wouldn't like the Planet Gway
Where people watch the news all day
And no one stops to talk to you
Because they've got Too Much to do.

I'd rather see the Planet Zwee.
(The pace is much more leisurely.)
The folks there say it isn't wrong
To stay in bed all morning long.

Planets, planets, everywhere,
Some are round, and some are square,
Some are ugly, some are nice,
Some I'd like to visit twice.

You won't believe the Planet Whyze
Where yogurt walks and butter flies
And muffins dress in silk and lace.
(It *is* a most peculiar place.)

But still it beats the Planet Traw
Where laughing is against the law
And children aren't allowed to play
Or smile more than once a day.

Planets, planets, all around,
Some are square, and some are round,
Some are big, and some are small,
Some I do not like at all.

I'll bet that you have never heard
Of people on the planet Squird,
And how they take their morning tea
A little bit too seriously.

You'd best avoid the Planet Kwight
Where people think they're always right,
And if your views aren't *apropos*
They're not afraid to tell you so.

Planets, planets, everywhere,
Some are round, and some are square,
Some are ugly, and some are nice,
Some I'd like to visit twice.

I once went to the Planet Flunn
(The 16th planet from the sun)
And there I searched from pole to pole
And never even met a soul.

From there I went to the Planet Plarrs
Where homes are built of candy bars
And there's a pond where you can wade
Up to your knees in lemonade.

Planets, planets, all around,
Some are square, and some are round,
Some are East, and some are West,
One is different from the rest.

Of course I mean the Planet Earth,
And my opinion, for what it's worth,
Is that it's lovely, through and through.

(But *I* prefer the planet Smoo.)

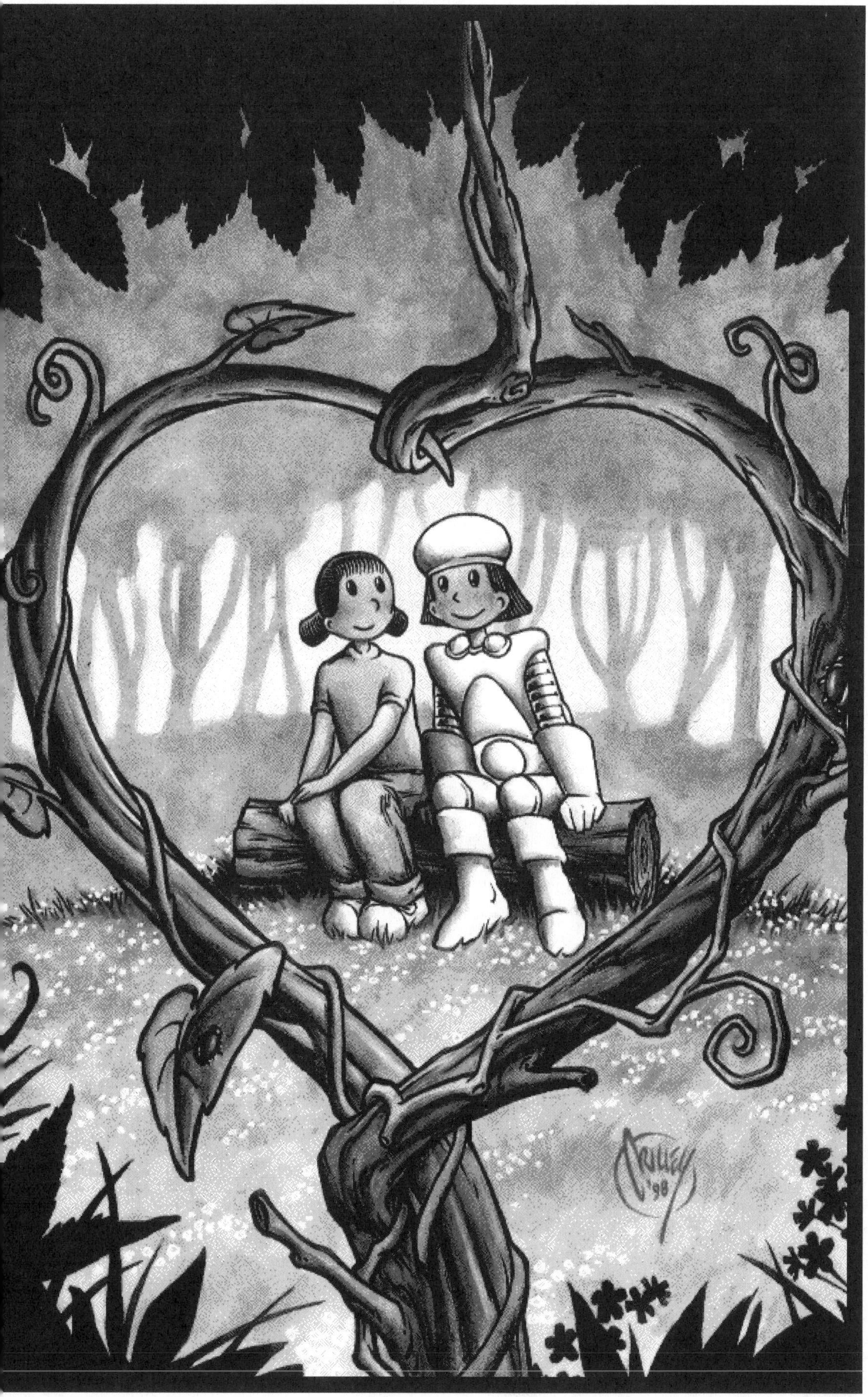

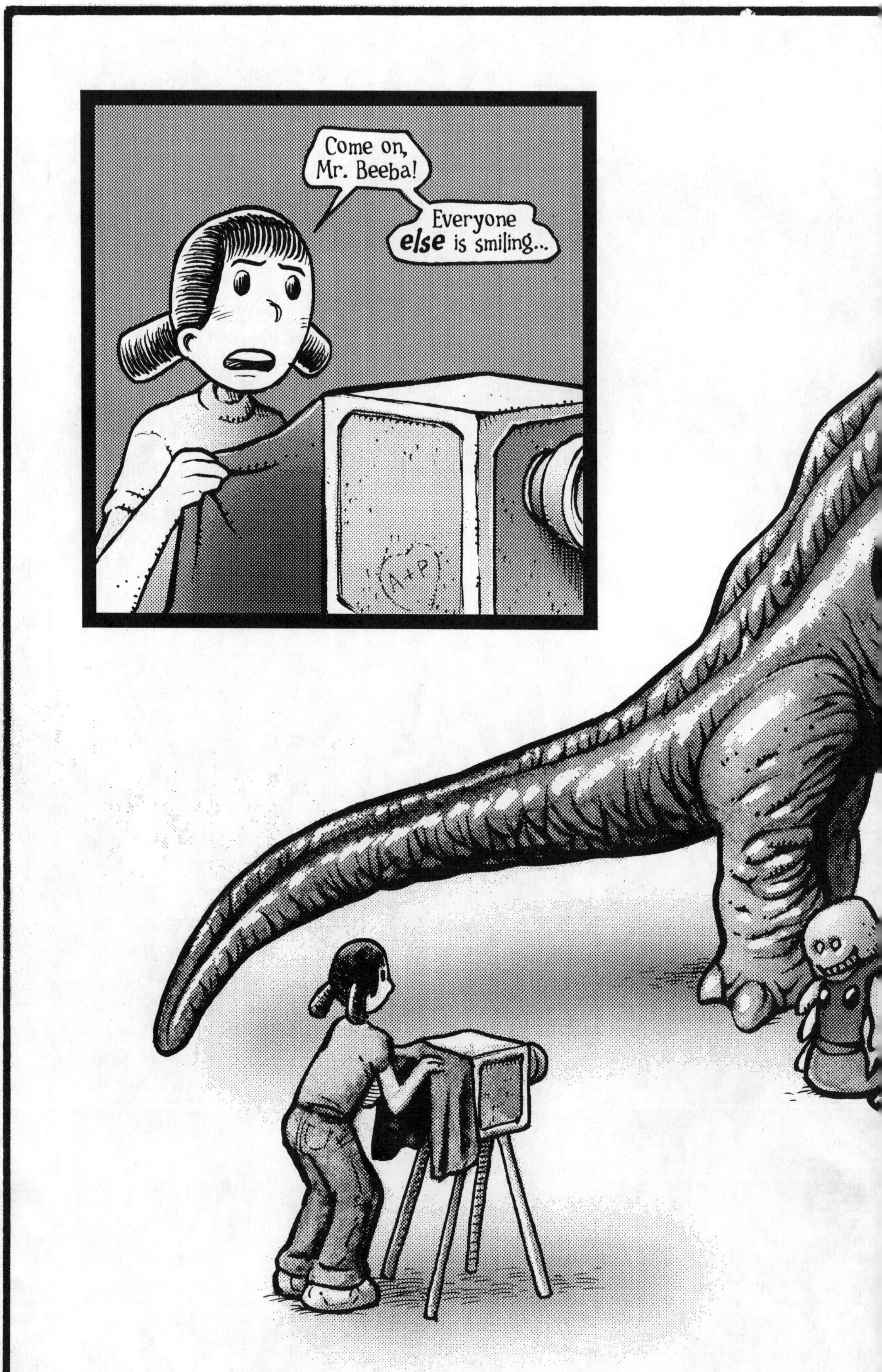
Come on, Mr. Beeba!
Everyone *else* is smiling...

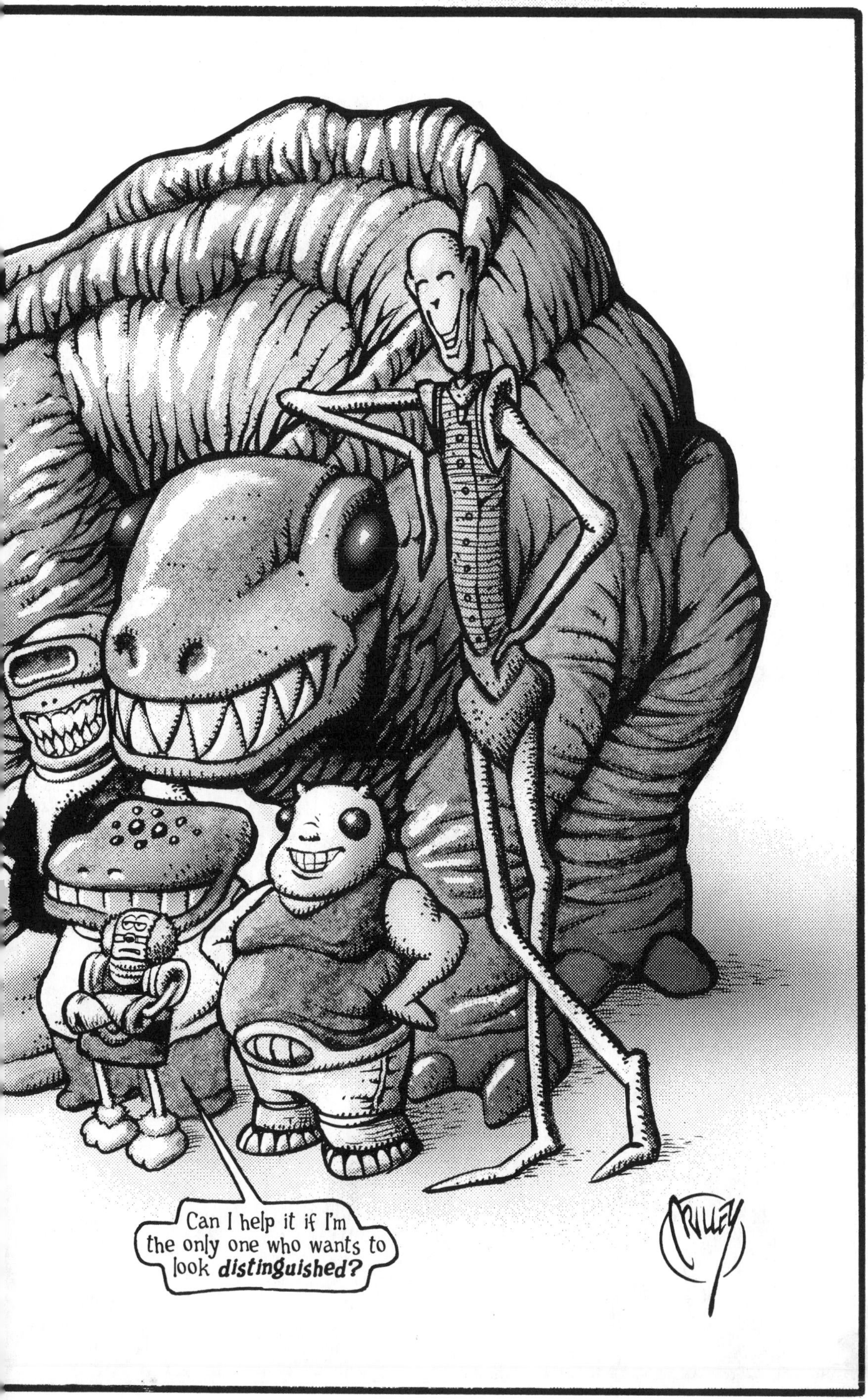
Can I help it if I'm the only one who wants to look distinguished?

Spuckler *in* "Spuckler vs. Spuckler"

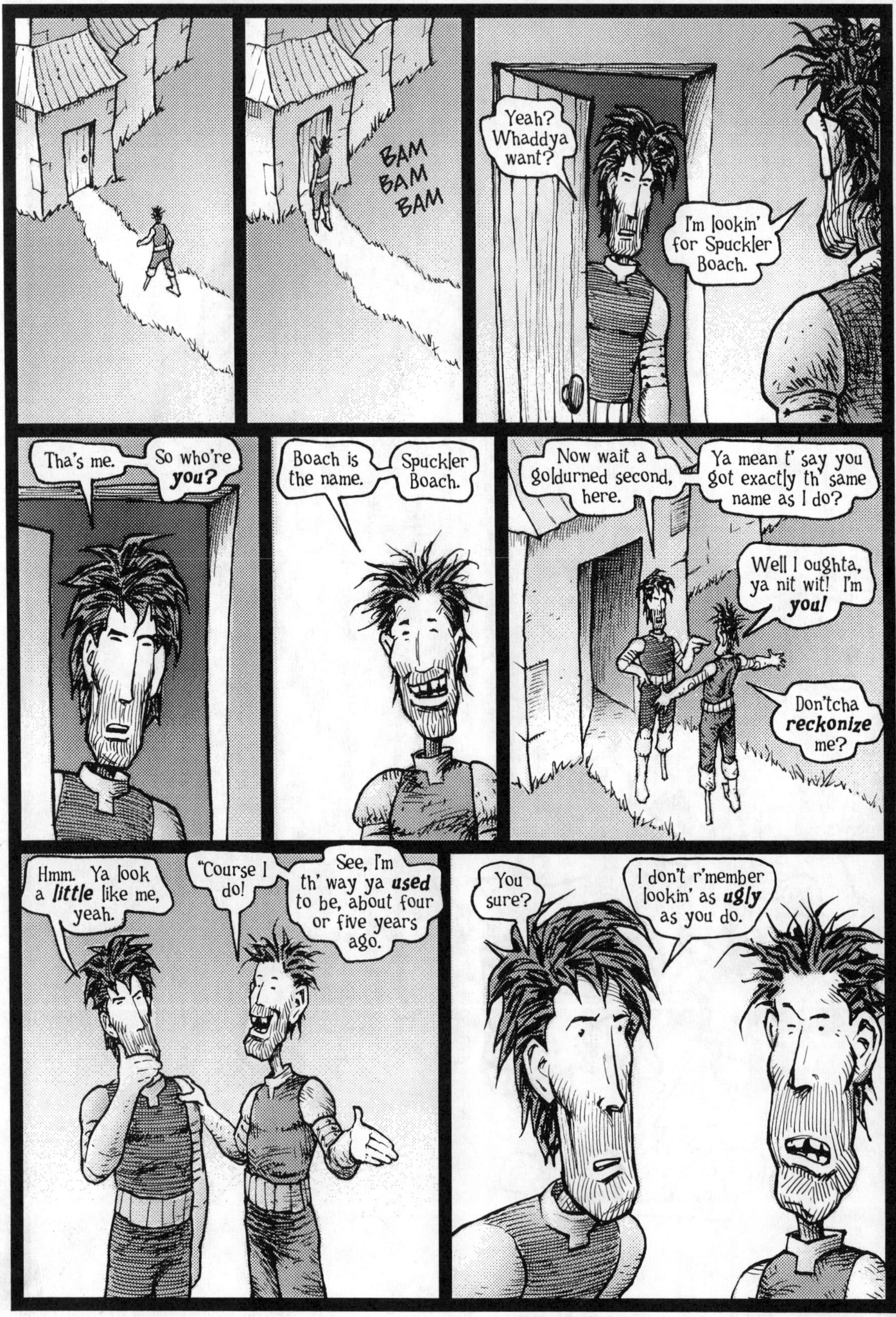

BAM
BAM
BAM
Yeah? Whaddya want?
I'm lookin' for Spuckler Boach.
Tha's me.
So who're *you?*
Boach is the name.
Spuckler Boach.
Now wait a goldurned second, here.
Ya mean t' say you got exactly th' same name as I do?
Well I oughta, ya nit wit! I'm *you!*
Don'tcha *reckonize* me?
Hmm. Ya look a *little* like me, yeah.
'Course I do!
See, I'm th' way ya *used* to be, about four or five years ago.
You sure?
I don't r'member lookin' as *ugly* as you do.

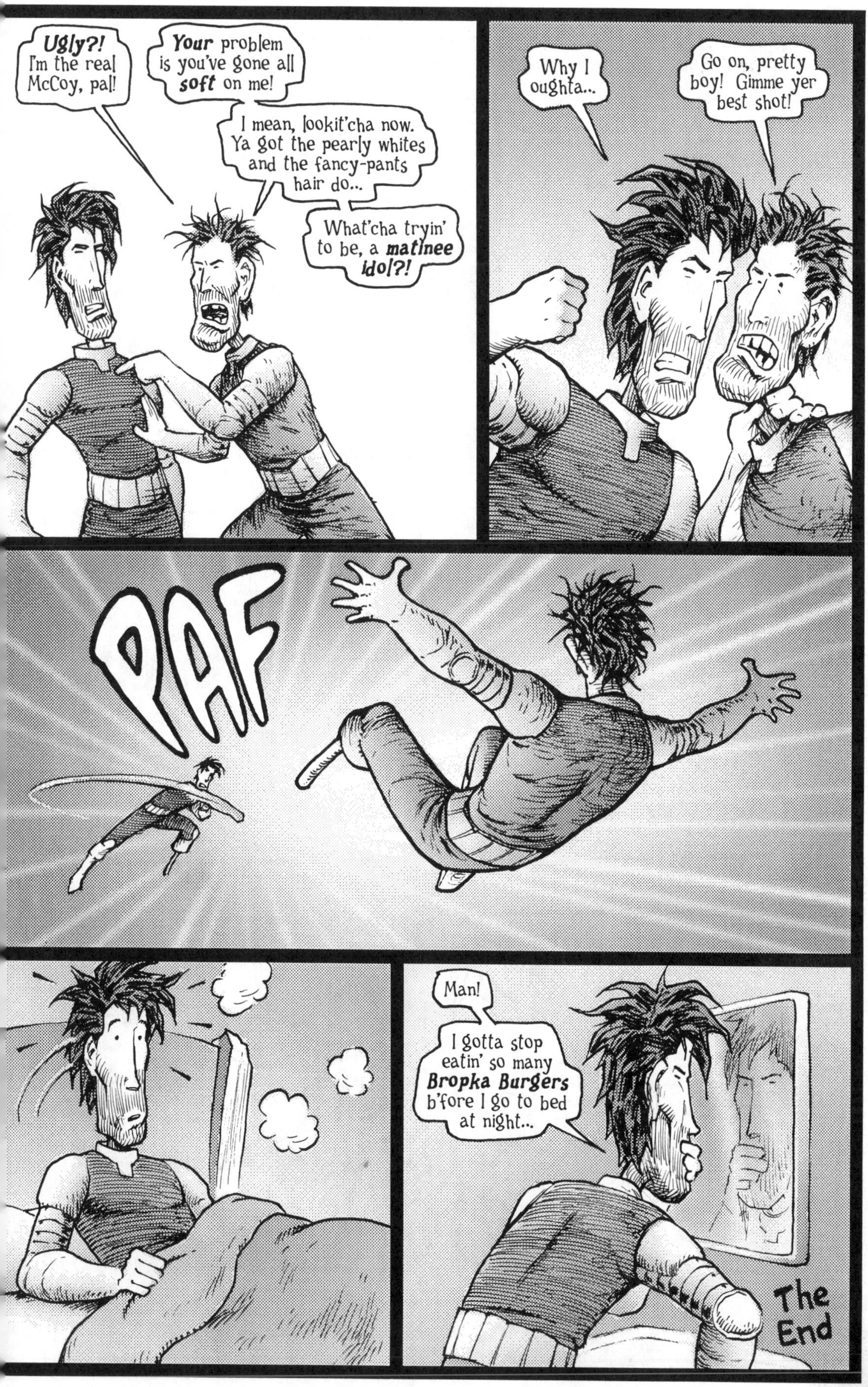
Ugly?! I'm the real McCoy, pal!
Your problem is you've gone all soft on me!
I mean, lookit'cha now. Ya got the pearly whites and the fancy-pants hair do...
What'cha tryin' to be, a matinee idol?!
Why I oughta...
Go on, pretty boy! Gimme yer best shot!
PAF
Man!
I gotta stop eatin' so many Bropka Burgers b'fore I go to bed at night...
The End

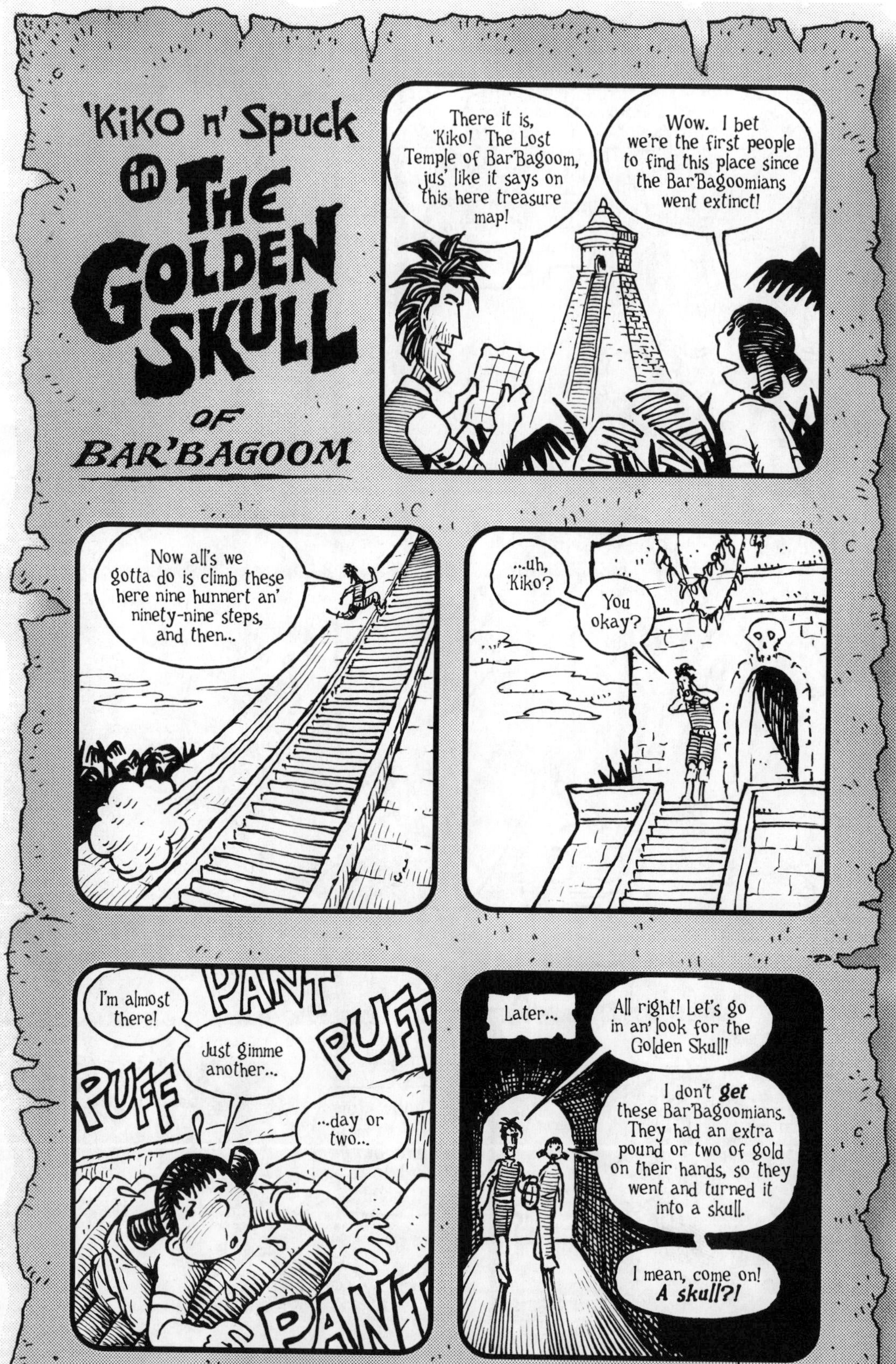
'KiKO n' Spuck in THE GOLDEN SKULL OF BAR'BAGOOM
There it is, 'Kiko! The Lost Temple of Bar'Bagoom, jus' like it says on this here treasure map!
Wow. I bet we're the first people to find this place since the Bar'Bagoomians went extinct!
Now all's we gotta do is climb these here nine hunnert an' ninety-nine steps, and then..
...uh, 'Kiko?
You okay?
I'm almost there!
PANT
Just gimme another...
PUFF
PUFF
...day or two...
PANT
Later...
All right! Let's go in an' look for the Golden Skull!
I don't **get** these Bar'Bagoomians. They had an extra pound or two of gold on their hands, so they went and turned it into a skull.
I mean, come on! ***A skull?!***

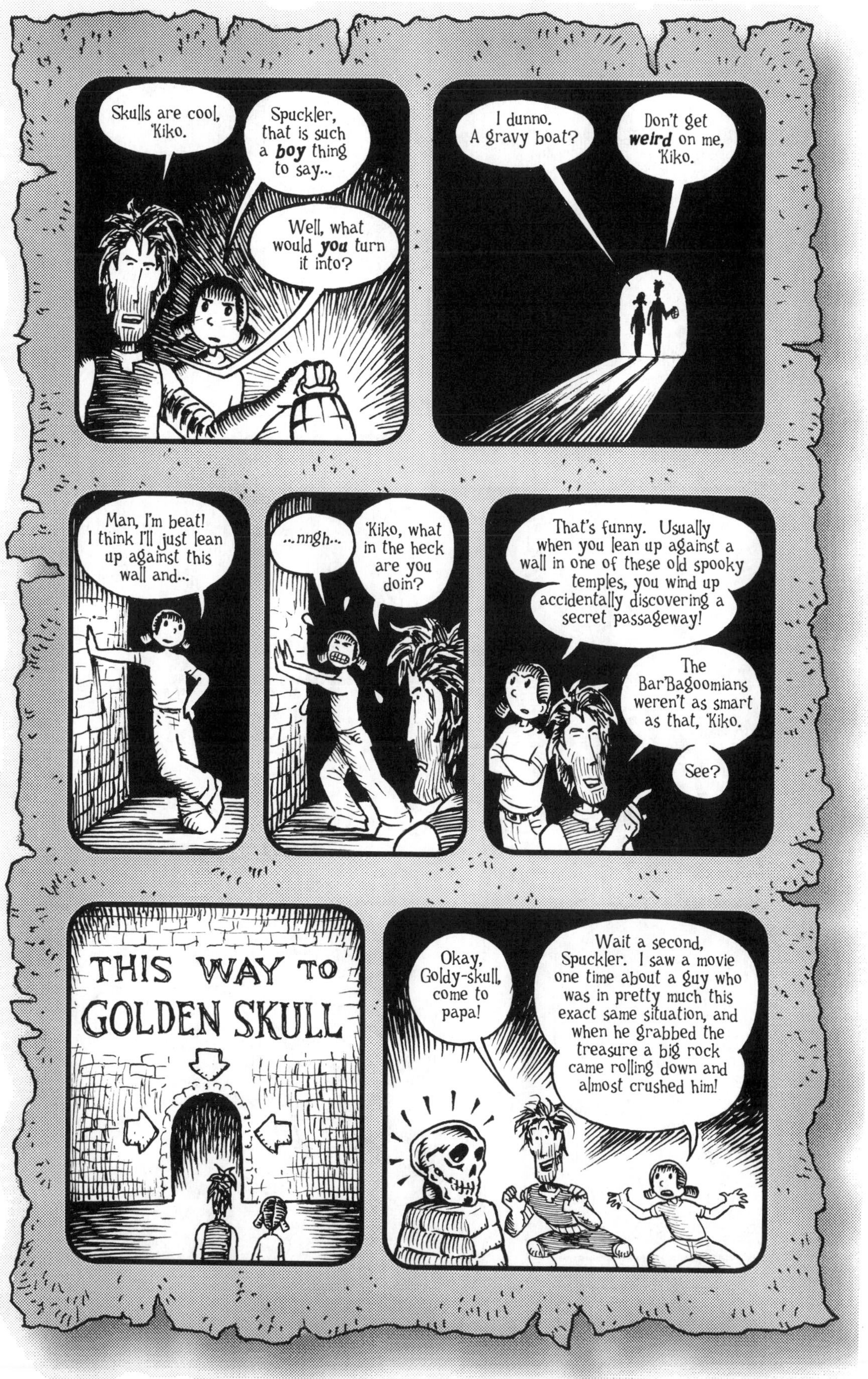

Skulls are cool, 'Kiko.
Spuckler, that is such a **boy** thing to say...
Well, what would **you** turn it into?
I dunno. A gravy boat?
Don't get **weird** on me, 'Kiko.
Man, I'm beat! I think I'll just lean up against this wall and...
...nngh...
'Kiko, what in the heck are you doin?
That's funny. Usually when you lean up against a wall in one of these old spooky temples, you wind up accidentally discovering a secret passageway!
The Bar'Bagoomians weren't as smart as that, 'Kiko.
See?
THIS WAY TO GOLDEN SKULL
Okay, Goldy-skull, come to papa!
Wait a second, Spuckler. I saw a movie one time about a guy who was in pretty much this exact same situation, and when he grabbed the treasure a big rock came rolling down and almost crushed him!

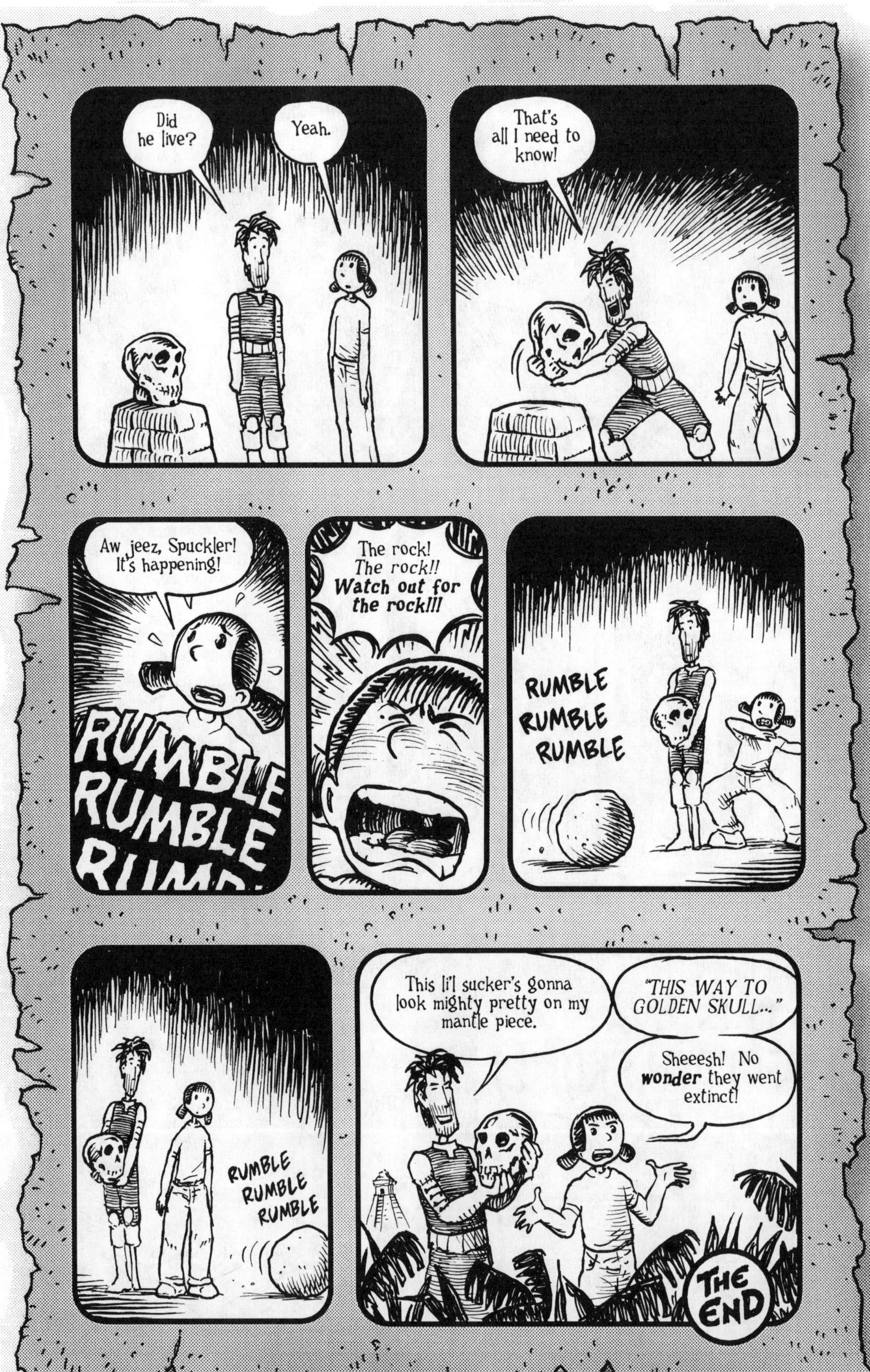
Did he live?
Yeah.
That's all I need to know!
Aw jeez, Spuckler! It's happening!
RUMBLE RUMBLE
The rock! The rock!! Watch out for the rock!!!
RUMBLE RUMBLE RUMBLE
RUMBLE RUMBLE RUMBLE
This li'l sucker's gonna look mighty pretty on my mantle piece.
"THIS WAY TO GOLDEN SKULL..."
Sheeesh! No wonder they went extinct!
THE END

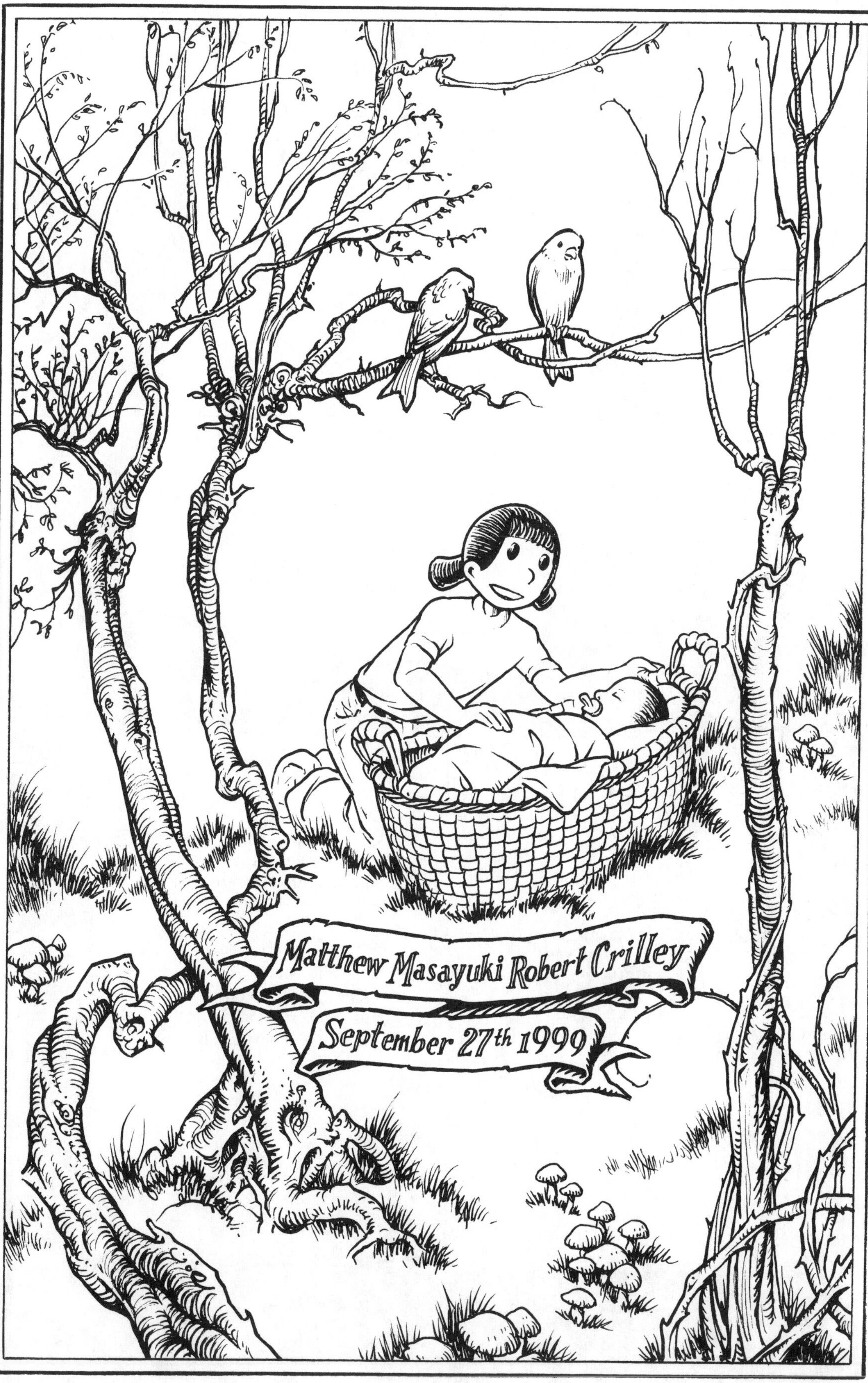
Matthew Masayuki Robert Crilley
September 27th 1999

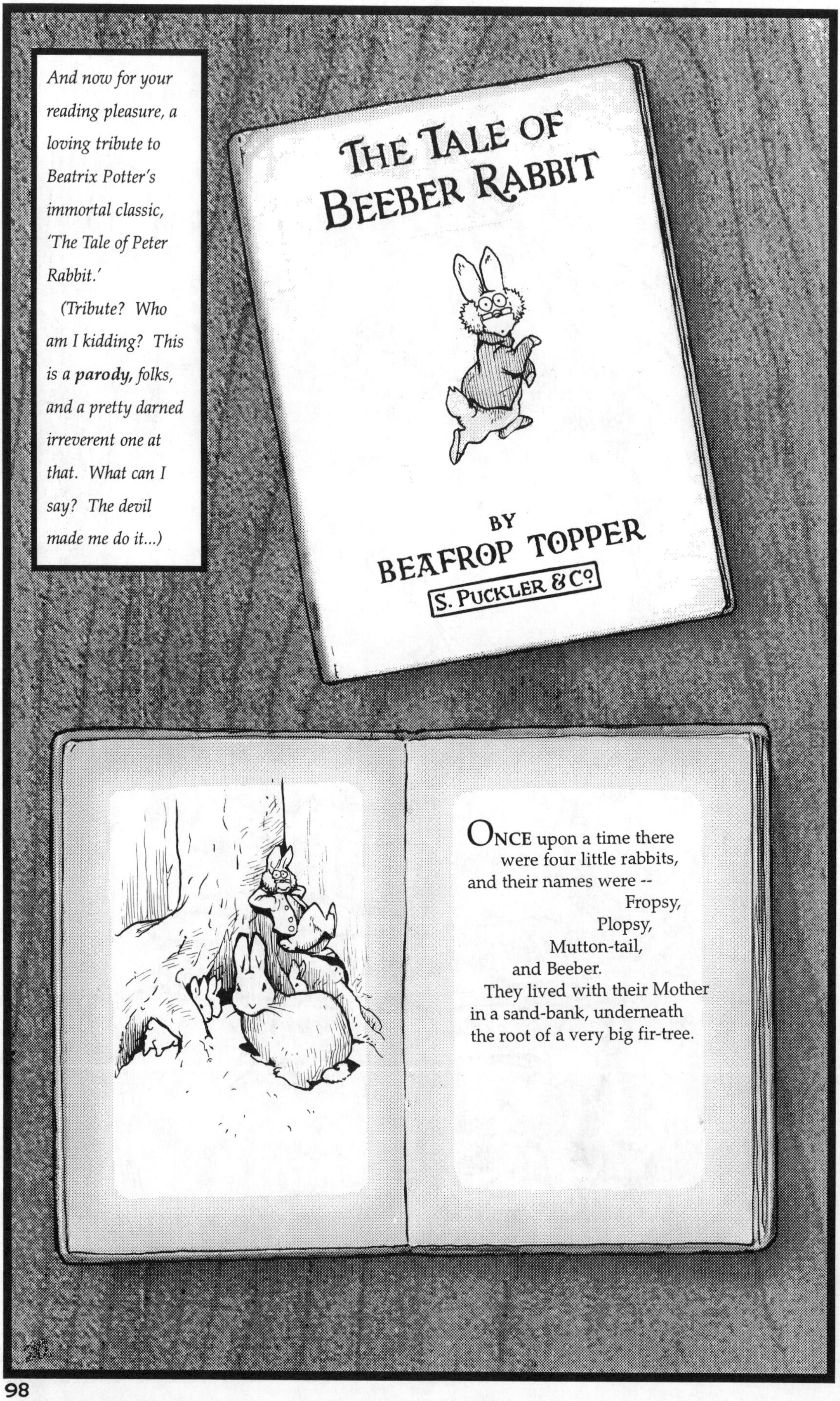

And now for your reading pleasure, a loving tribute to Beatrix Potter's immortal classic, 'The Tale of Peter Rabbit.'
(Tribute? Who am I kidding? This is a **parody,** folks, and a pretty darned irreverent one at that. What can I say? The devil made me do it...)
THE TALE OF BEEBER RABBIT
BY
BEAFROP TOPPER
S. PUCKLER & Co.
ONCE upon a time there were four little rabbits, and their names were --
Fropsy,
Plopsy,
Mutton-tail,
and Beeber.
They lived with their Mother in a sand-bank, underneath the root of a very big fir-tree.

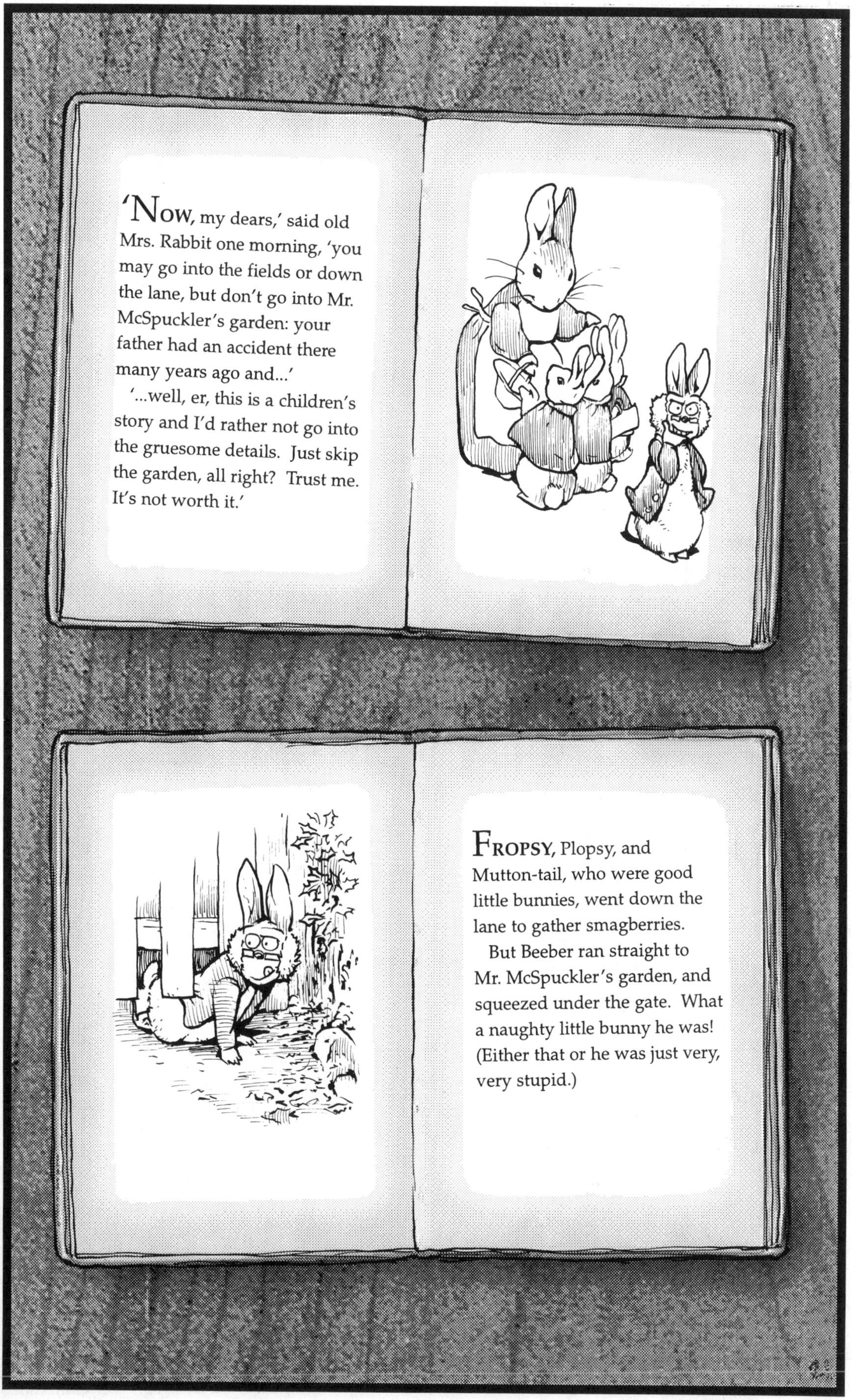
'Now, my dears,' said old Mrs. Rabbit one morning, 'you may go into the fields or down the lane, but don't go into Mr. McSpuckler's garden: your father had an accident there many years ago and...'
'...well, er, this is a children's story and I'd rather not go into the gruesome details. Just skip the garden, all right? Trust me. It's not worth it.'
Fropsy, Plopsy, and Mutton-tail, who were good little bunnies, went down the lane to gather smagberries.
But Beeber ran straight to Mr. McSpuckler's garden, and squeezed under the gate. What a naughty little bunny he was! (Either that or he was just very, very stupid.)

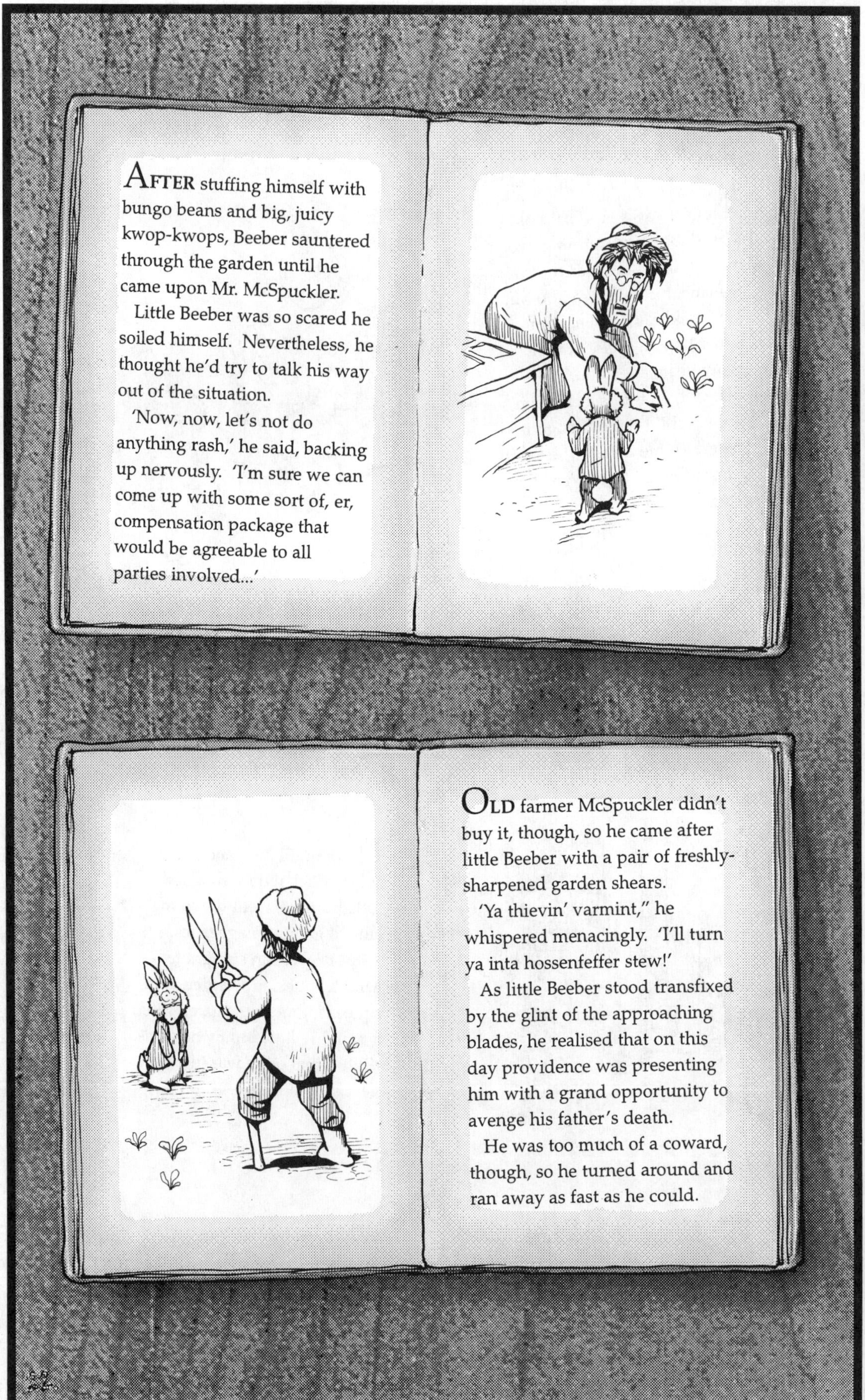
AFTER stuffing himself with bungo beans and big, juicy kwop-kwops, Beeber sauntered through the garden until he came upon Mr. McSpuckler.
Little Beeber was so scared he soiled himself. Nevertheless, he thought he'd try to talk his way out of the situation.
'Now, now, let's not do anything rash,' he said, backing up nervously. 'I'm sure we can come up with some sort of, er, compensation package that would be agreeable to all parties involved...'
OLD farmer McSpuckler didn't buy it, though, so he came after little Beeber with a pair of freshly-sharpened garden shears.
'Ya thievin' varmint," he whispered menacingly. 'I'll turn ya inta hossenfeffer stew!'
As little Beeber stood transfixed by the glint of the approaching blades, he realised that on this day providence was presenting him with a grand opportunity to avenge his father's death.
He was too much of a coward, though, so he turned around and ran away as fast as he could.

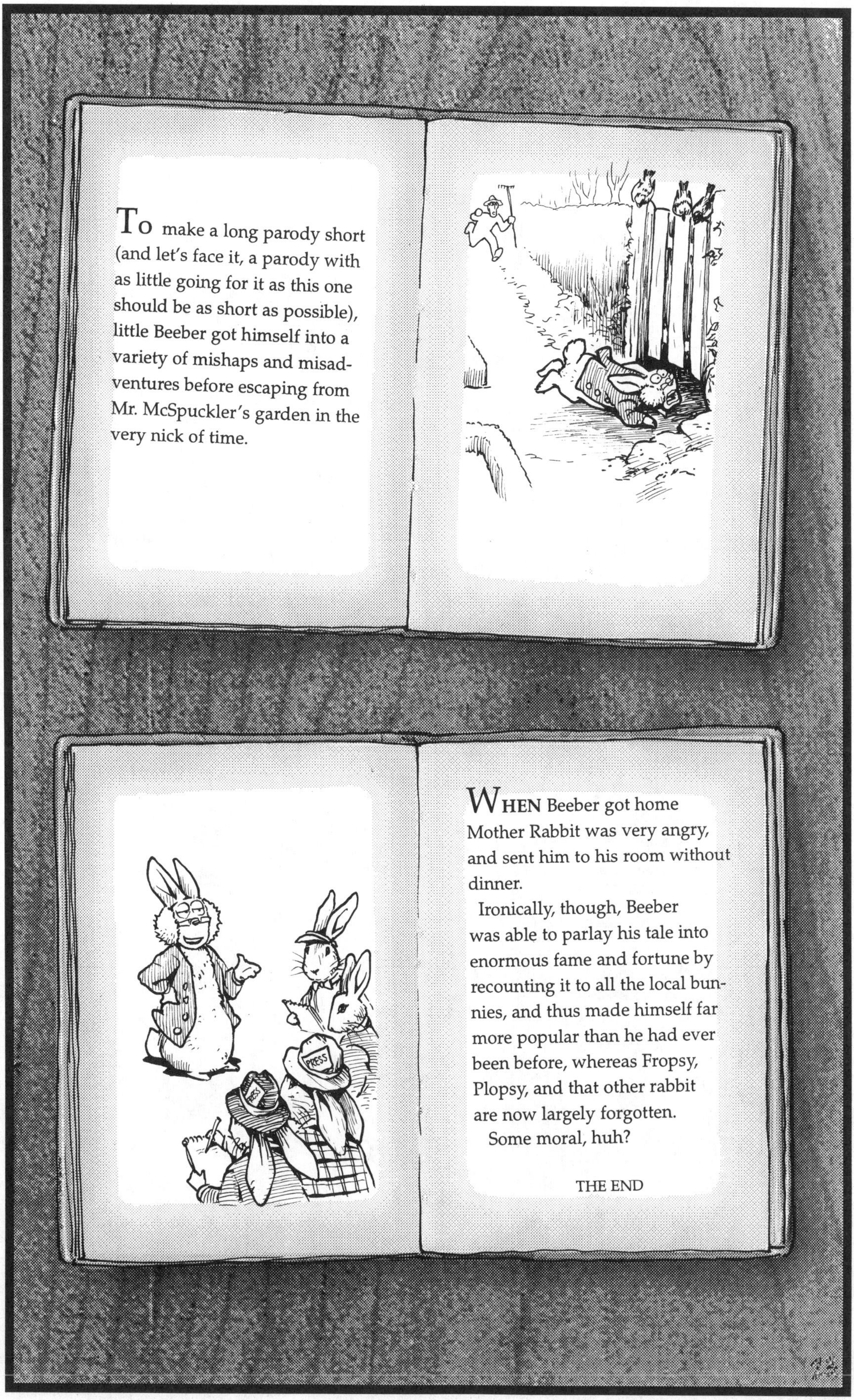
To make a long parody short (and let's face it, a parody with as little going for it as this one should be as short as possible), little Beeber got himself into a variety of mishaps and misadventures before escaping from Mr. McSpuckler's garden in the very nick of time.
PRESS
PRESS
WHEN Beeber got home Mother Rabbit was very angry, and sent him to his room without dinner.
Ironically, though, Beeber was able to parlay his tale into enormous fame and fortune by recounting it to all the local bunnies, and thus made himself far more popular than he had ever been before, whereas Fropsy, Plopsy, and that other rabbit are now largely forgotten.
Some moral, huh?
THE END

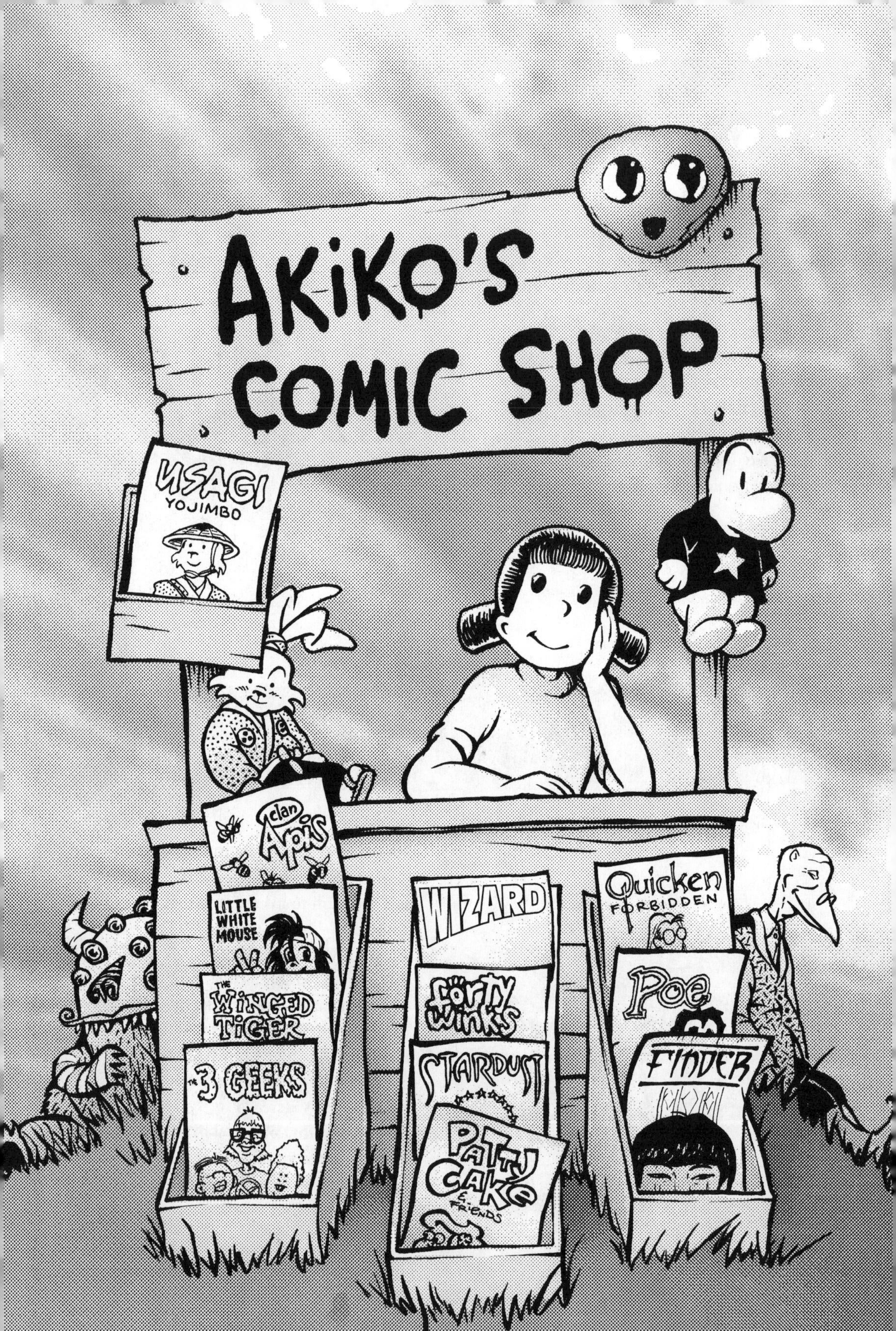
AKIKO'S
COMIC SHOP
USAGI
YOJIMBO
clan
Apis
LITTLE
WHITE
MOUSE
THE
WINGED
TIGER
THE 3 GEEKS
WIZARD
Forty
Winks
STARDUST
PATTY
CAKE
& FRIENDS
Quicken
FORBIDDEN
Poe
FINDER

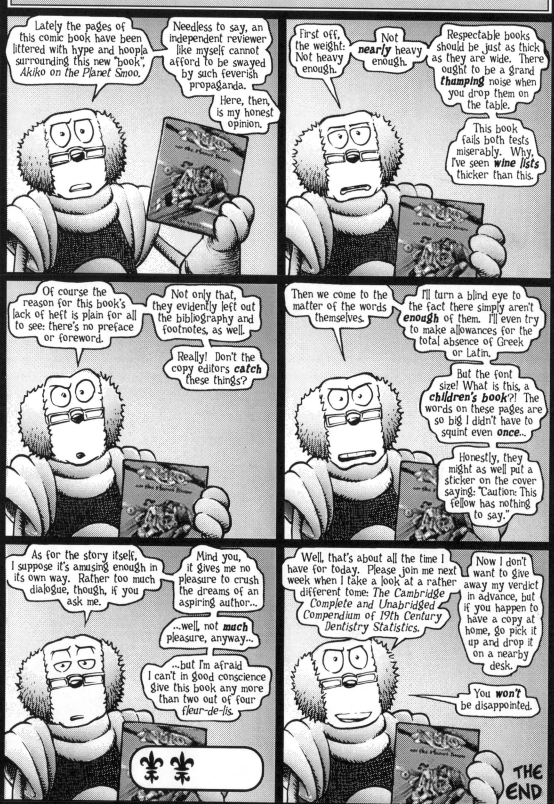

THIS STORY IS DEDICATED TO MY PARENTS-IN-LAW, KOJI & MINAE HIRABAYASHI

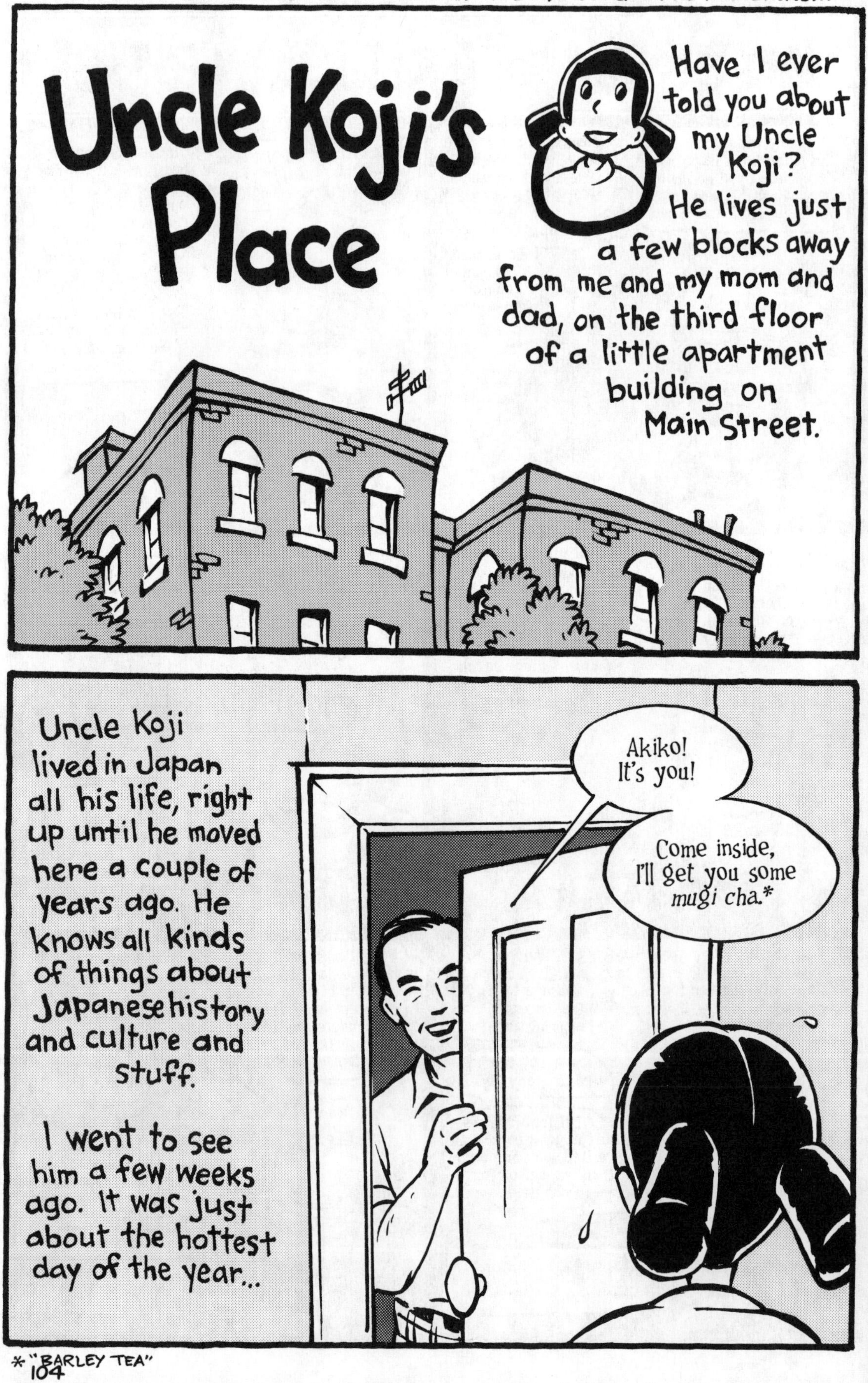
Uncle Koji's Place
Have I ever told you about my Uncle Koji? He lives just a few blocks away from me and my mom and dad, on the third floor of a little apartment building on Main Street.
Uncle Koji lived in Japan all his life, right up until he moved here a couple of years ago. He knows all kinds of things about Japanese history and culture and stuff.
I went to see him a few weeks ago. It was just about the hottest day of the year...
Akiko! It's you!
Come inside, I'll get you some *mugi cha*.*

* "BARLEY TEA"

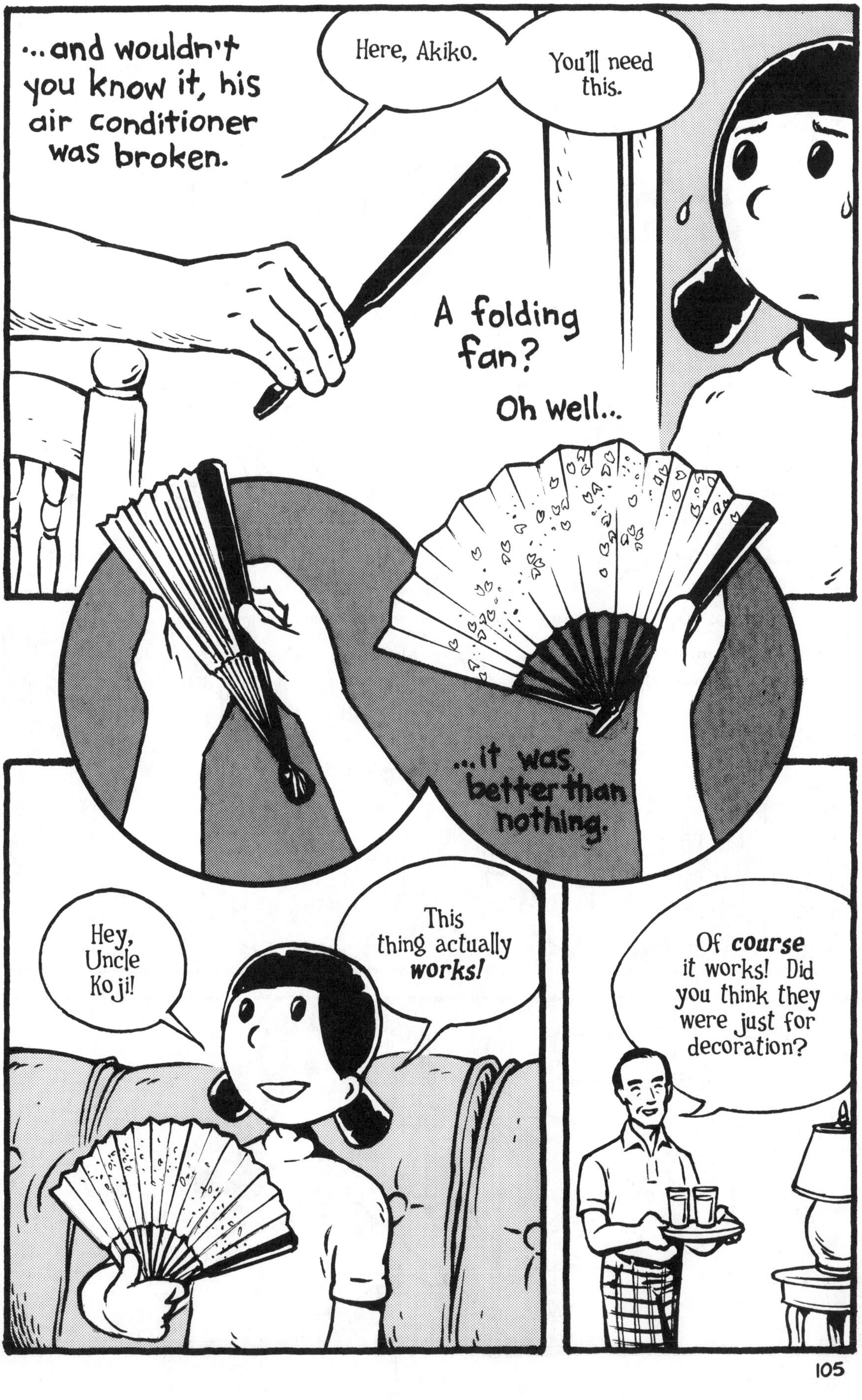
...and wouldn't you know it, his air conditioner was broken.
Here, Akiko.
You'll need this.
A folding fan?
Oh well...
...it was better than nothing.
Hey, Uncle Koji!
This thing actually ***works!***
Of ***course*** it works! Did you think they were just for decoration?

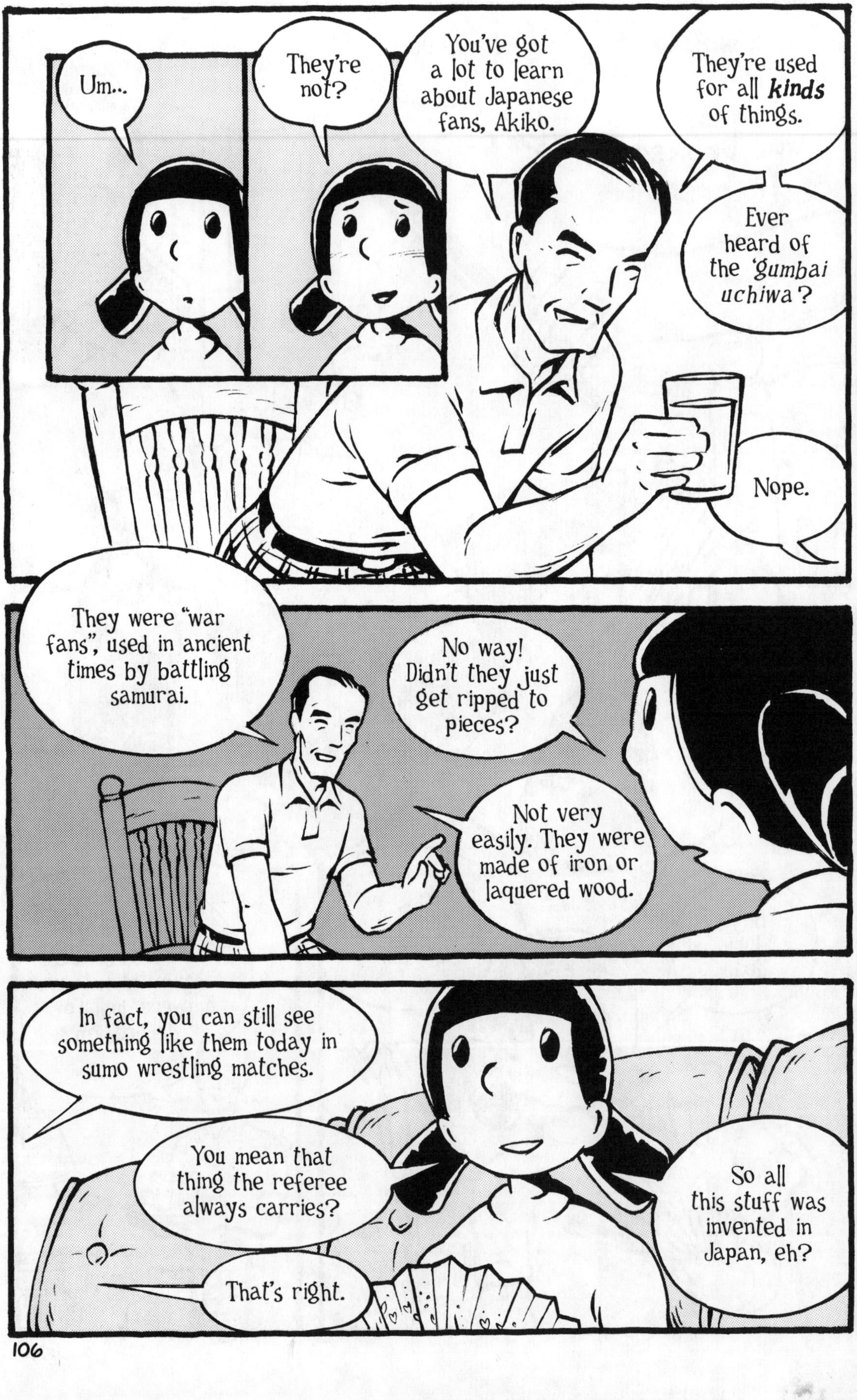

Um...
They're not?
You've got a lot to learn about Japanese fans, Akiko.
They're used for all *kinds* of things.
Ever heard of the 'gumbai uchiwa'?
Nope.
They were "war fans", used in ancient times by battling samurai.
No way! Didn't they just get ripped to pieces?
Not very easily. They were made of iron or laquered wood.
In fact, you can still see something like them today in sumo wrestling matches.
You mean that thing the referee always carries?
That's right.
So all this stuff was invented in Japan, eh?

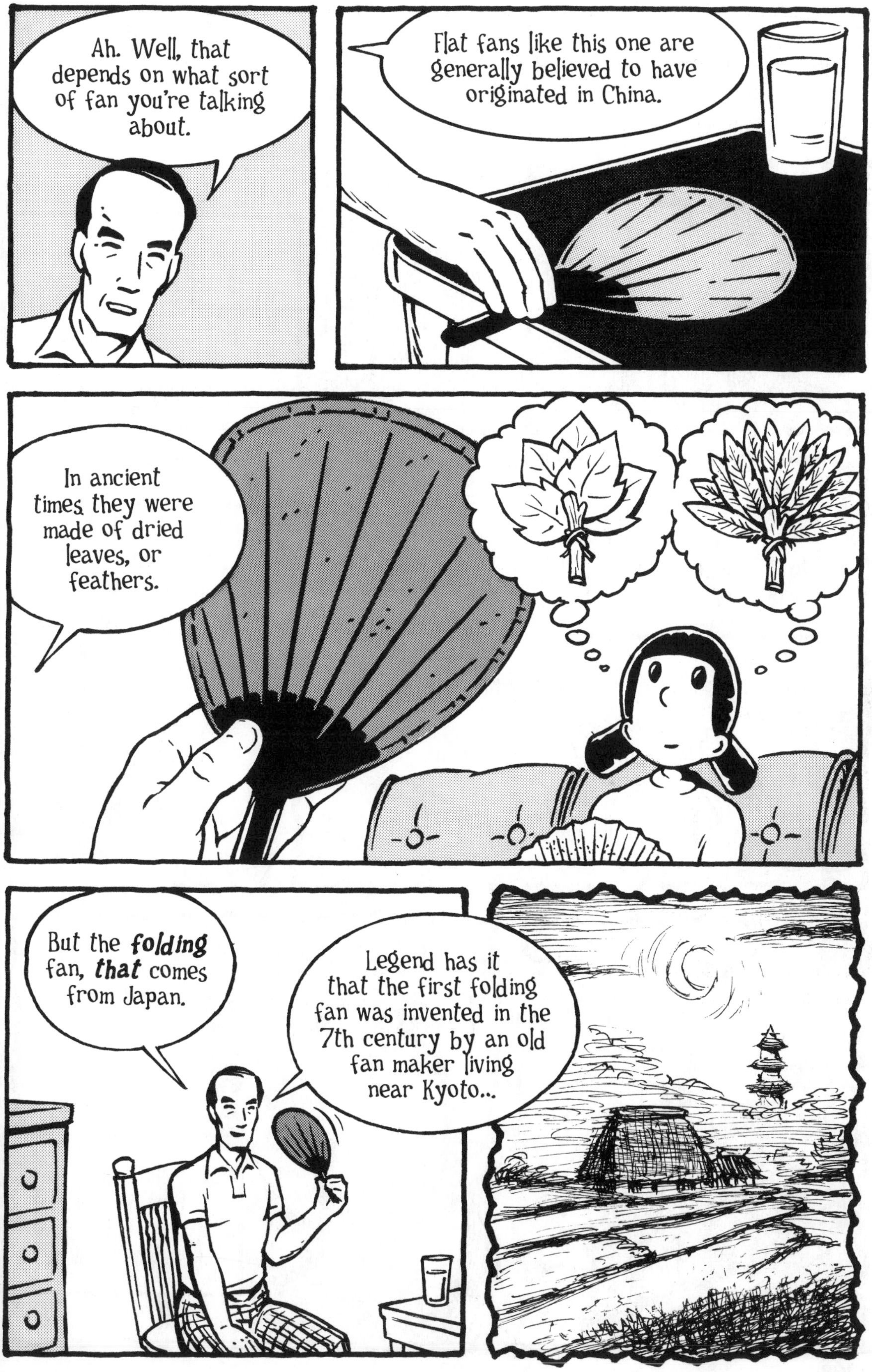
Ah. Well, that depends on what sort of fan you're talking about.
Flat fans like this one are generally believed to have originated in China.
In ancient times they were made of dried leaves, or feathers.
But the **folding** fan, **that** comes from Japan.
Legend has it that the first folding fan was invented in the 7th century by an old fan maker living near Kyoto...

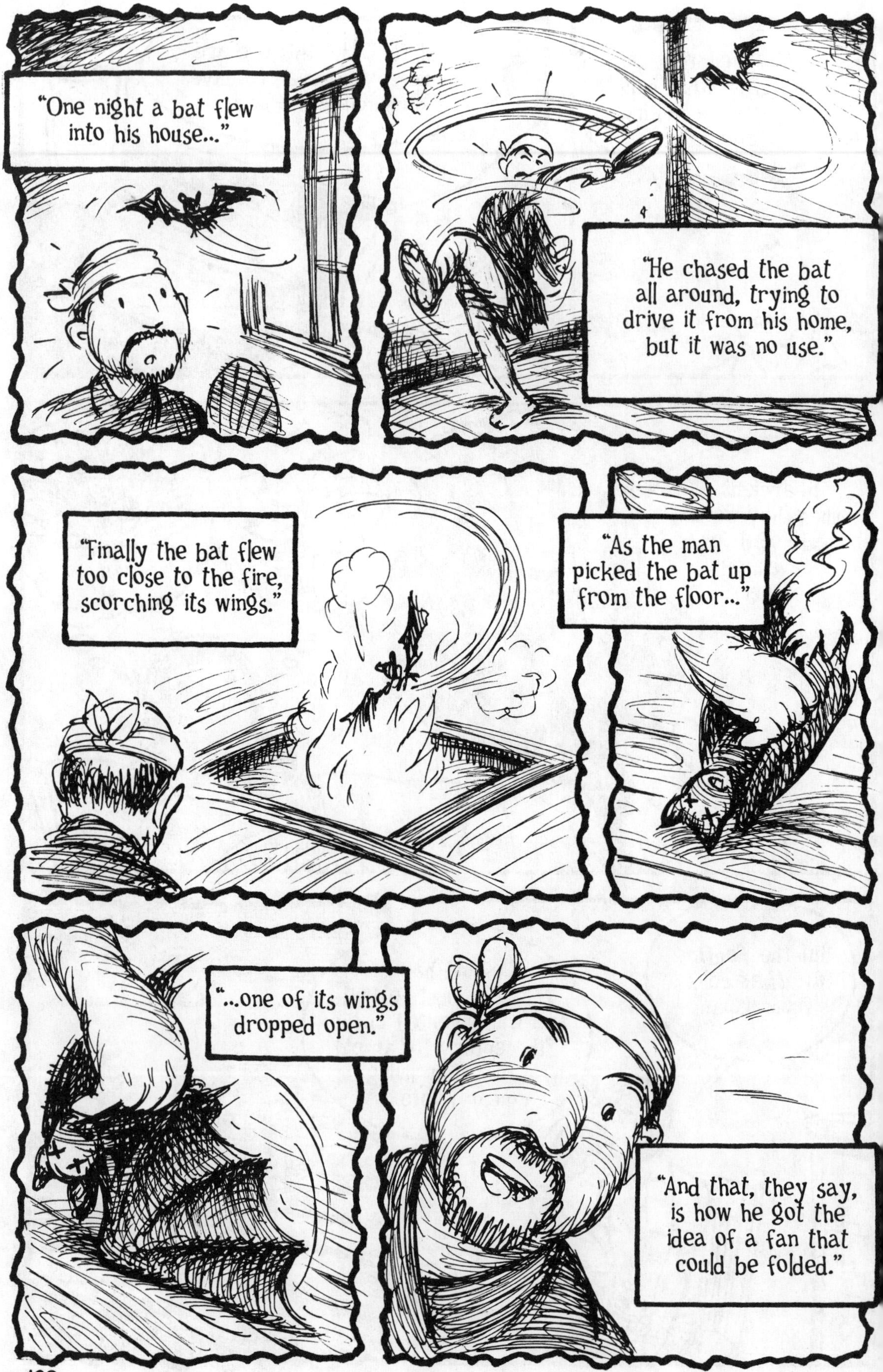
"One night a bat flew into his house..."
"He chased the bat all around, trying to drive it from his home, but it was no use."
"Finally the bat flew too close to the fire, scorching its wings."
"As the man picked the bat up from the floor..."
"...one of its wings dropped open."
"And that, they say, is how he got the idea of a fan that could be folded."

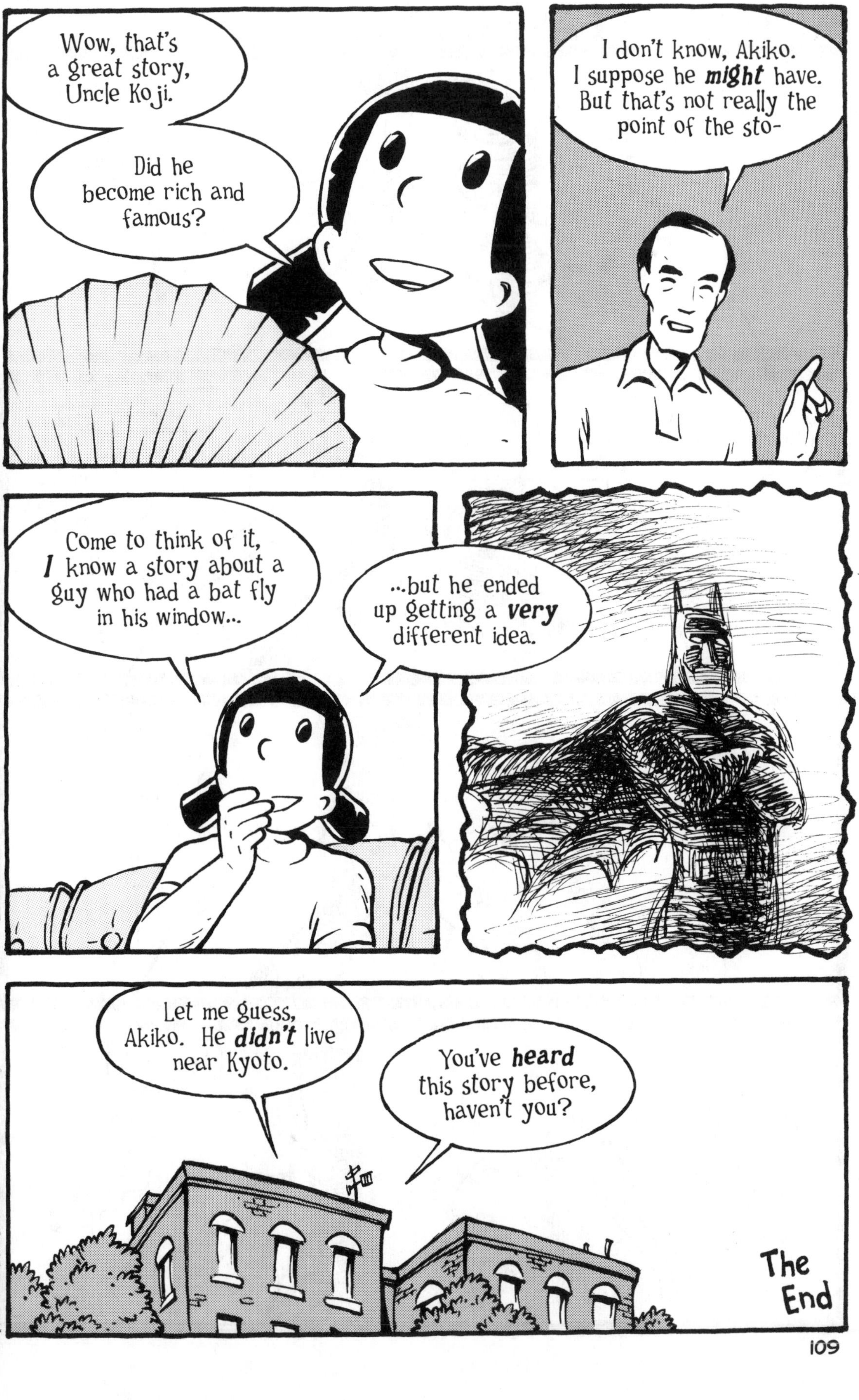
Wow, that's a great story, Uncle Koji.
Did he become rich and famous?
I don't know, Akiko. I suppose he **might** have. But that's not really the point of the sto-
Come to think of it, *I* know a story about a guy who had a bat fly in his window...
...but he ended up getting a **very** different idea.
Let me guess, Akiko. He **didn't** live near Kyoto.
You've **heard** this story before, haven't you?
The End

AKIKO'S PLAYHOUSE

Hi Spuckler! You're looking very, um, *splendiferous* today!
You ain't foolin' nobody, Beebs. There's no such word as "splendiferous".
But of **course** there is, Spuckler. It's a combination of the word "splendid" and, um, "ferocious".
Yeah, whatever.
Hey, here comes Gax!
HELLO, SIR... MY NAME IS GAX... I AM A ROBOT.
I know you're a robot, Gax! What are ya, crazy?
NO SIR. I WAS JUST...
...um...
...TESTING YOU.
Some test.
Hey, here comes Poog!

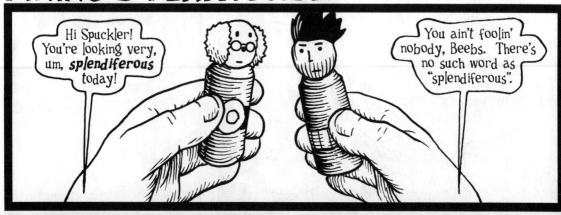

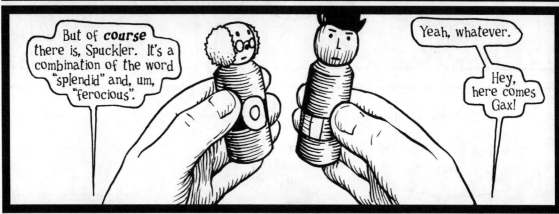

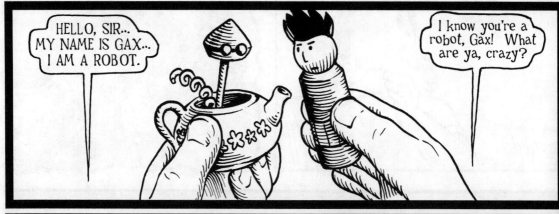

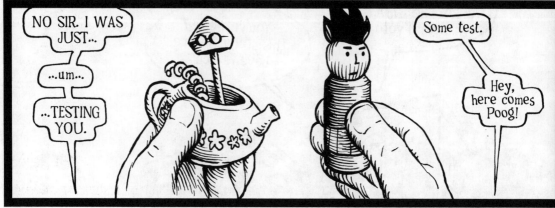

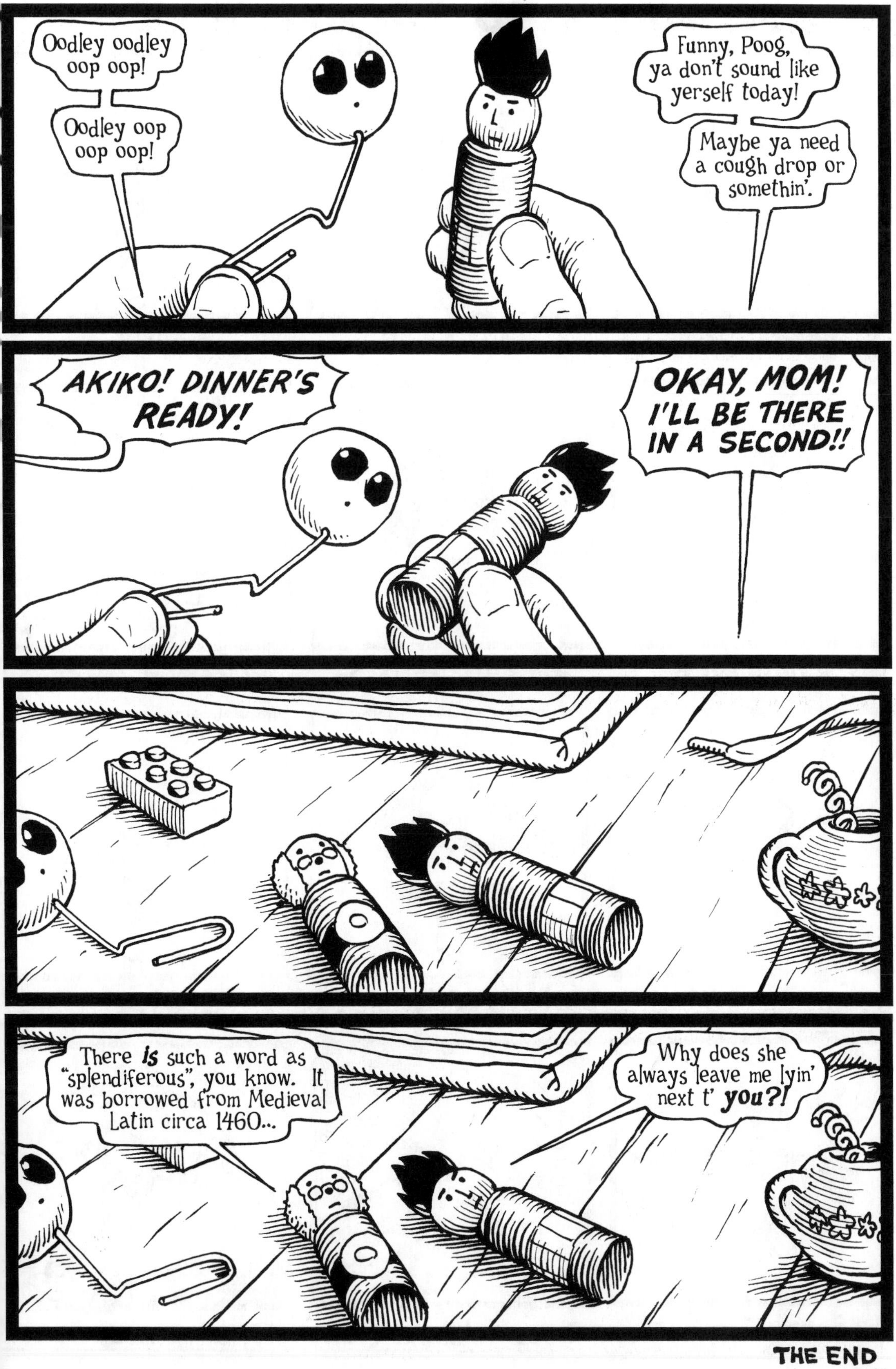

Oodley oodley oop oop!
Oodley oop oop oop!
Funny, Poog, ya don't sound like yerself today!
Maybe ya need a cough drop or somethin'.
AKIKO! DINNER'S READY!
OKAY, MOM! I'LL BE THERE IN A SECOND!!
There *is* such a word as "splendiferous", you know. It was borrowed from Medieval Latin circa 1460...
Why does she always leave me lyin' next t' ***you?!***

THE END

24 WAYS TO DRAW GAX

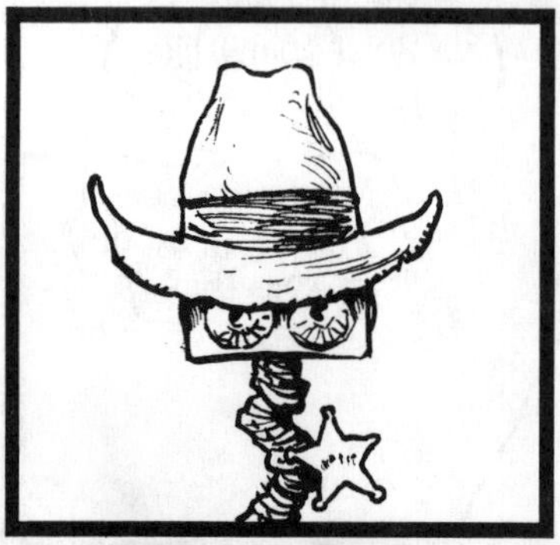

Sheriff Gax

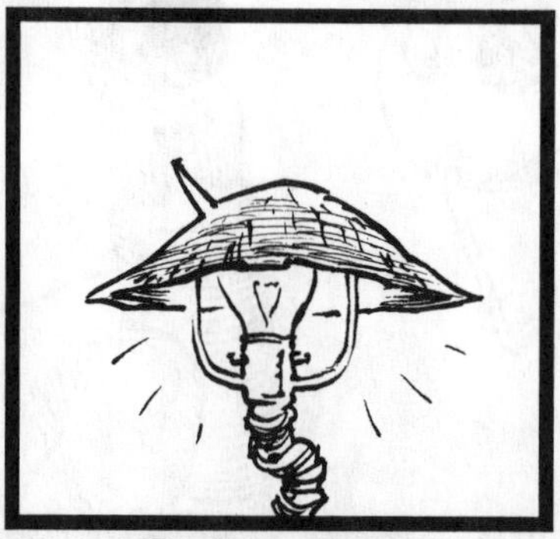

Gax Lamp

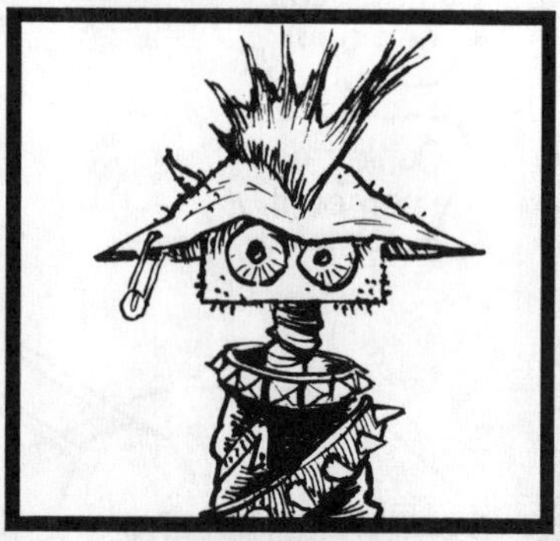

Punk Gax

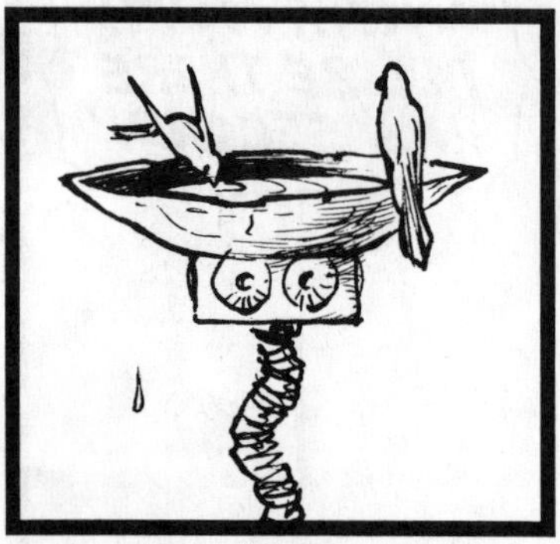

Bird Bath Gax

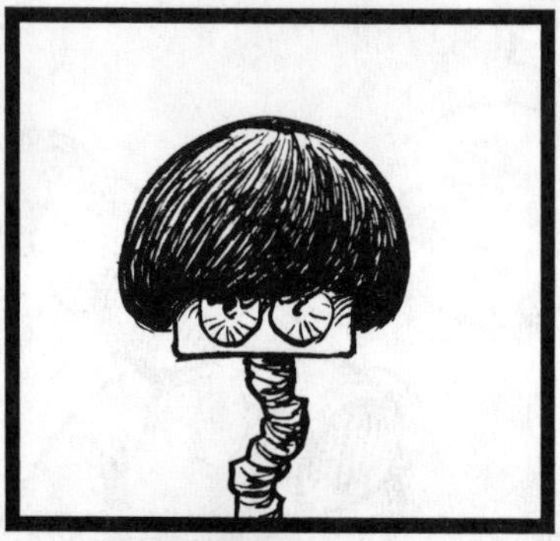

Beatle Gax

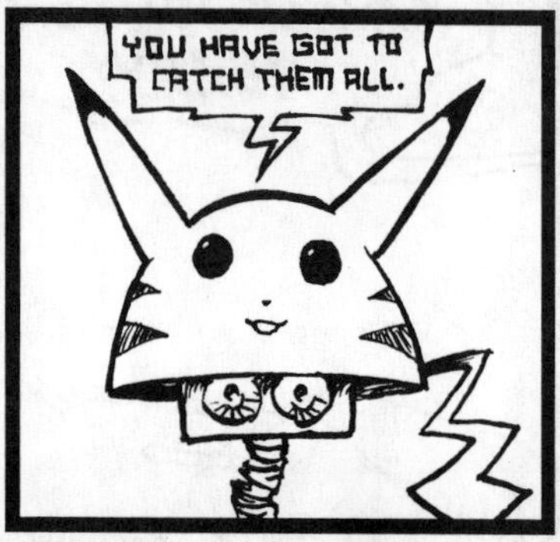
YOU HAVE GOT TO CATCH THEM ALL.

Pokémon Gax

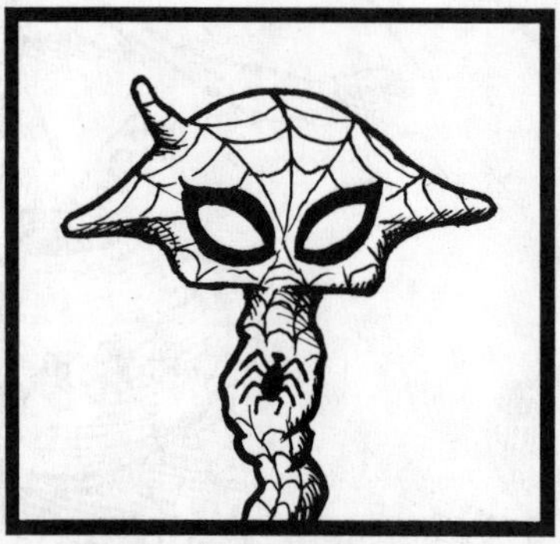

Spidergax

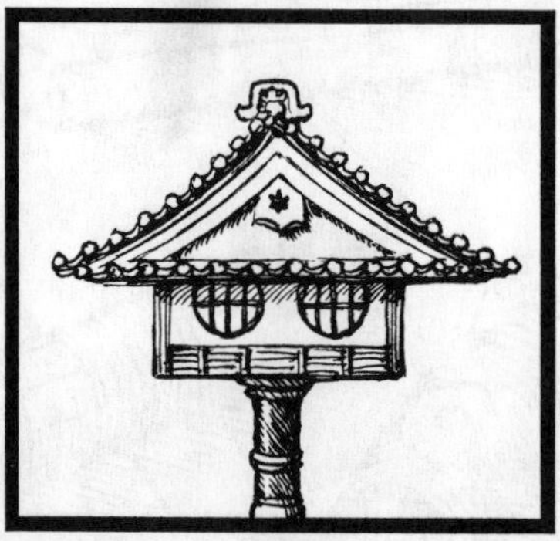

Eastern Architecture Gax

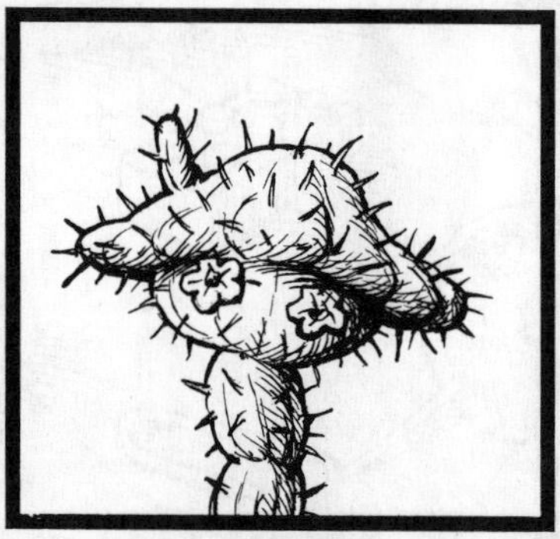

Gactus

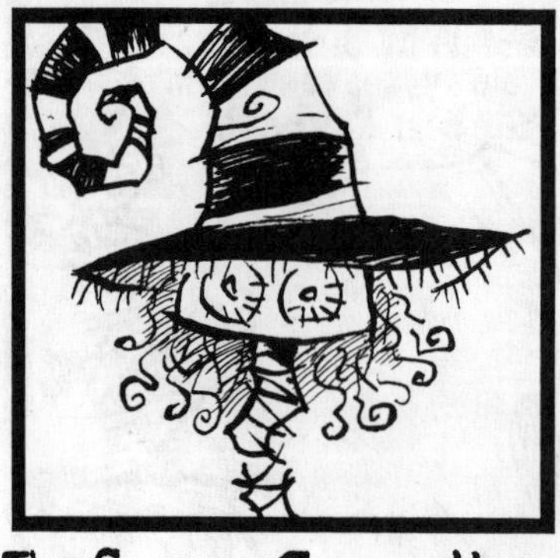

The Scary Gaxmother

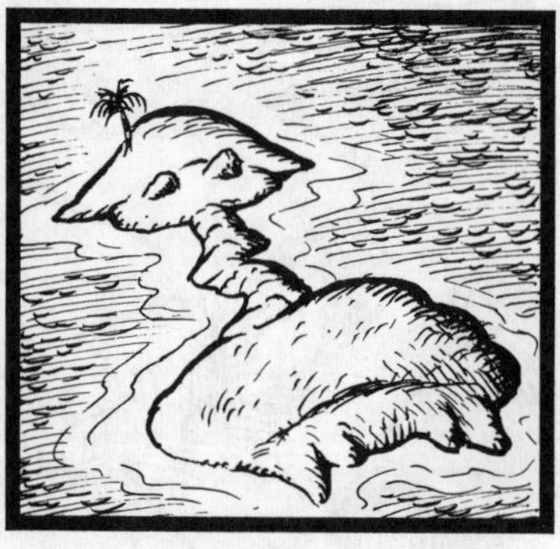

Desert Island Gax

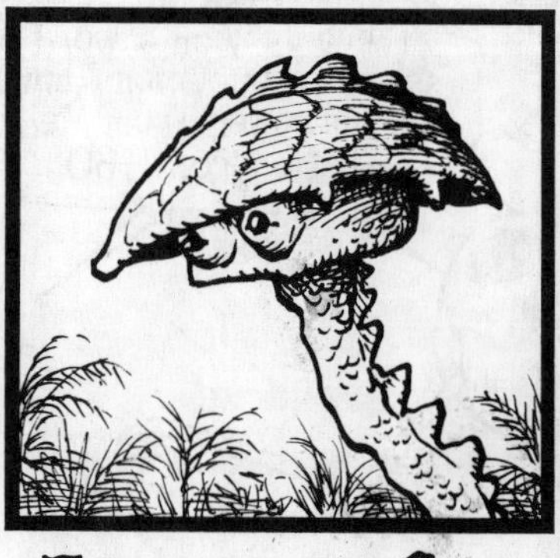

Tyrannosaurus Gax

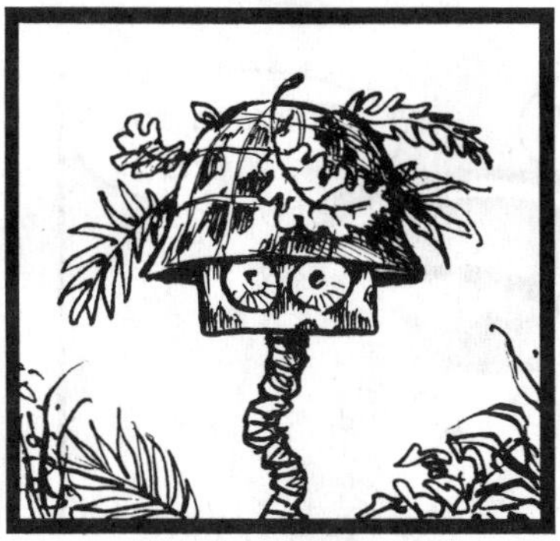
G.I. Gax

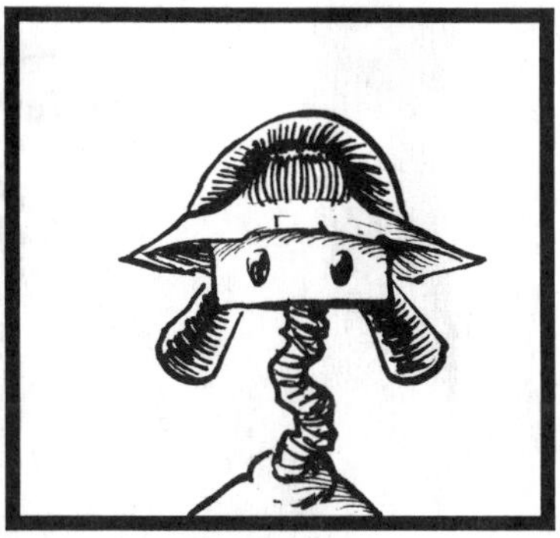
'Kiko Gax

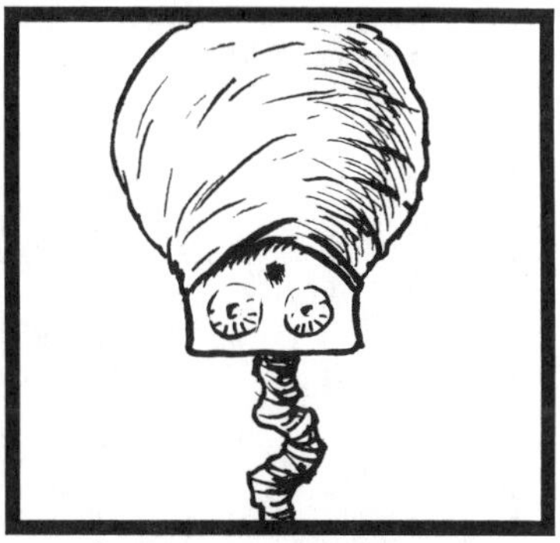
Indian Gax

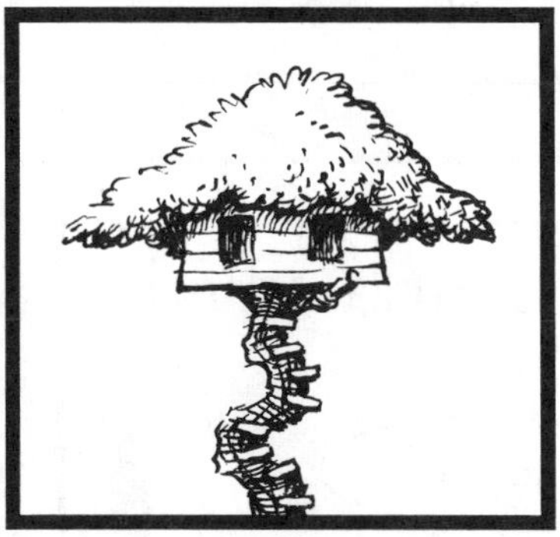
Treehouse Gax

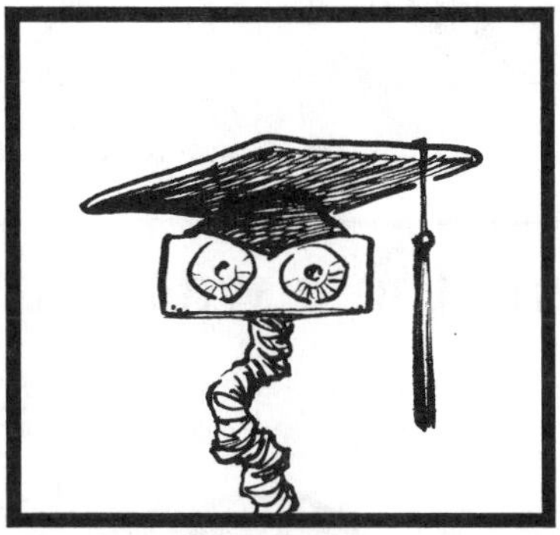
College Grad Gax

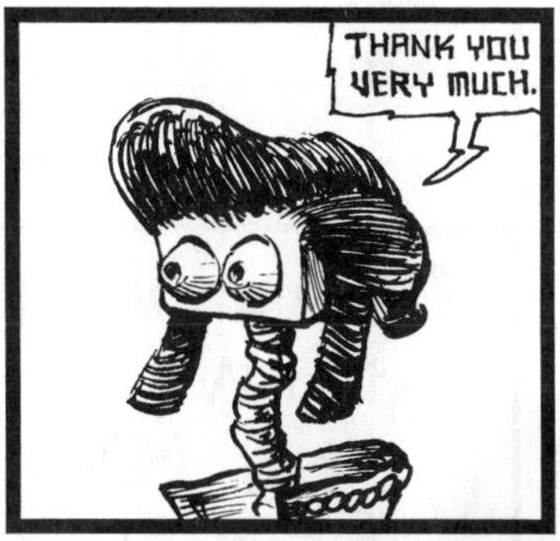
THANK YOU VERY MUCH.
Elvis Gaxley

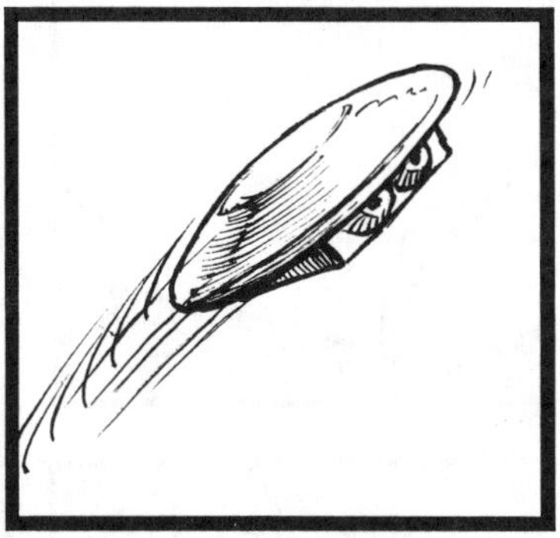
Frisbee Gax

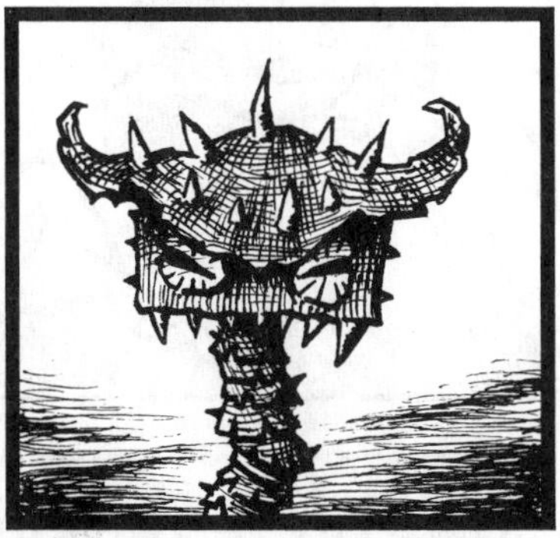
Evil Scary Gax

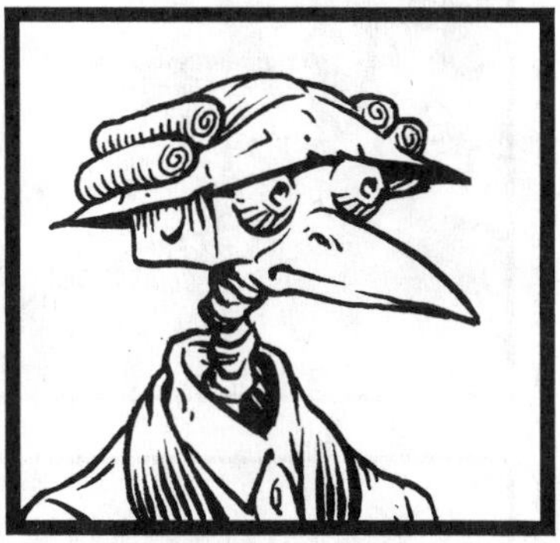
Gaxham Adjutant

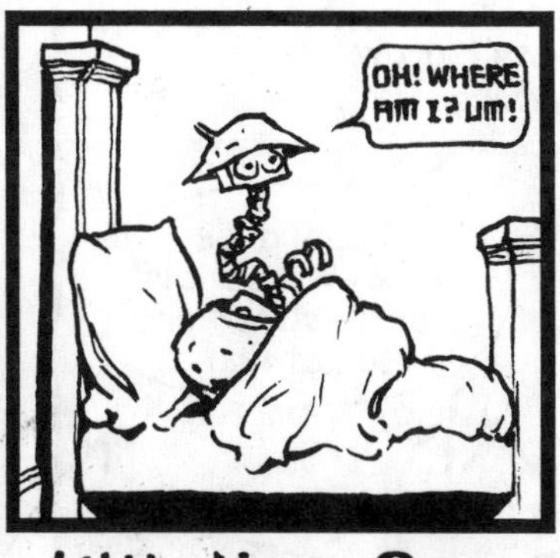
OH! WHERE AM I? UM!
Little Nemo Gax

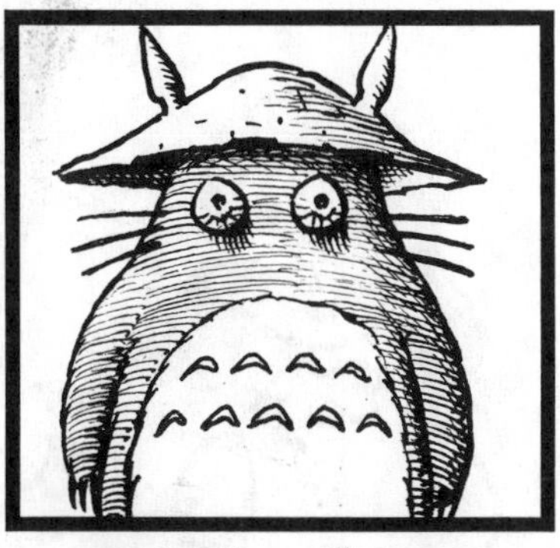
Totoro Gax

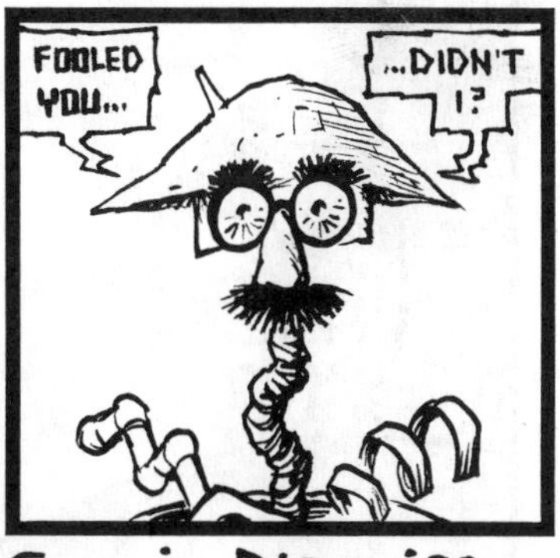
FOOLED YOU...
...DIDN'T I?
Gax in Disguise

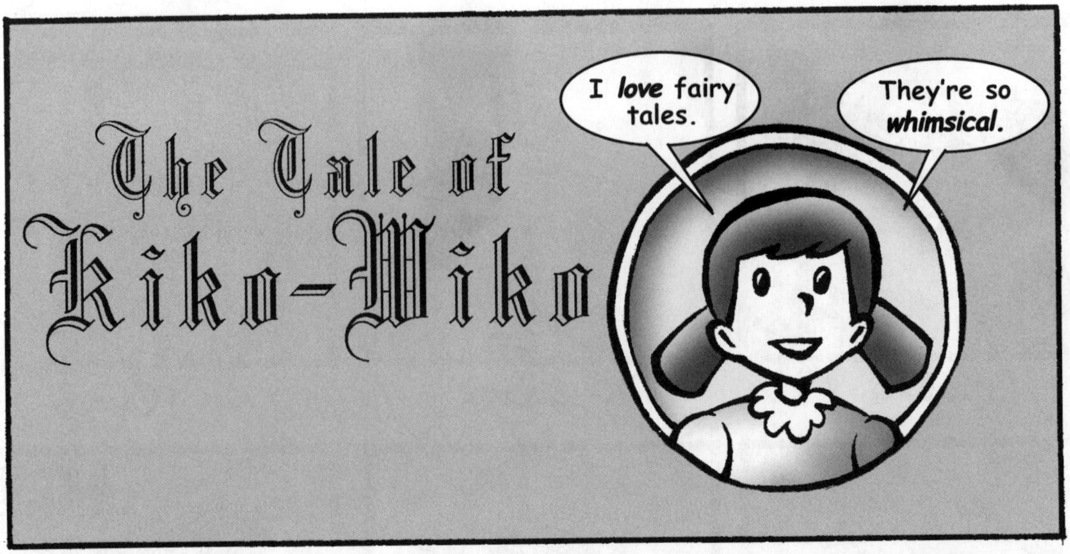
The Tale of Kiko-Wiko
I *love* fairy tales.
They're so *whimsical*.

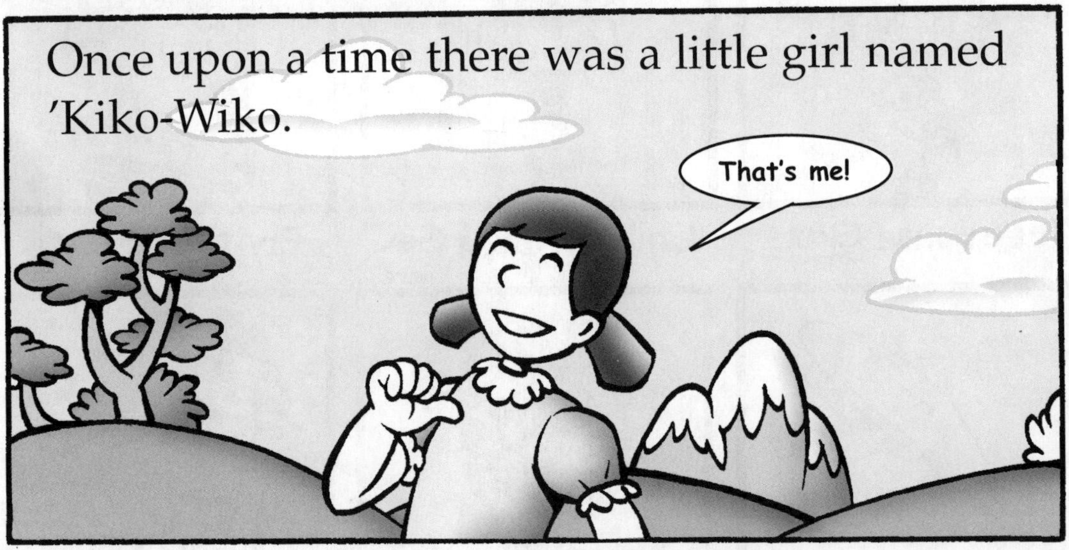
Once upon a time there was a little girl named 'Kiko-Wiko.
That's me!

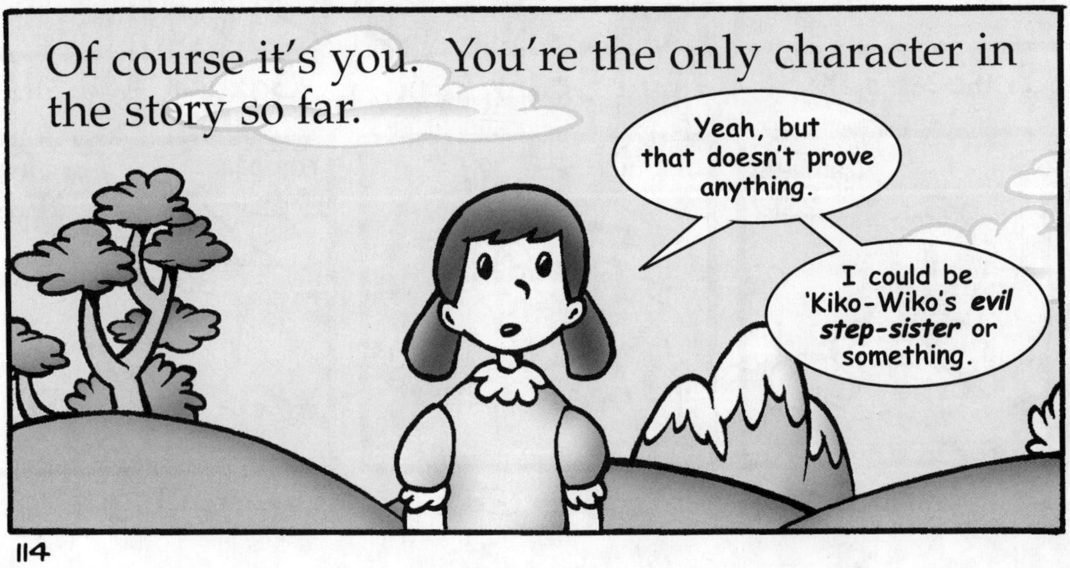
Of course it's you. You're the only character in the story so far.
Yeah, but that doesn't prove anything.
I could be 'Kiko-Wiko's *evil step-sister* or something.

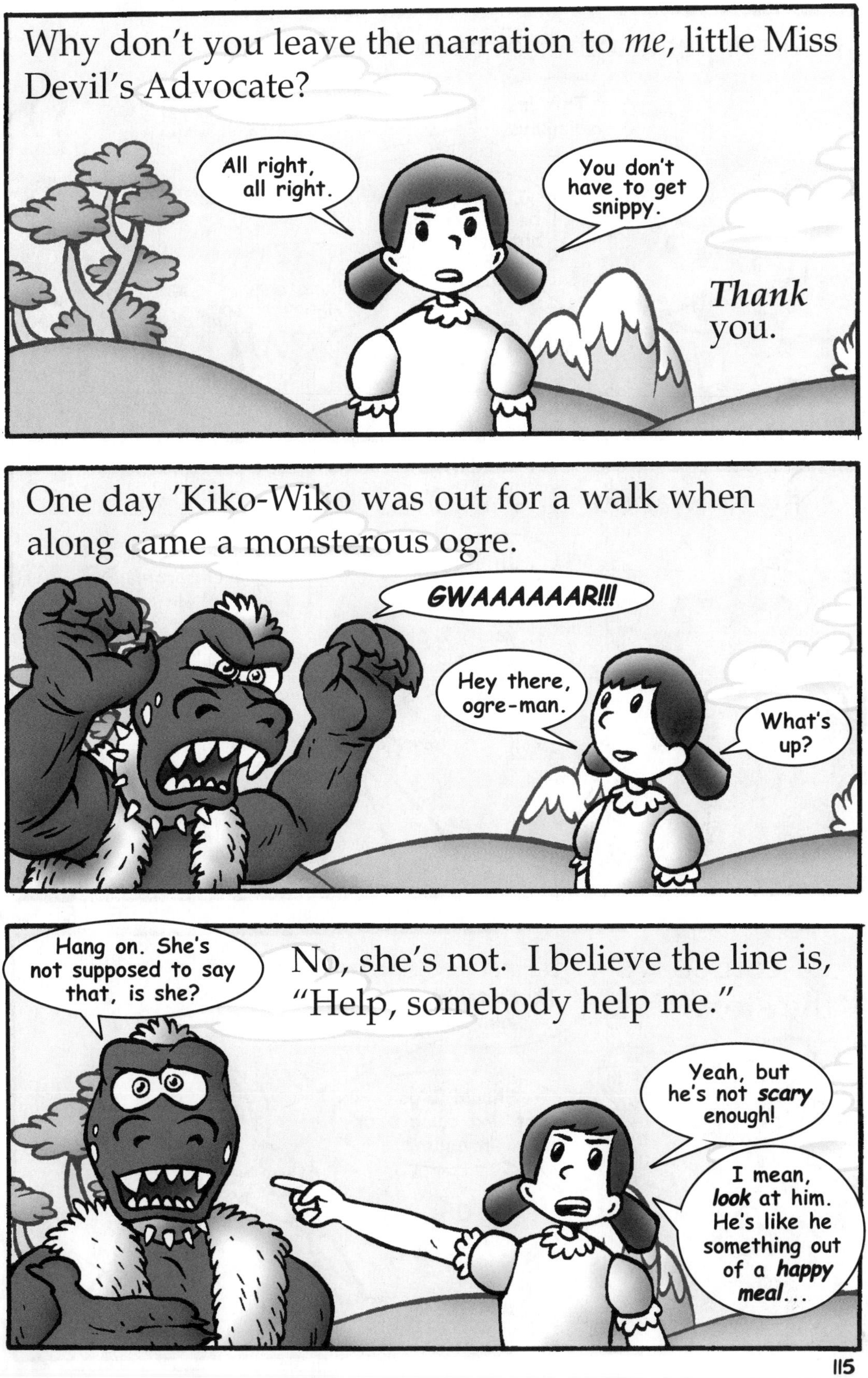
Why don't you leave the narration to *me*, little Miss Devil's Advocate?
All right, all right.
You don't have to get snippy.
Thank you.
One day 'Kiko-Wiko was out for a walk when along came a monsterous ogre.
GWAAAAAAR!!!
Hey there, ogre-man.
What's up?
Hang on. She's not supposed to say that, is she?
No, she's not. I believe the line is, "Help, somebody help me."
Yeah, but he's not *scary* enough!
I mean, *look* at him. He's like he something out of a *happy meal*...

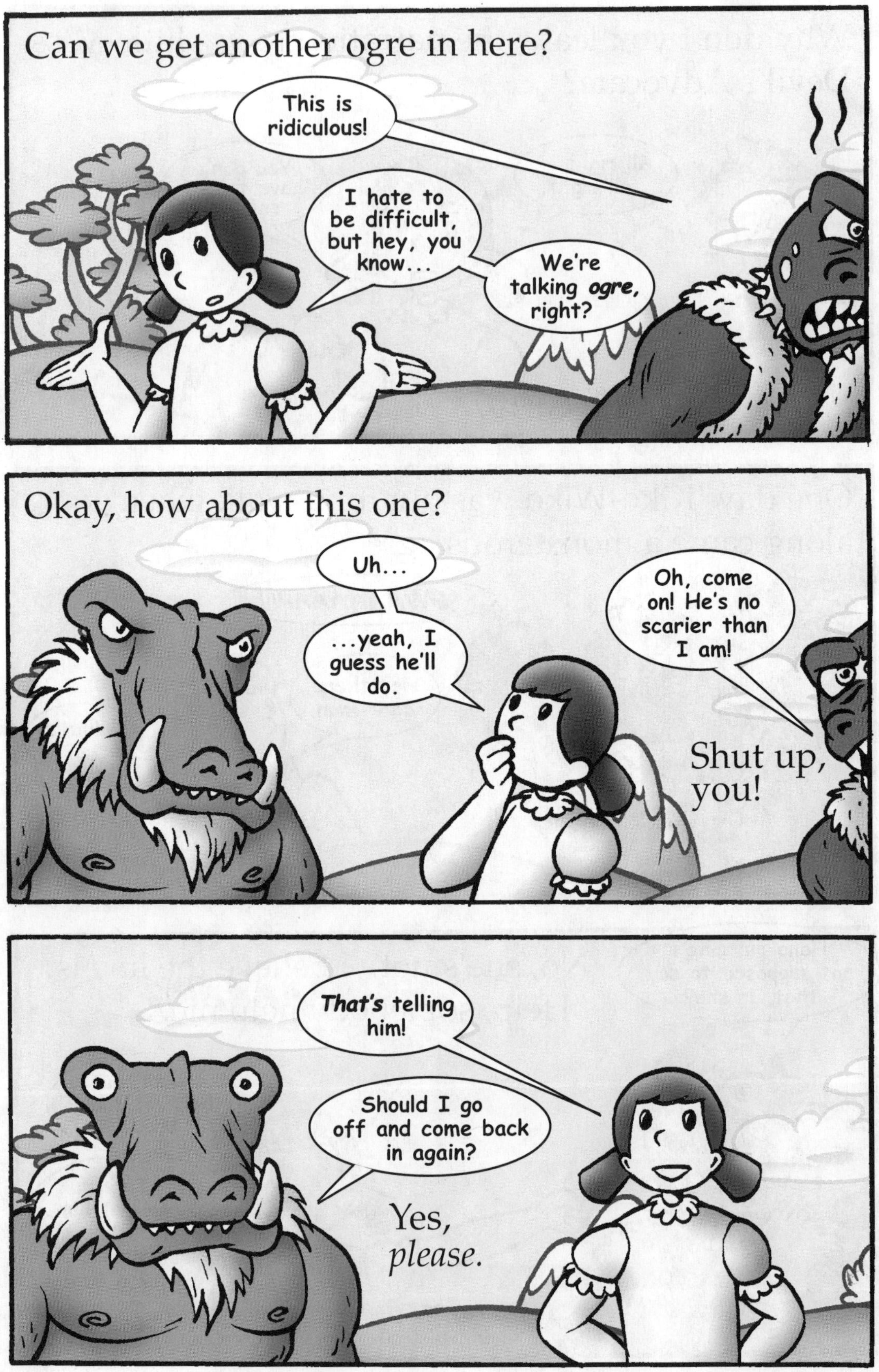
Can we get another ogre in here?
This is ridiculous!
I hate to be difficult, but hey, you know...
We're talking *ogre*, right?
Okay, how about this one?
Uh...
...yeah, I guess he'll do.
Oh, come on! He's no scarier than I am!
Shut up, you!
That's telling him!
Should I go off and come back in again?
Yes, *please*.

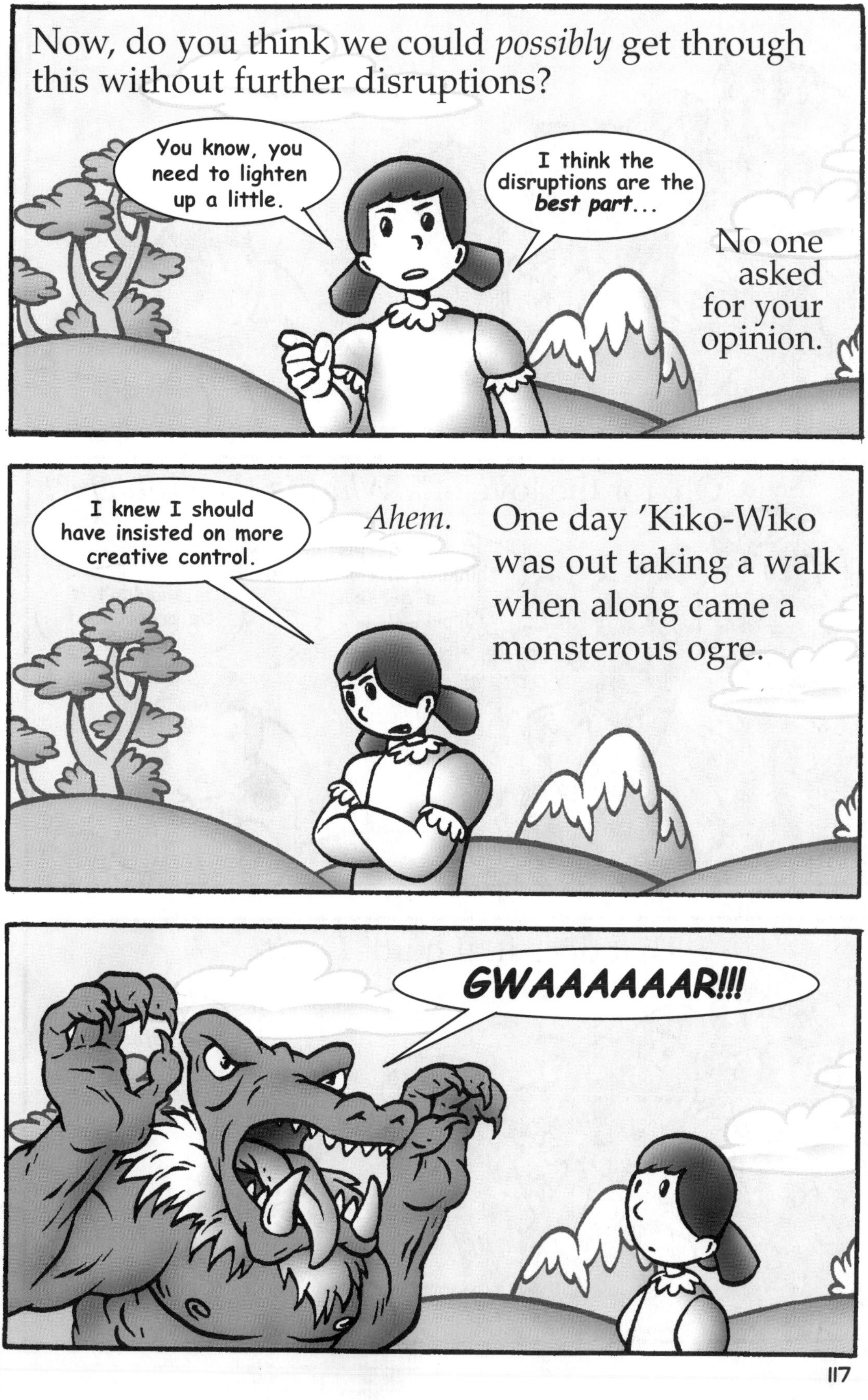
Now, do you think we could *possibly* get through this without further disruptions?
You know, you need to lighten up a little.
I think the disruptions are the ***best part***...
No one asked for your opinion.
I knew I should have insisted on more creative control.
Ahem.
One day 'Kiko-Wiko was out taking a walk when along came a monsterous ogre.
GWAAAAAAR!!!

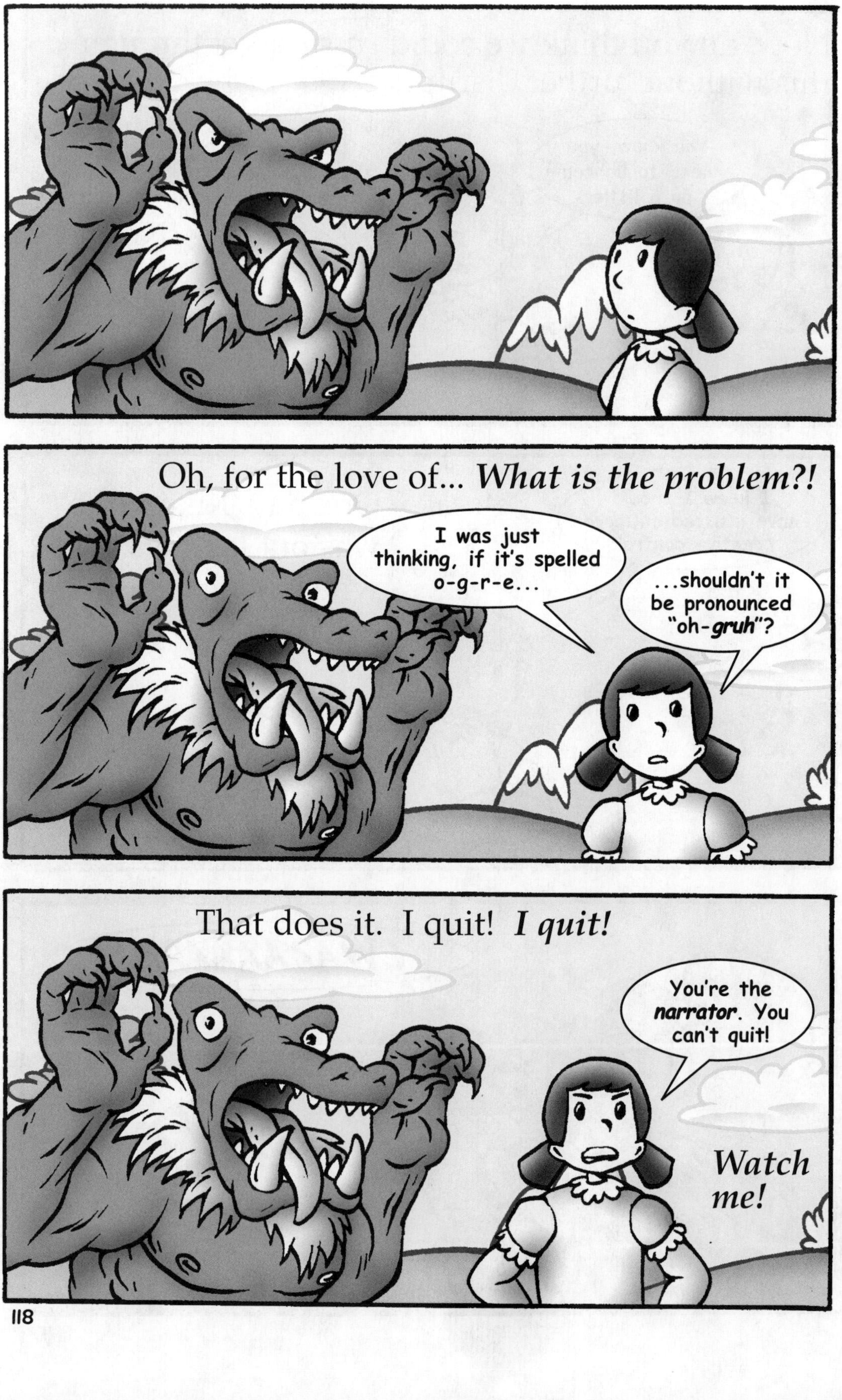
Oh, for the love of... *What is the problem?!*
I was just thinking, if it's spelled o-g-r-e...
...shouldn't it be pronounced "oh-*gruh*"?
That does it. I quit! *I quit!*
You're the ***narrator***. You can't quit!
Watch me!

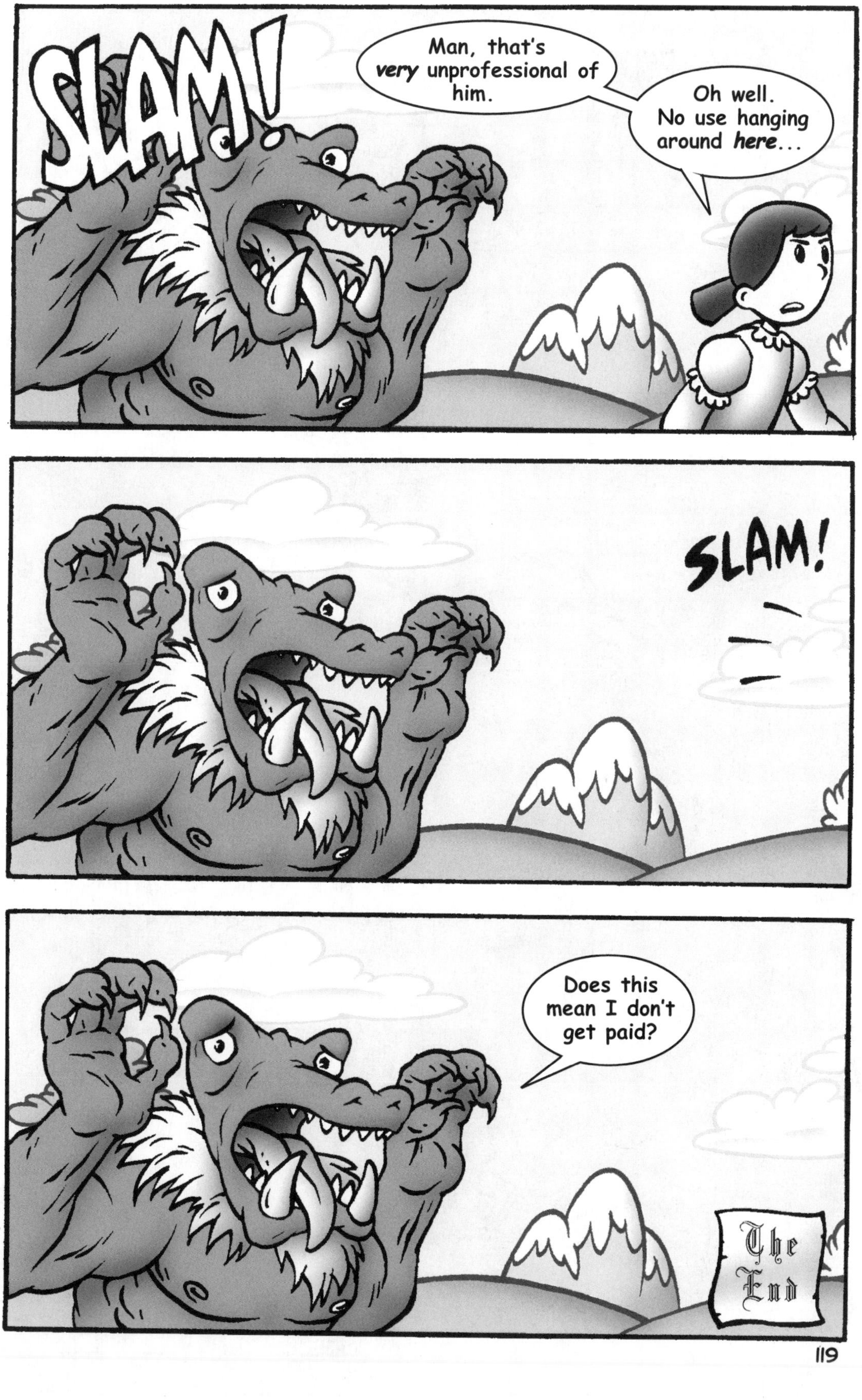
SLAM!
Man, that's *very* unprofessional of him.
Oh well. No use hanging around *here*...
SLAM!
Does this mean I don't get paid?
The End

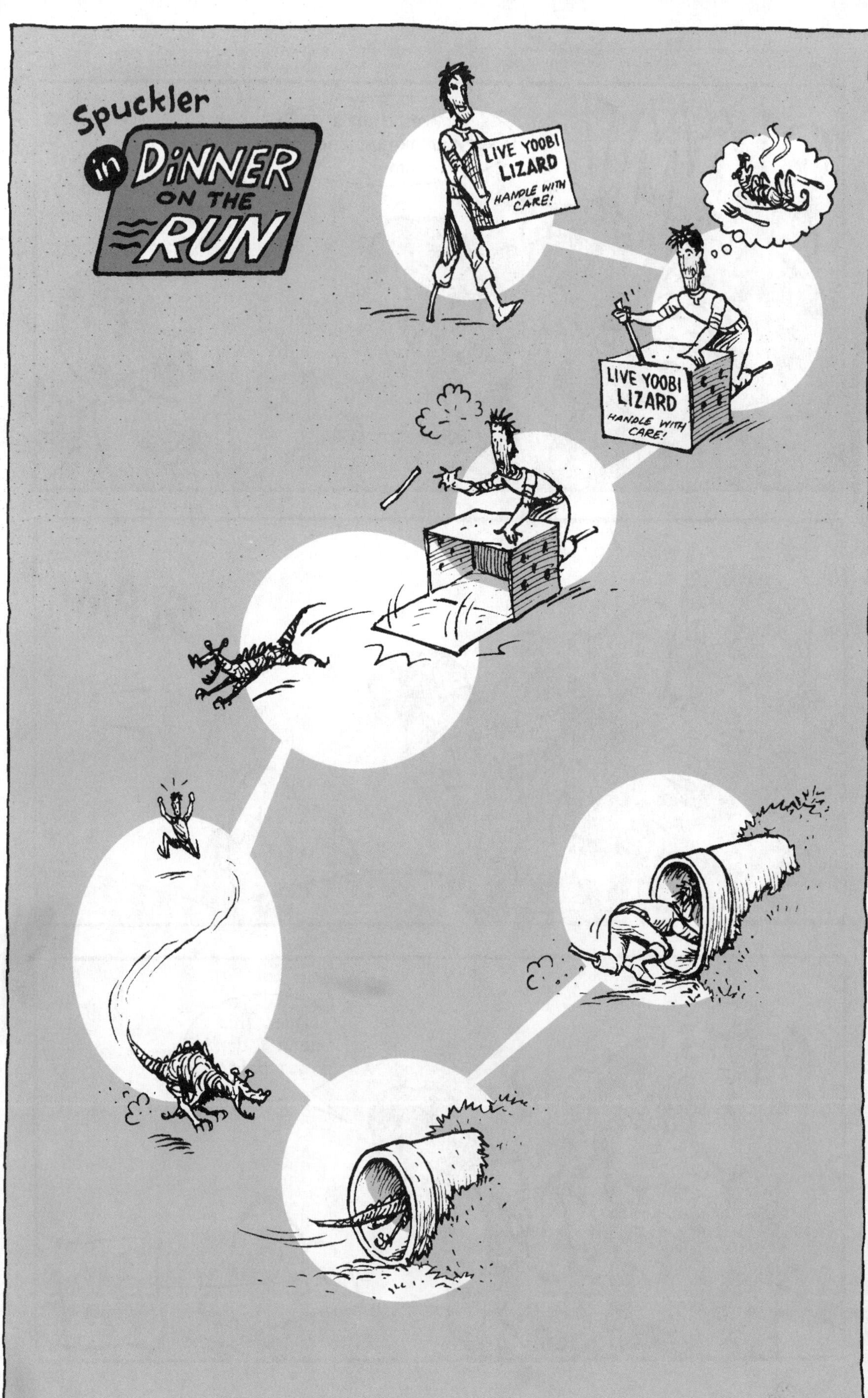
Spuckler
in DiNNER ON THE RUN
LIVE YOOBI LIZARD
HANDLE WITH CARE!
LIVE YOOBI LIZARD
HANDLE WITH CARE!

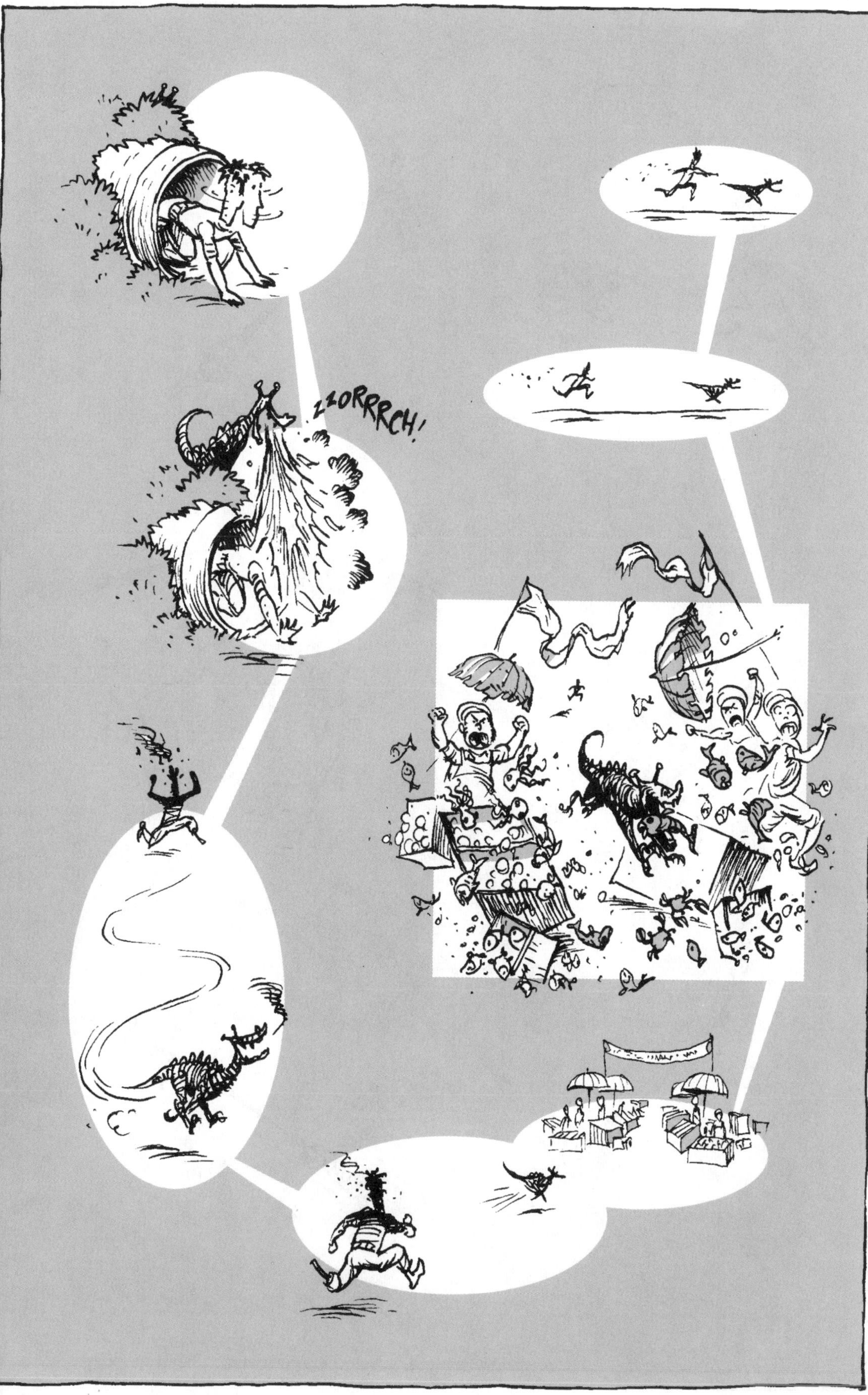
ZZORRRCH!

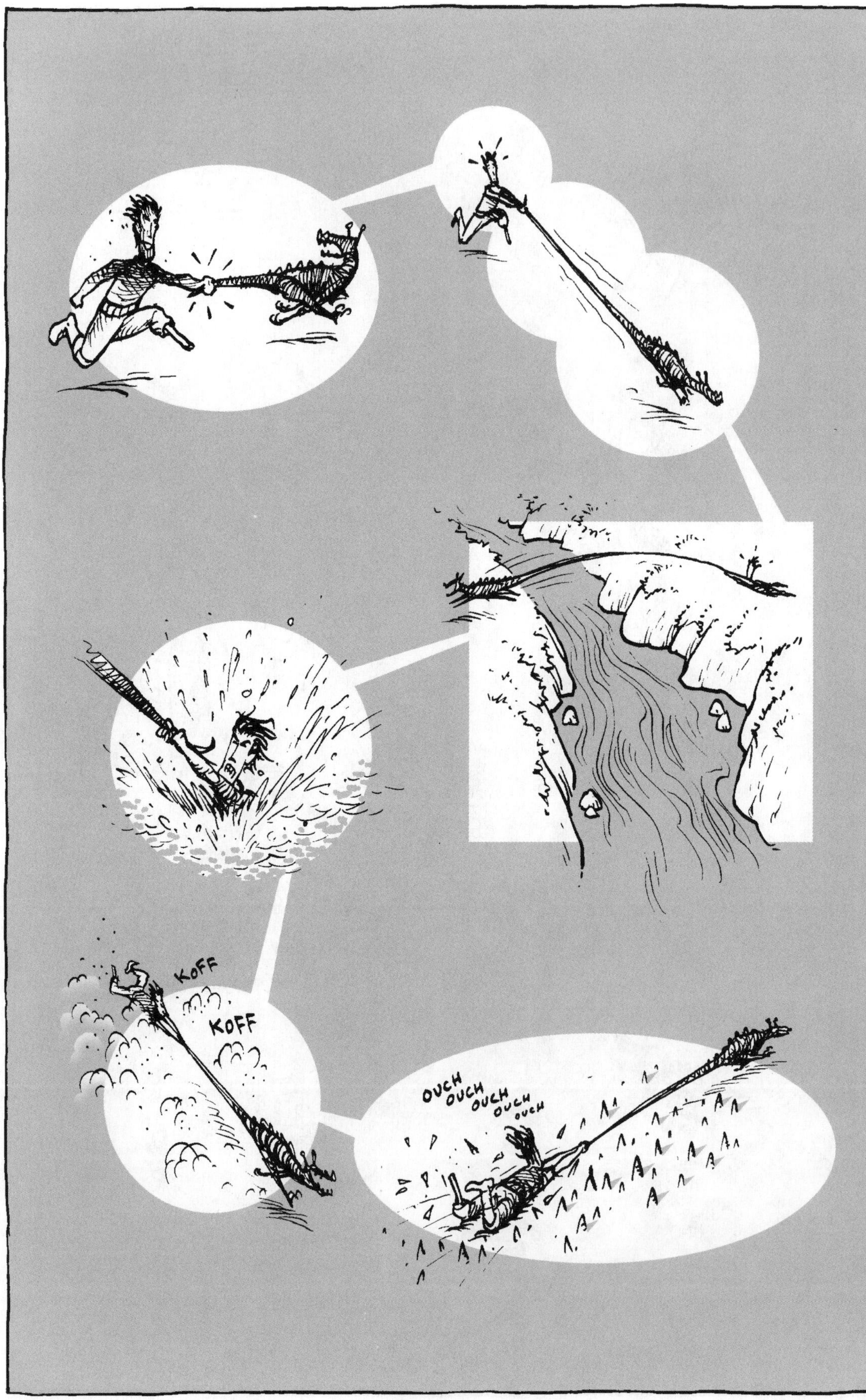
KOFF
KOFF
OUCH
OUCH
OUCH
OUCH

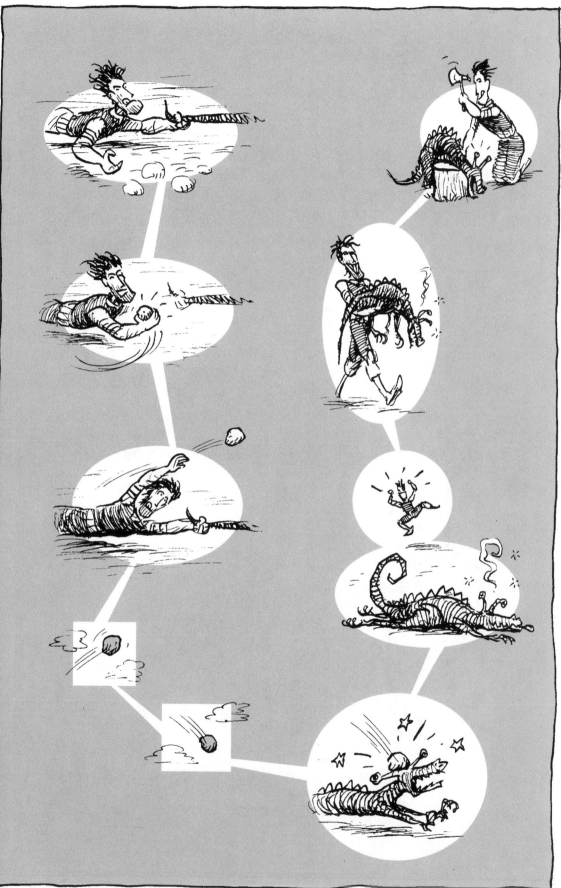

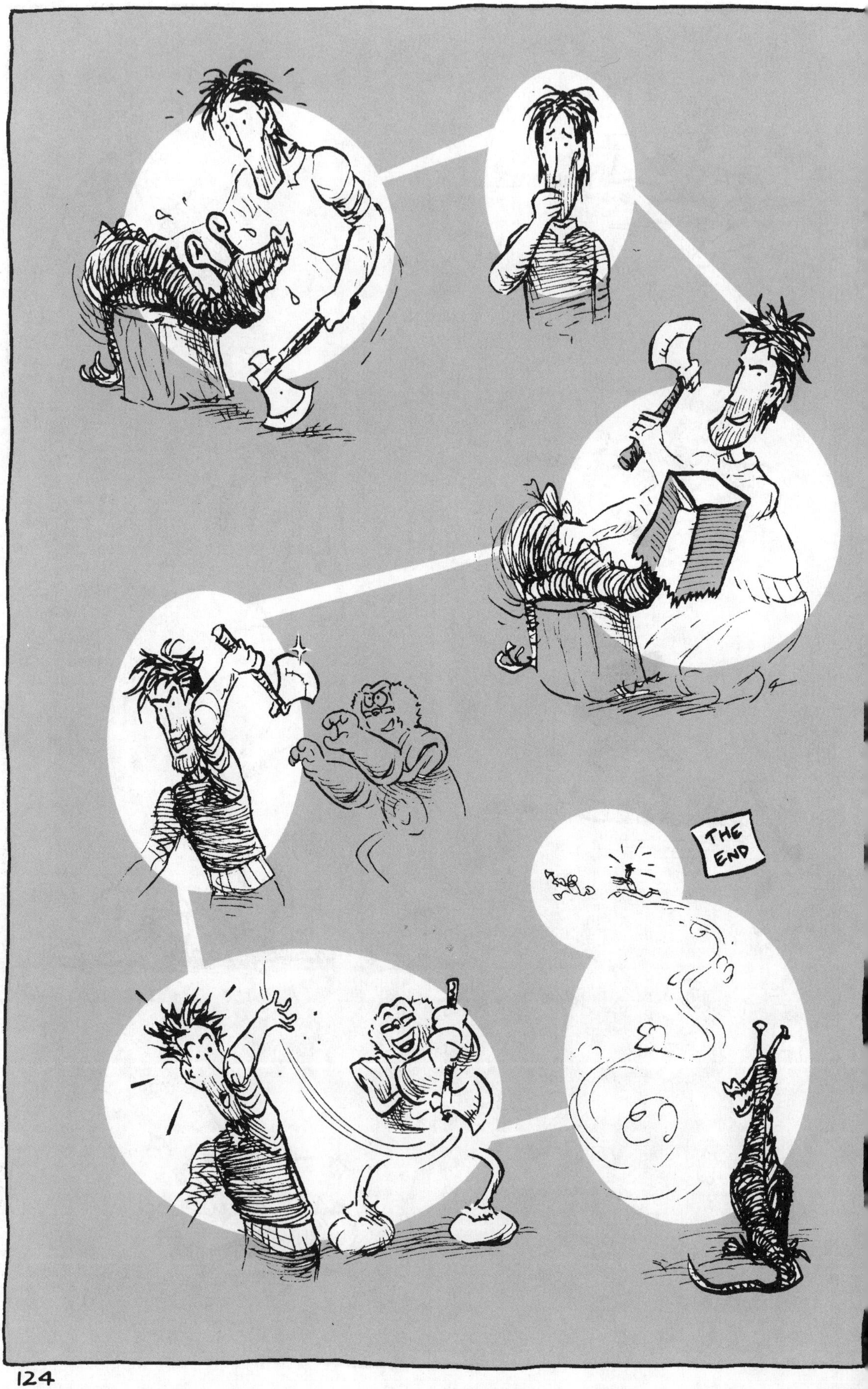
THE END

The Critical Critic Returns

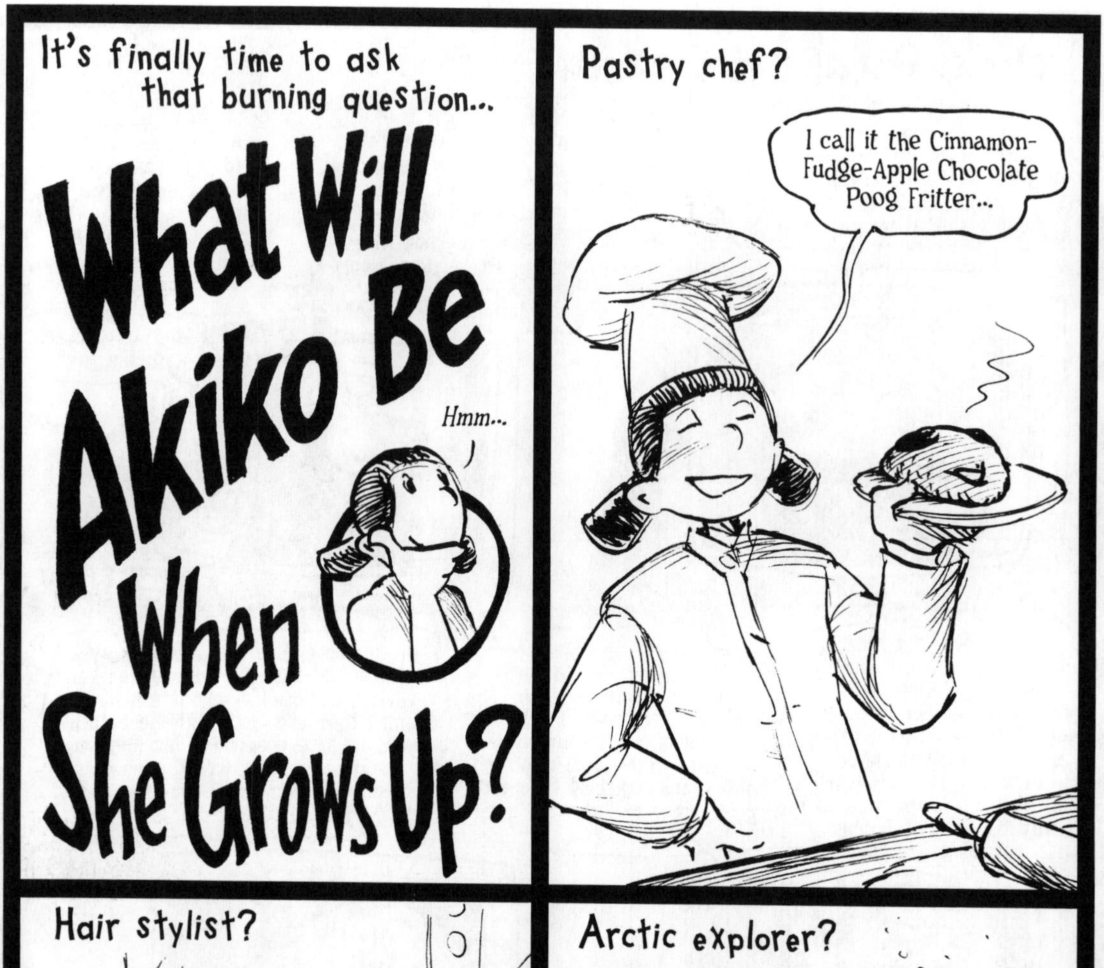
It's finally time to ask that burning question...
What Will Akiko Be When She Grows Up?
Hmm...
Pastry chef?
I call it the Cinnamon-Fudge-Apple Chocolate Poog Fritter...
Hair stylist?
It's you.
It's **really** you...
Do you *think* so?
Arctic explorer?
I know there were supposed to be penguins at **one** of these poles...
NORTH POLE

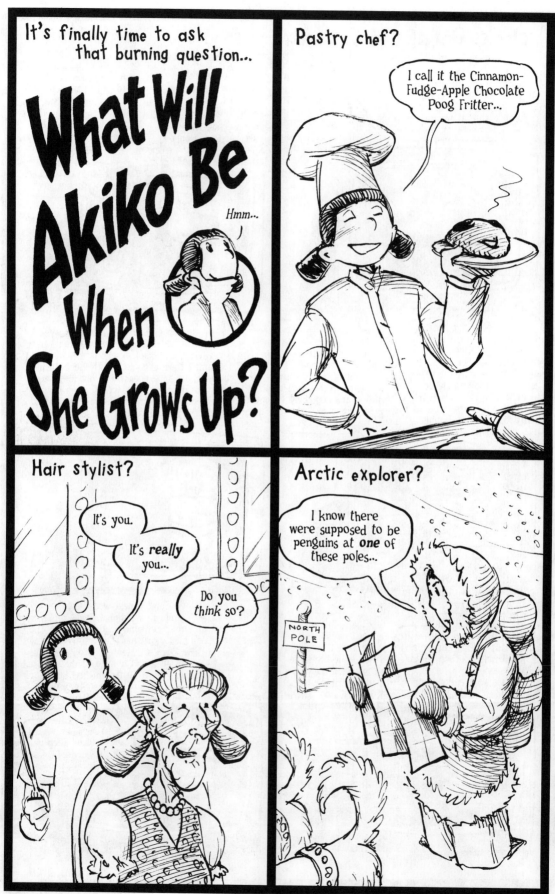

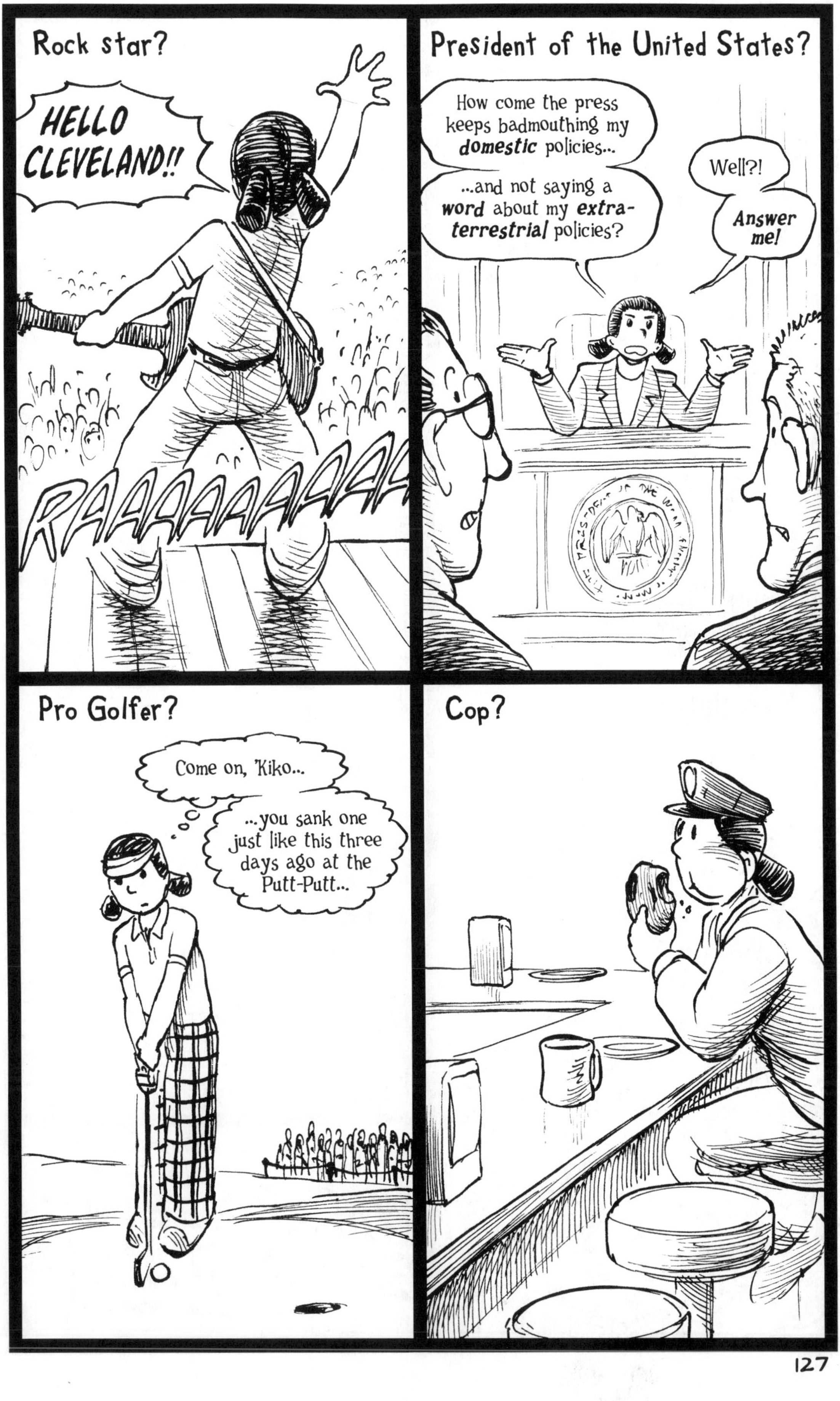
Rock star?
HELLO CLEVELAND!!
RAAAAAAAAAA
President of the United States?
How come the press keeps badmouthing my domestic policies...
...and not saying a word about my extra-terrestrial policies?
Well?!
Answer me!
Pro Golfer?
Come on, 'Kiko...
...you sank one just like this three days ago at the Putt-Putt...
Cop?

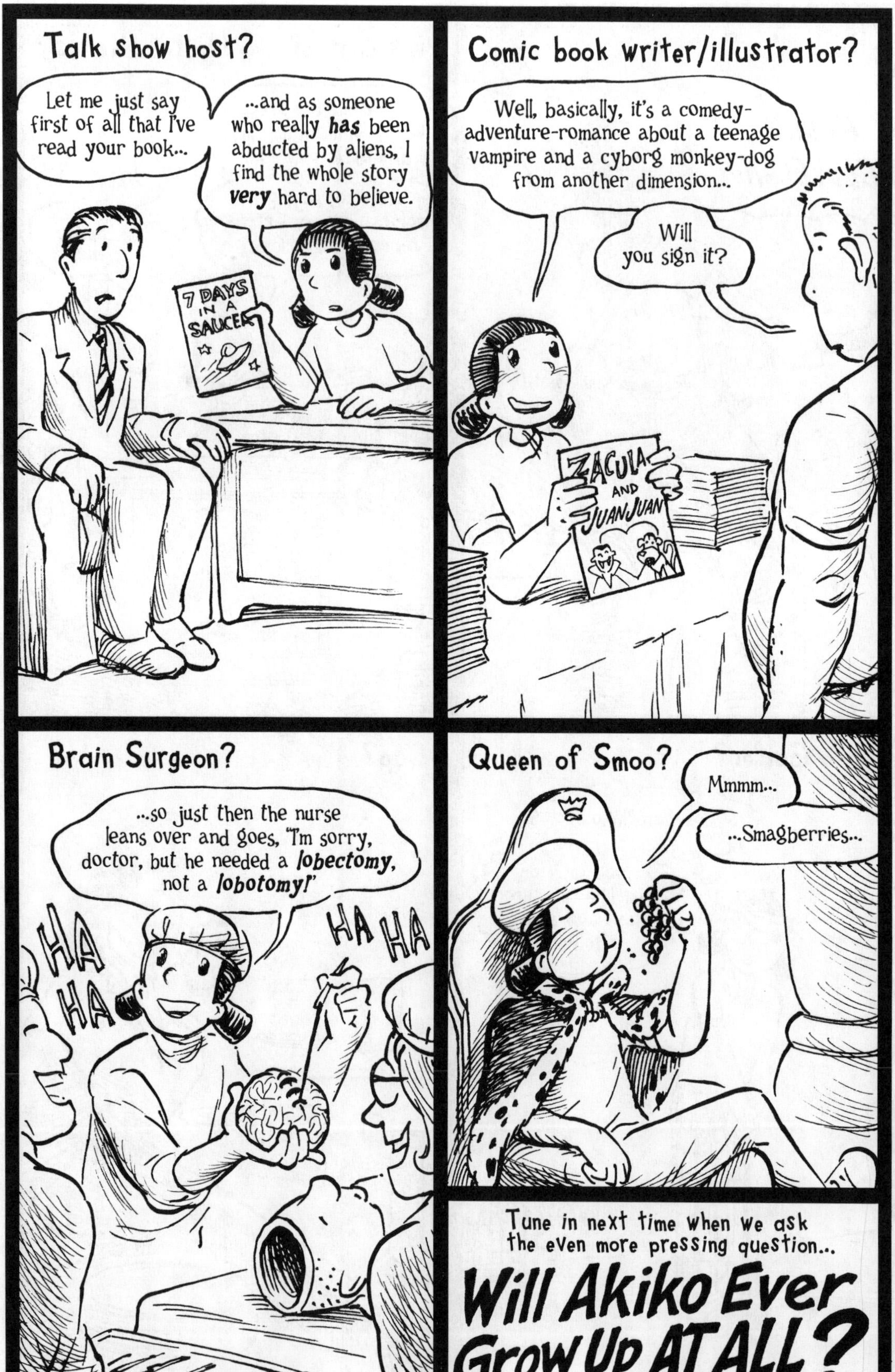
Talk show host?
Let me just say first of all that I've read your book...
...and as someone who really **has** been abducted by aliens, I find the whole story **very** hard to believe.
7 DAYS IN A SAUCER
Comic book writer/illustrator?
Well, basically, it's a comedy-adventure-romance about a teenage vampire and a cyborg monkey-dog from another dimension...
Will you sign it?
ZACULA AND JUANJUAN
Brain Surgeon?
...so just then the nurse leans over and goes, "I'm sorry, doctor, but he needed a *lobectomy*, not a *lobotomy!*"
HA HA HA
HA HA
Queen of Smoo?
Mmmm...
...Smagberries...
Tune in next time when we ask the even more pressing question...
Will Akiko Ever Grow Up AT ALL?

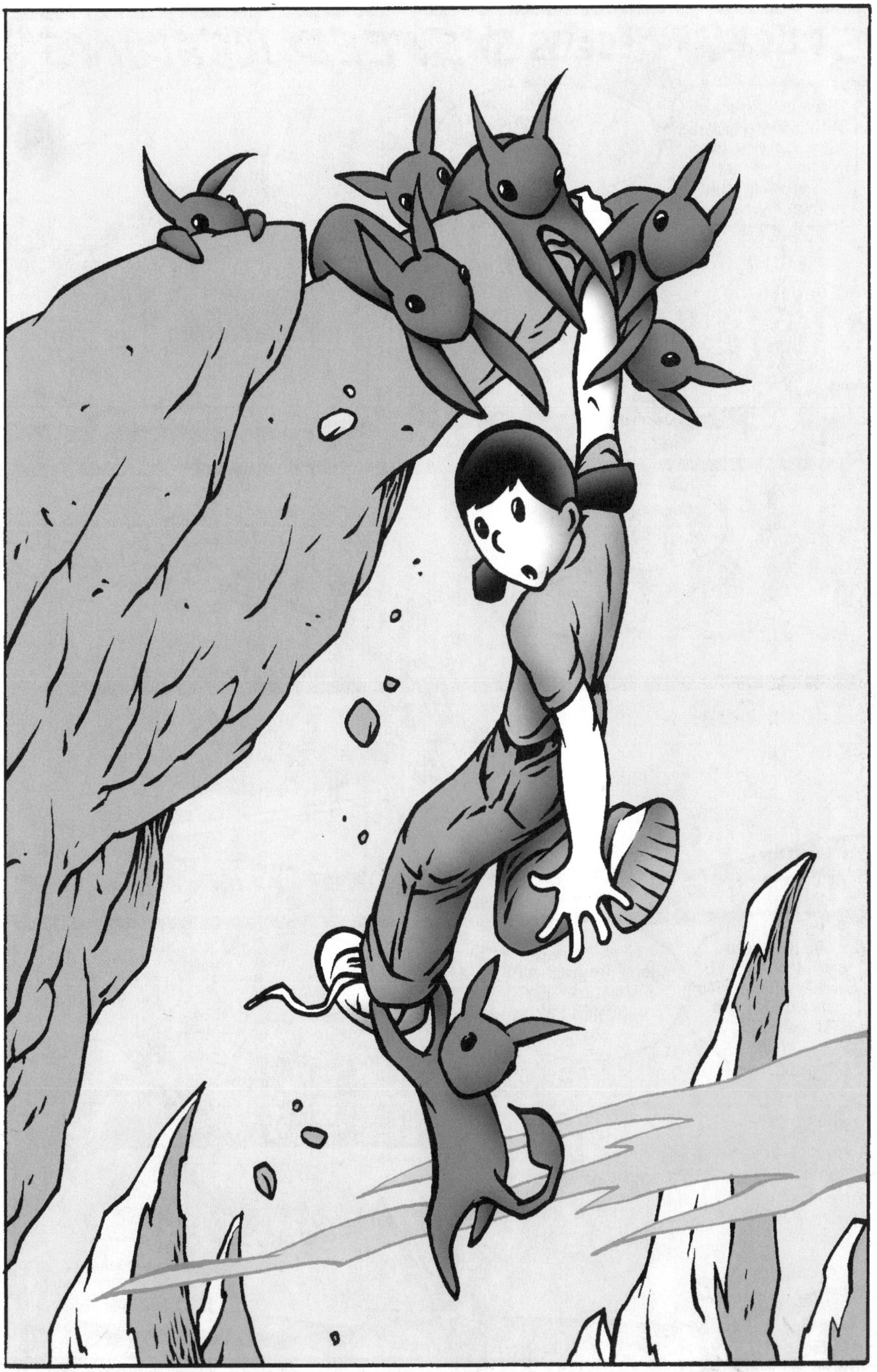

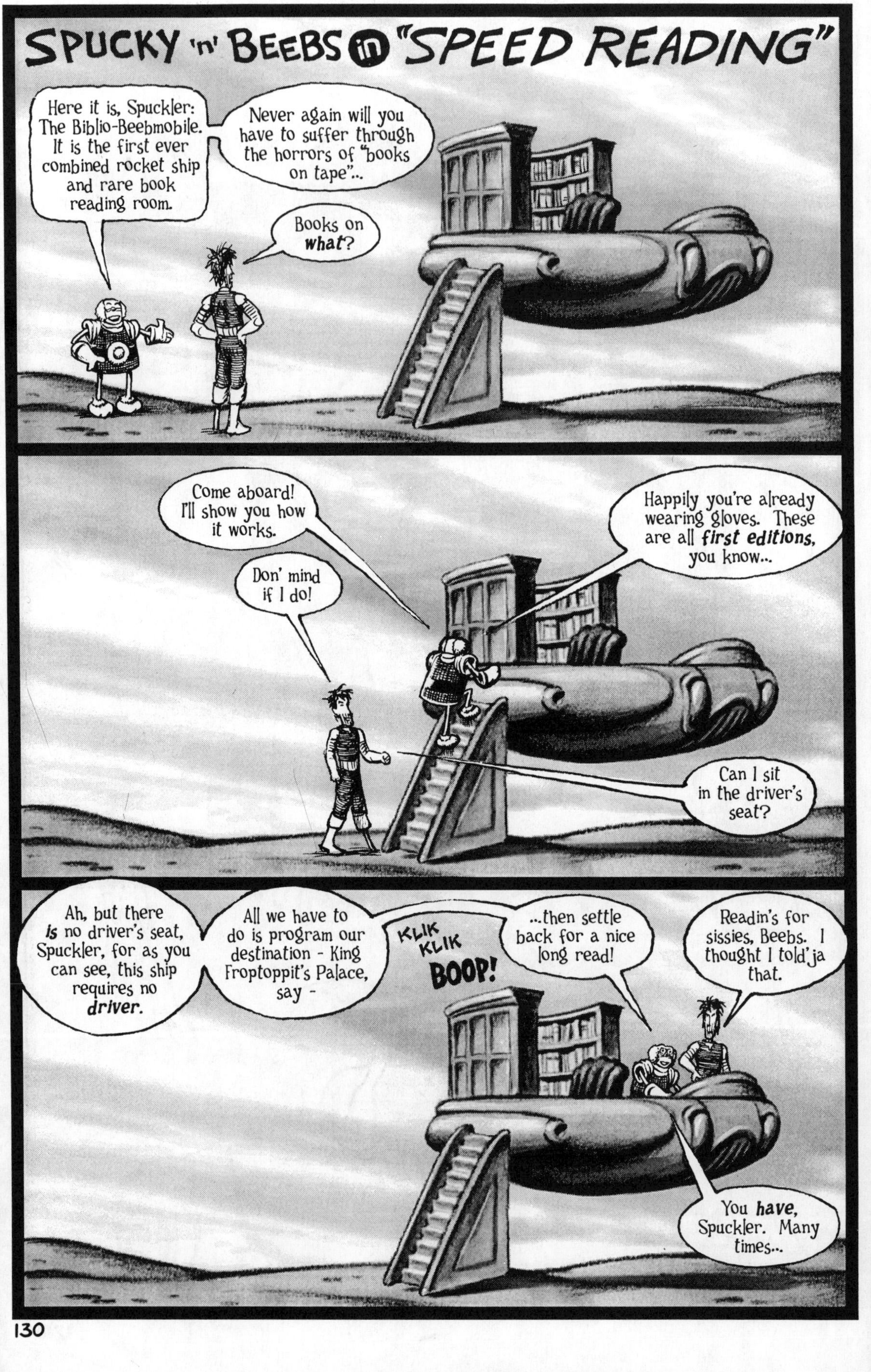

SPUCKY 'n' BEEBS in "SPEED READING"
Here it is, Spuckler: The Biblio-Beebmobile. It is the first ever combined rocket ship and rare book reading room.
Never again will you have to suffer through the horrors of "books on tape"...
Books on **what**?
Come aboard! I'll show you how it works.
Happily you're already wearing gloves. These are all **first editions**, you know...
Don' mind if I do!
Can I sit in the driver's seat?
Ah, but there **is** no driver's seat, Spuckler, for as you can see, this ship requires no **driver**.
All we have to do is program our destination - King Froptoppit's Palace, say -
KLIK KLIK
BOOP!
...then settle back for a nice long read!
Readin's for sissies, Beebs. I thought I told'ja that.
You **have**, Spuckler. Many times...

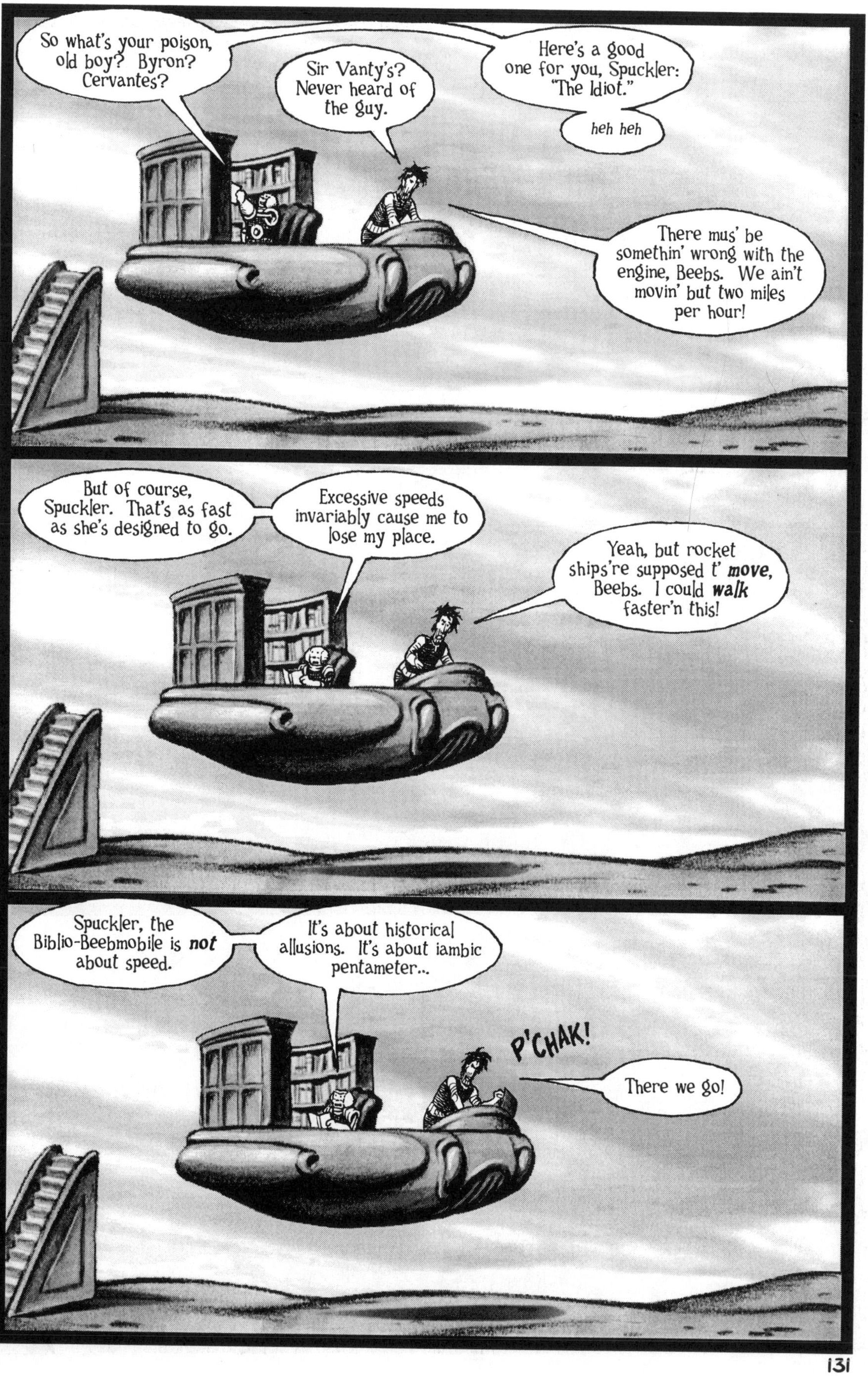
So what's your poison, old boy? Byron? Cervantes?
Sir Vanty's? Never heard of the guy.
Here's a good one for you, Spuckler: "The Idiot."
heh heh
There mus' be somethin' wrong with the engine, Beebs. We ain't movin' but two miles per hour!
But of course, Spuckler. That's as fast as she's designed to go.
Excessive speeds invariably cause me to lose my place.
Yeah, but rocket ships're supposed t' **move**, Beebs. I could **walk** faster'n this!
Spuckler, the Biblio-Beebmobile is **not** about speed.
It's about historical allusions. It's about iambic pentameter...
P'CHAK!
There we go!

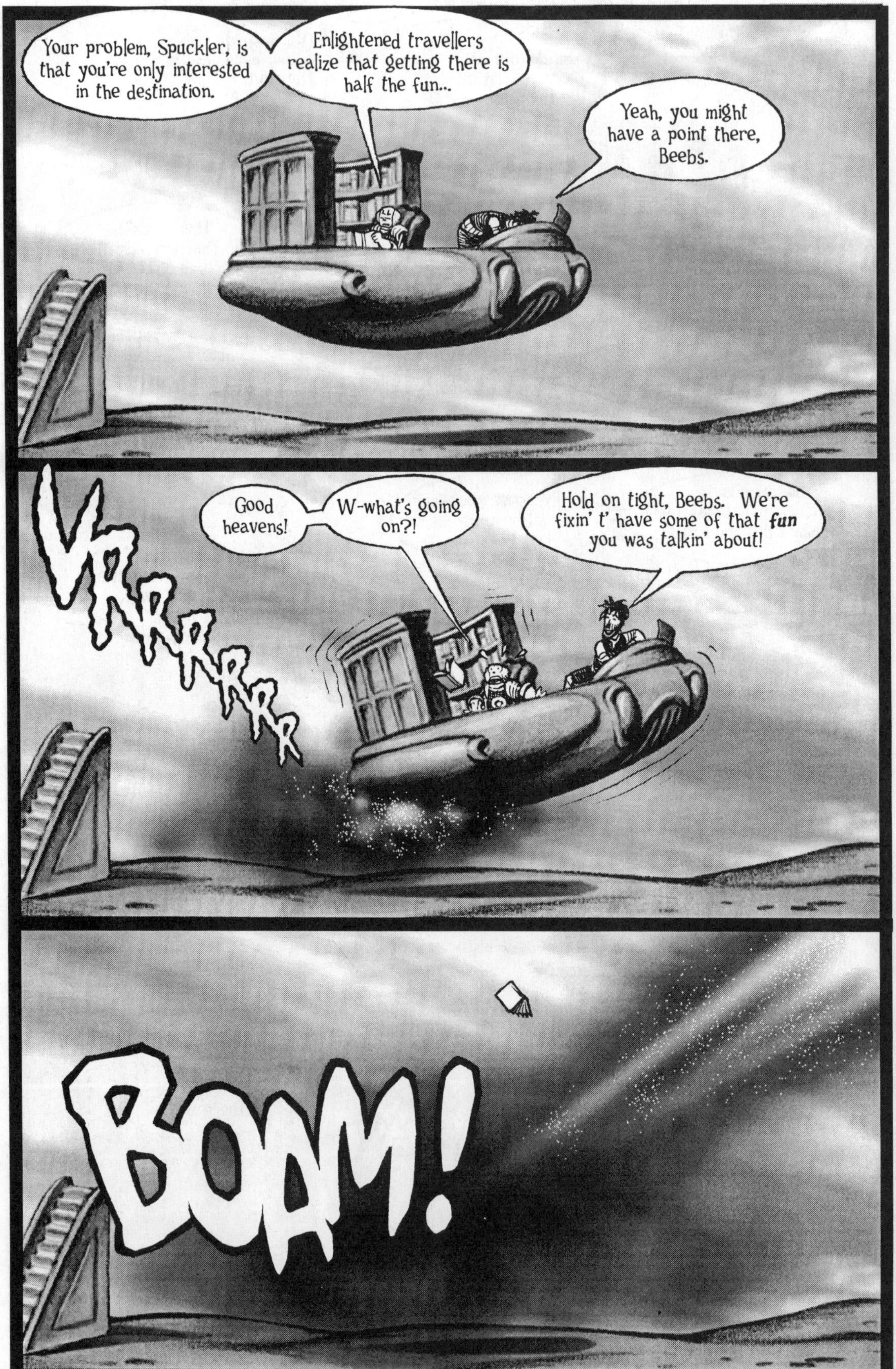
Your problem, Spuckler, is that you're only interested in the destination.
Enlightened travellers realize that getting there is half the fun...
Yeah, you might have a point there, Beebs.
VRRRRRRR
Good heavens!
W-what's going on?!
Hold on tight, Beebs. We're fixin' t' have some of that **fun** you was talkin' about!
BOAM!

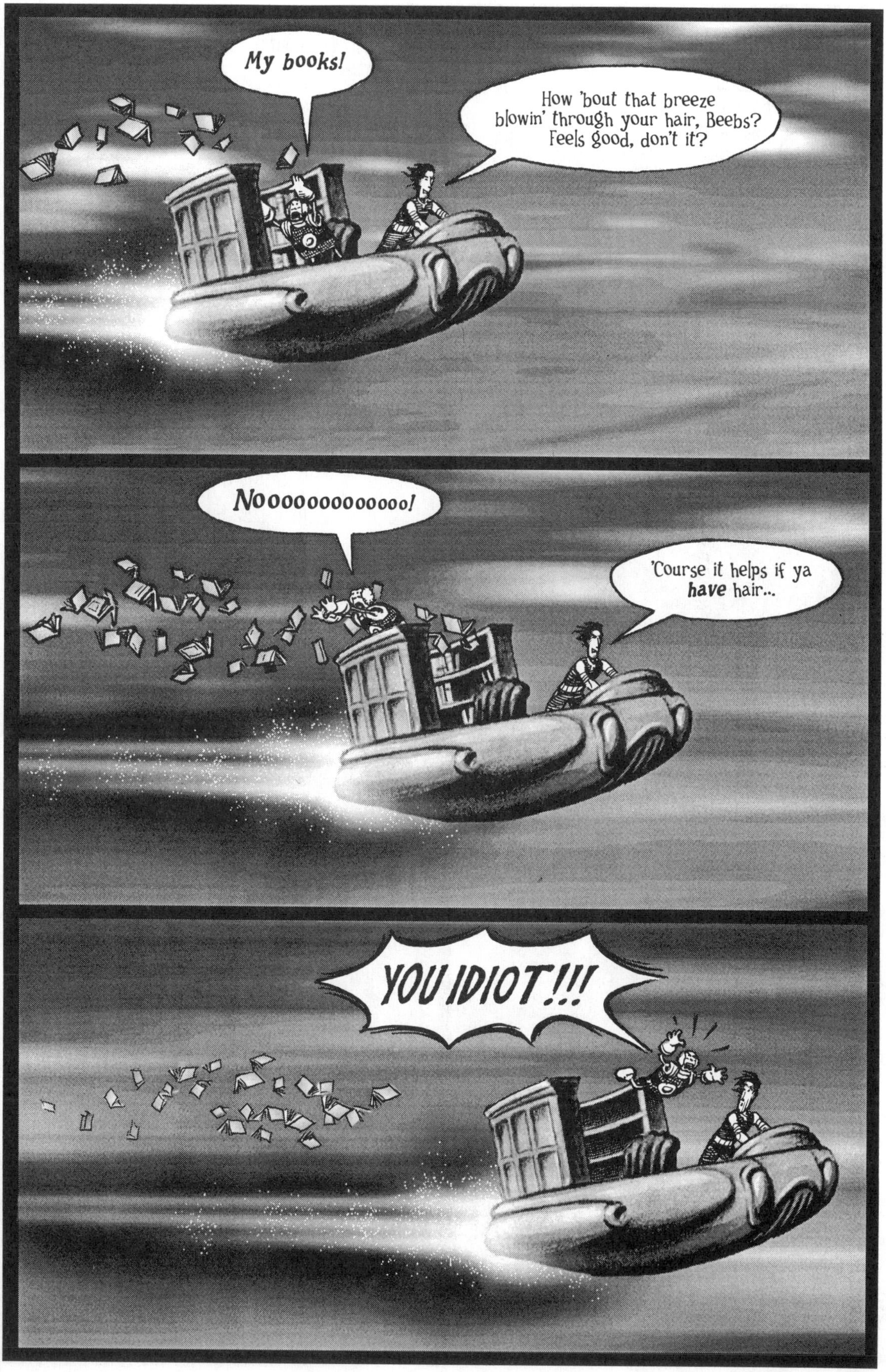

My books!
How 'bout that breeze blowin' through your hair, Beebs? Feels good, don't it?
Noooooooooooooo!
'Course it helps if ya **have** hair...
YOU IDIOT!!!

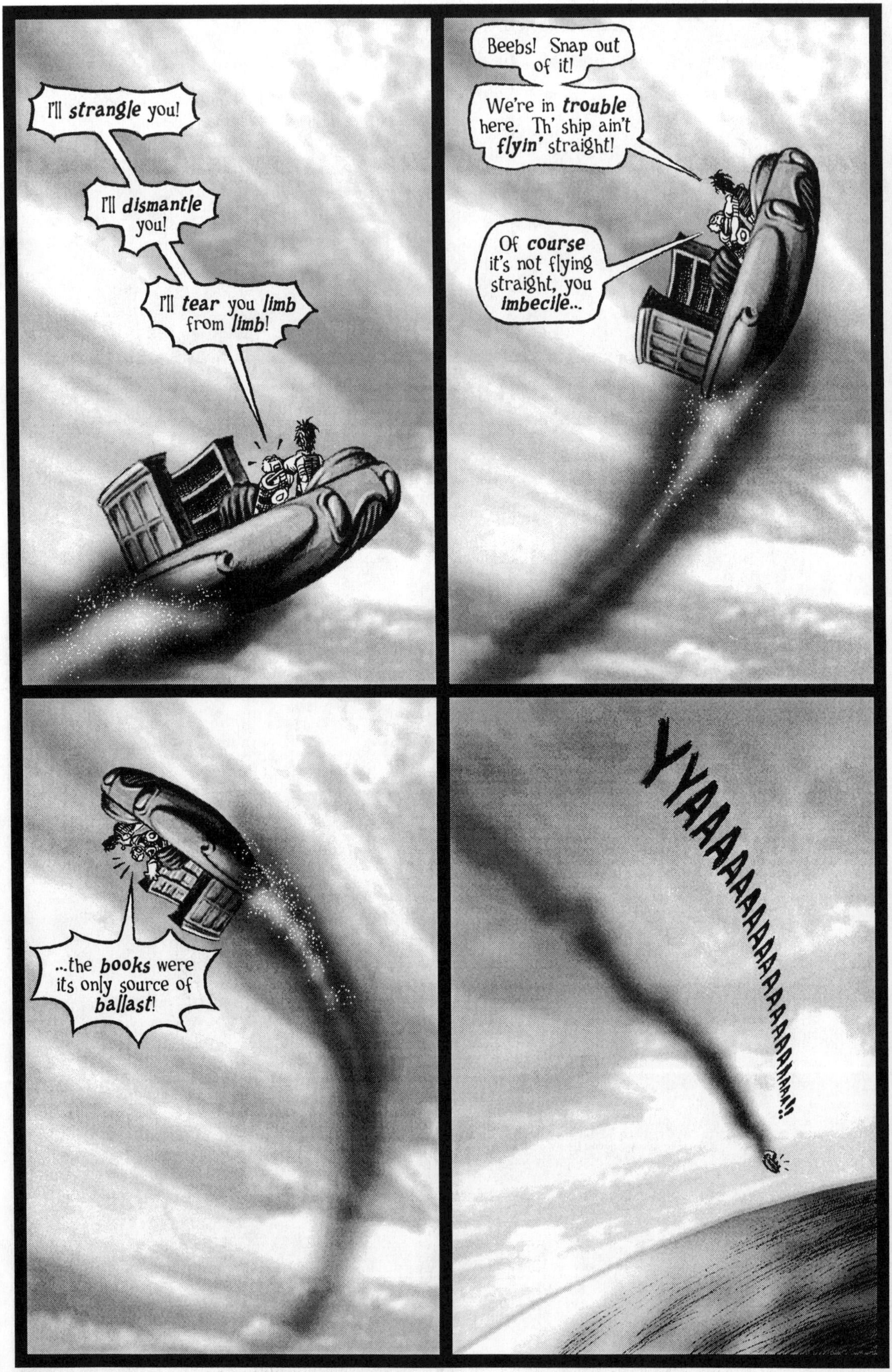
I'll strangle you!
I'll dismantle you!
I'll tear you limb from limb!
Beebs! Snap out of it!
We're in trouble here. Th' ship ain't flyin' straight!
Of course it's not flying straight, you imbecile...
...the books were its only source of ballast!
YYAAAAAAAAAAAAAAAAAAAAAAAAAAAAAAAAAA!!

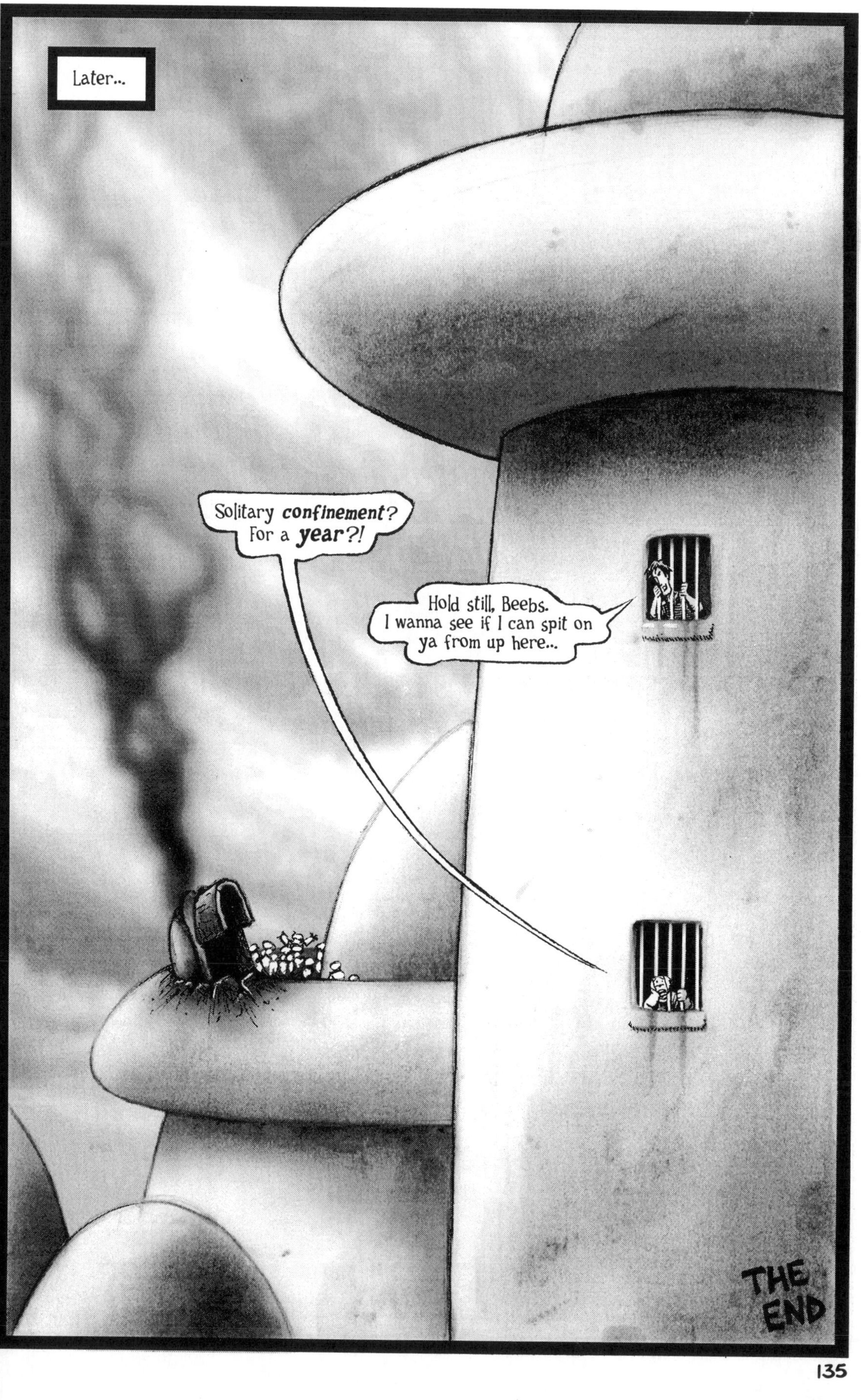
Later...
Solitary *confinement*? For a **year**?!
Hold still, Beebs. I wanna see if I can spit on ya from up here...
THE END

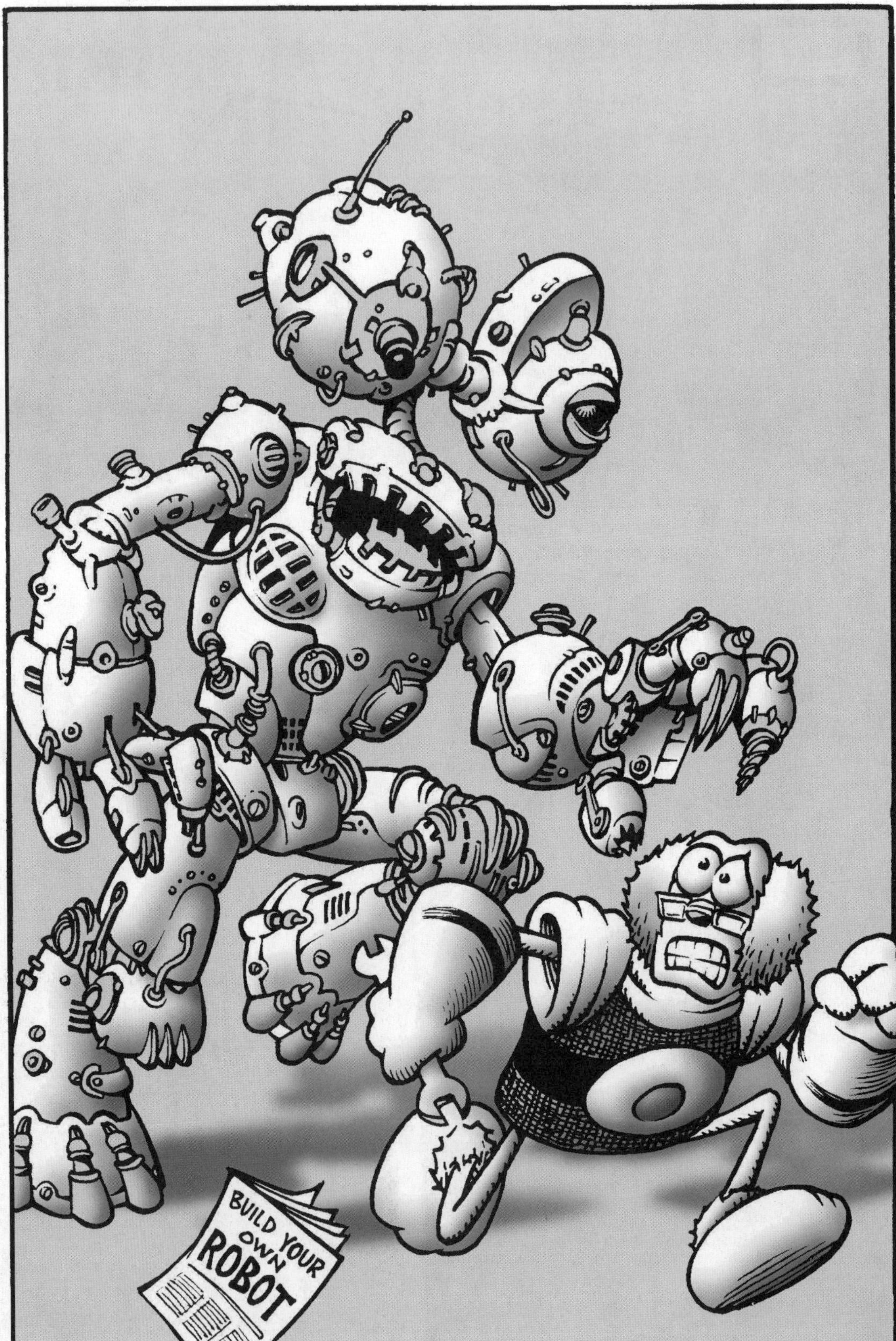
BUILD YOUR OWN ROBOT

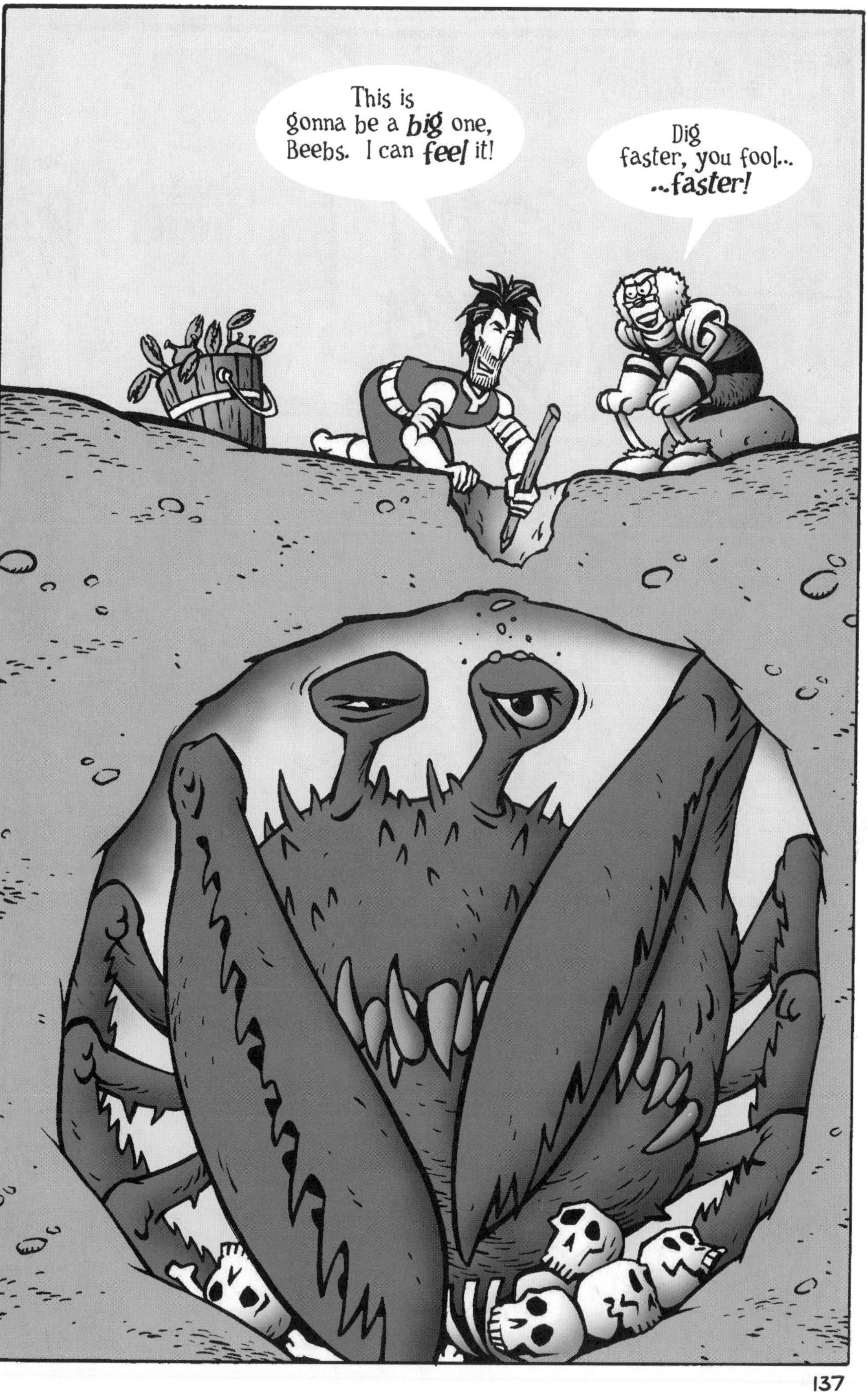
This is gonna be a big one, Beebs. I can feel it!
Dig faster, you fool... ...faster!

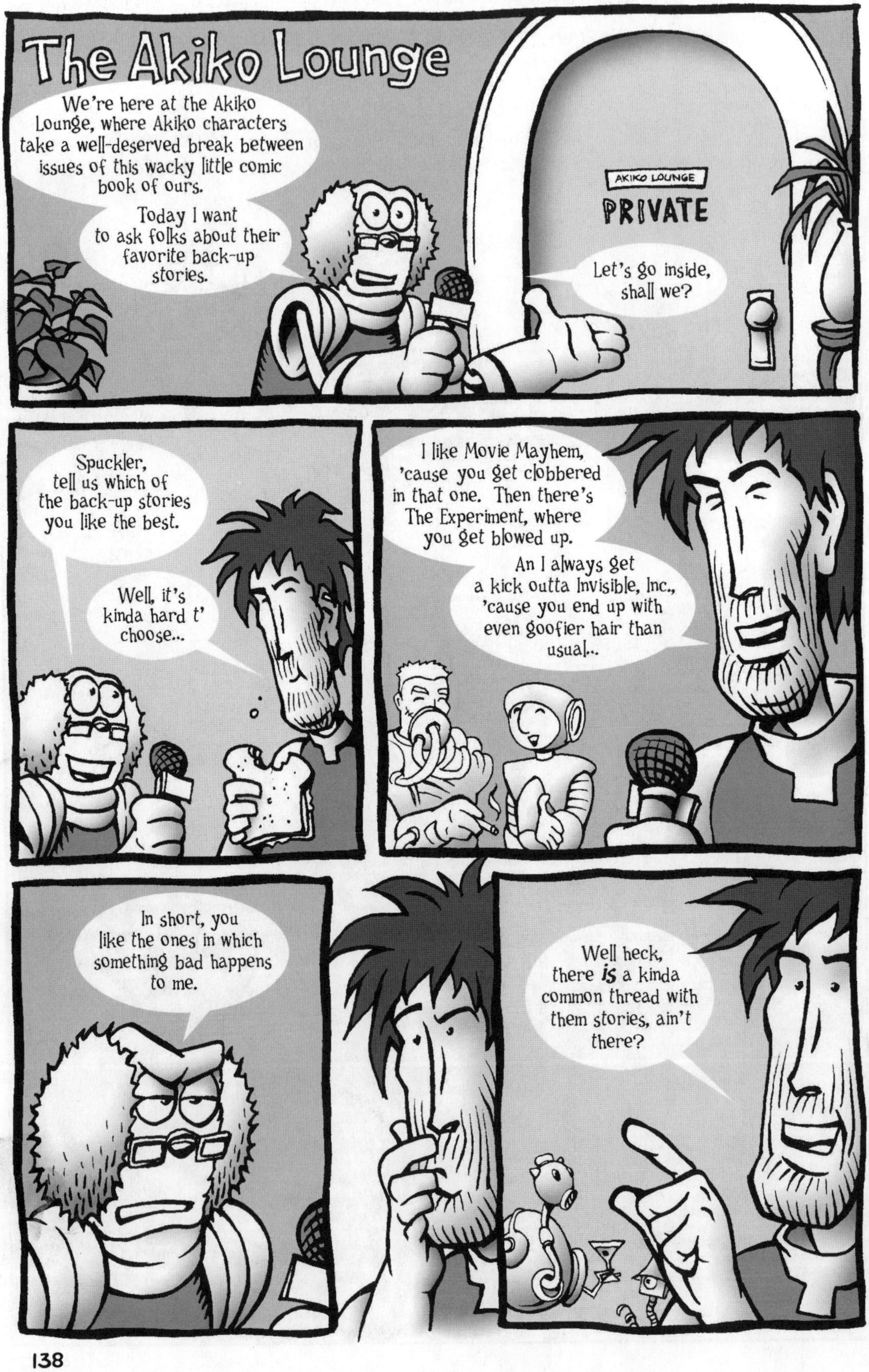
The Akiko Lounge
We're here at the Akiko Lounge, where Akiko characters take a well-deserved break between issues of this wacky little comic book of ours.
Today I want to ask folks about their favorite back-up stories.
AKIKO LOUNGE
PRIVATE
Let's go inside, shall we?
Spuckler, tell us which of the back-up stories you like the best.
Well, it's kinda hard t' choose...
I like Movie Mayhem, 'cause you get clobbered in that one. Then there's The Experiment, where you get blowed up.
An I always get a kick outta Invisible, Inc., 'cause you end up with even goofier hair than usual...
In short, you like the ones in which something bad happens to me.
Well heck, there *is* a kinda common thread with them stories, ain't there?

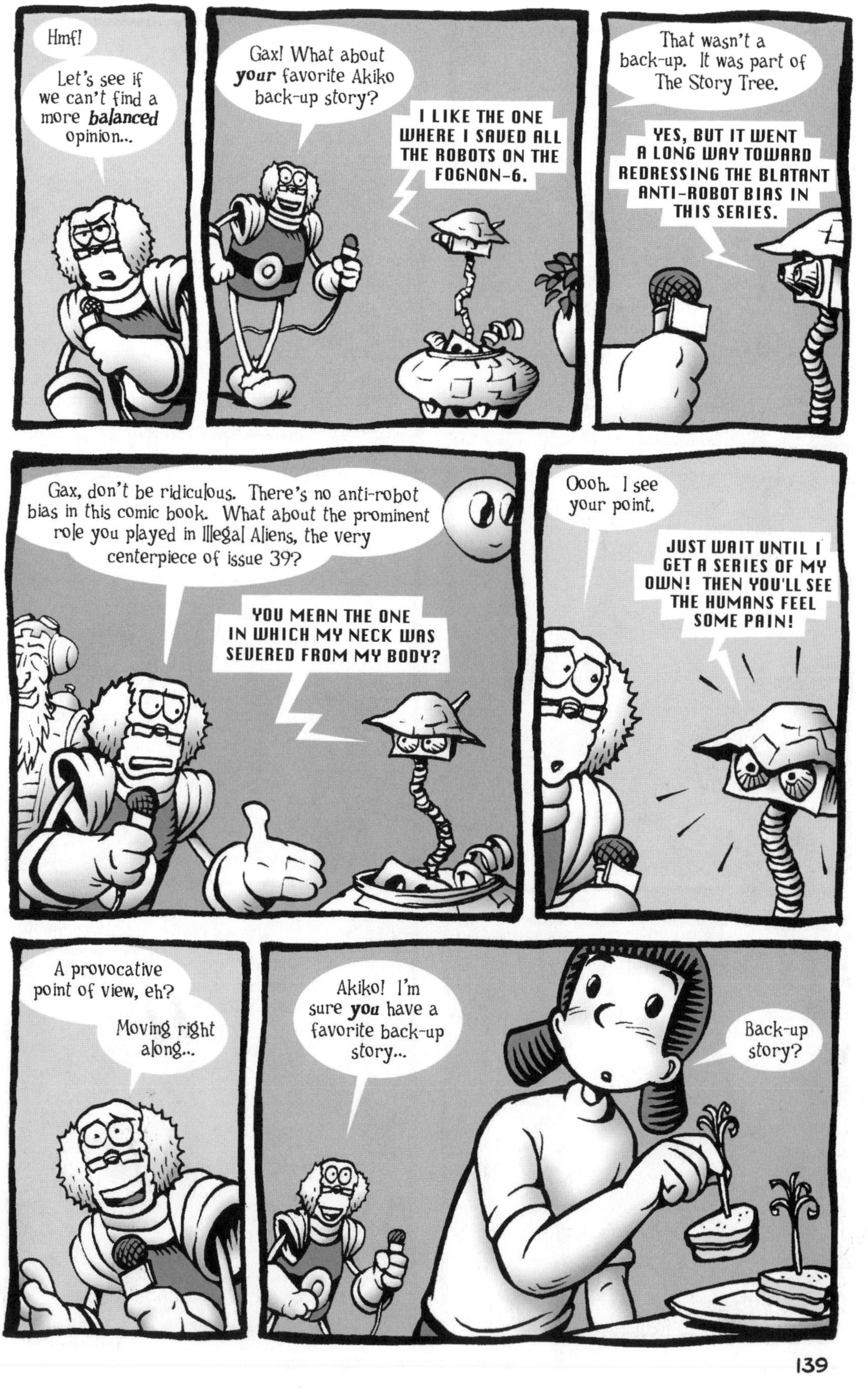

Hmf!
Let's see if we can't find a more *balanced* opinion...
Gax! What about *your* favorite Akiko back-up story?
I LIKE THE ONE WHERE I SAVED ALL THE ROBOTS ON THE FOGNON-6.
That wasn't a back-up. It was part of The Story Tree.
YES, BUT IT WENT A LONG WAY TOWARD REDRESSING THE BLATANT ANTI-ROBOT BIAS IN THIS SERIES.
Gax, don't be ridiculous. There's no anti-robot bias in this comic book. What about the prominent role you played in Illegal Aliens, the very centerpiece of issue 39?
YOU MEAN THE ONE IN WHICH MY NECK WAS SEVERED FROM MY BODY?
Oooh. I see your point.
JUST WAIT UNTIL I GET A SERIES OF MY OWN! THEN YOU'LL SEE THE HUMANS FEEL SOME PAIN!
A provocative point of view, eh?
Moving right along...
Akiko! I'm sure *you* have a favorite back-up story...
Back-up story?

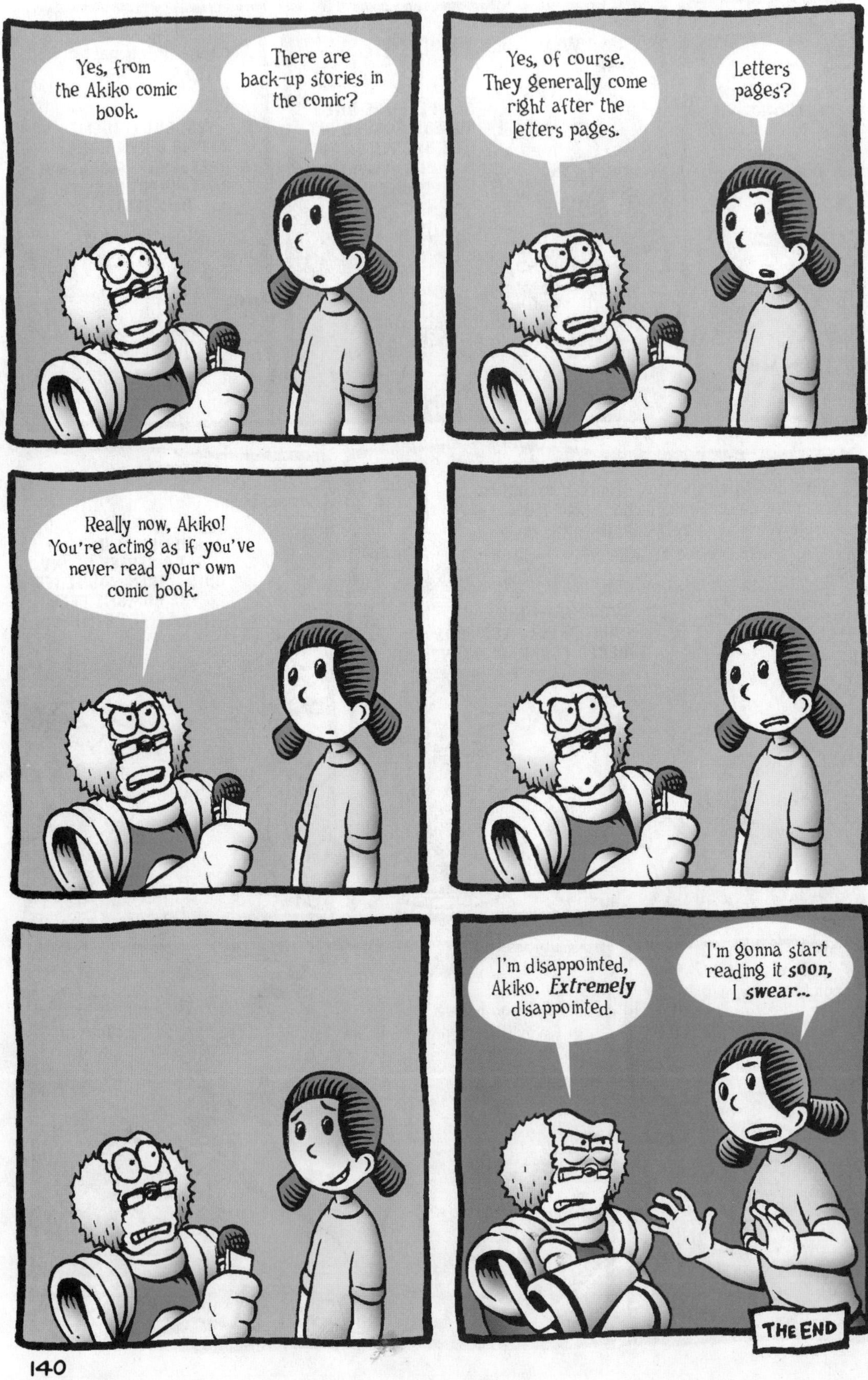
Yes, from the Akiko comic book.
There are back-up stories in the comic?
Yes, of course. They generally come right after the letters pages.
Letters pages?
Really now, Akiko! You're acting as if you've never read your own comic book.
I'm disappointed, Akiko. *Extremely* disappointed.
I'm gonna start reading it *soon*, I *swear...*
THE END